Hell in An Loc

The 1972 Easter Invasion
and the Battle that Saved South Viet Nam

Lam Quang Thi

University of North Texas Press
Denton, Texas

10 9 8 7 6 5 4 3 2 1

Permissions:
University of North Texas Press
1155 Union Circle #311336
Denton, TX 76203-5017

The paper used in this book meets the minimum requirements of the American
National Standard for Permanence of Paper for Printed Library Materials,
z39.48.1984. Binding materials have been chosen for durability.

Library of Congress Cataloging-in-Publication Data
Lam, Quang Thi, 1932-
Hell in An Loc : the 1972 Easter Invasion and the battle that saved South Viet
Nam / Lam Quang Thi ; foreword by Andrew Wiest. -- 1st ed.
p. cm.
Includes bibliographical references and index.
ISBN 978-1-57441-276-5 (cloth : alk. paper)
1. Lam, Quang Thi, 1932- 2. An Loc, Battle of, An Loc, Vietnam,
1972--Personal narratives, Vietnamese. 3. Easter Offensive, 1972--Personal
narratives, Vietnamese. 4. Vietnam War, 1961-1975--Campaigns--Vietnam--
An Loc--Personal narratives, Vietnamese. 5. Vietnam War, 1961-1975--Aerial
operations, American--Personal narratives, Vietnamese. 6. Vietnam War,
1961-1975--Regimental histories--Vietnam (Republic). I. Title.
DS557.8.A5L36 2009
959.704'34--dc22
2009020095

Contents

Illustrations

Foreword

by Andrew Wiest

The American tragedy that was the Vietnam War is the subject of seemingly endless fascination in both U.S. academic and popular circles. Efforts to interpret the war range from big screen portrayals, including Tom Hanks in *Forrest Gump* and Mel Gibson in *We Were Soldiers*, to well-documented tomes on the military prosecution of the war, such as John Nagl's *Learning to Eat Soup with a Knife*, that heavily influence present-day tactics in the ongoing Global War on Terror. Any attempts to explain this national fixation on or the ongoing influence of the Vietnam War leads back to the same uncomfortably dark riddle. How did the United States, history's greatest superpower and a nation that presumably stands for good, on one hand lose a war to a third-rate power like North Vietnam and on the other lose its soul amidst a cacophony of protests, war crimes trials, and assassinations?

The arbiters of America's past, whether they be film directors, novelists, historians, or reporters, have provided a dizzying array of potential answers, some controversial and others taken as dogma, to explain American failure in the Vietnam War. President Lyndon Johnson was too distracted by his Great Society. The American media subverted the mission of the military. American society was too fractured, and the nation's will was too weak. General William Westmoreland never understood the war that was his to command. The U.S. military relied on overly traditional tactics. The U.S. military did not rely enough on traditional tactics. The power of the U.S. Air Force was never truly unleashed. Airpower was used too indiscriminately. The ignominious roll call is, indeed, quite long, leaving no shortage of villainous characters contending for the leading part in the American morality play that is the history of the Vietnam War.

Much of the historical and cultural debate that swirls around the failure of the American war in Vietnam is complicated by the very fact that its participants all too often view the conflict simply as an *American* war. Arguably perpetuating the fatal flaw of the U.S. military effort in Vietnam, the American popular and historical consciousness regularly omits the Vietnamese from the story of their own war. What for Americans was but part of a much wider geopolitical chess match was for Vietnam a brutal civil war that fractured the nation along ethnic, social, religious, geographic, and economic fault lines the roots of which extended well beyond the transitory motivations and concerns of the Cold War. While popular portrayal concedes that the conflict in Vietnam can be dated back to 1945 and the re-imposition of French colonialism, actually the struggle can be seen as a part of a broader Vietnamese dynamic of south vs. north competition that extends back at least as far as the 1500s. Viewing such a complex conflict only from the perspective of its final foreign interloper is overly simplistic. A full understanding of the Vietnam War, and of America's failed crusade, requires coming to terms with Vietnam's Vietnam War.

The only Vietnamese who seem to register in the American public consciousness, and who receive coverage in most popular accounts of the war, are America's enemies—Victor Charlie—the cunning V.C., and the hard-bitten warriors of North Vietnam. Allowing time for and praise of enemy forces in Vietnam makes perfect historical sense, for facing such stalwart adversaries—the inheritors of a martial tradition that had bested everyone from the Mongols to the Chinese—makes America's failure in its Vietnamese adventure somehow more palatable. By comparison, America's allies, the South Vietnamese, receive little notice and have become very nearly historically invisible. When not totally ignored in western accounts of the conflict, the South Vietnamese usually receive only damning reference as a collection of cowards and incompetents who served a fatally flawed government that had little connection to Vietnam's glorious past. In the popular historical mind, then, geopolitical fate forced the United States to back the wrong horse in the Vietnam War, setting the stage for all that followed in America's great tragedy.

In recent years, though, western scholars have devoted an increased level of academic scrutiny to South Vietnam that has begun to reshape the history of the conflict. While the new history admits that South Vietnam and its military were flawed instruments, it maintains that the South had a deep connection to Vietnam's past and was not simply predisposed to failure. Even the briefest of accounts of the South Vietnamese experience of war draw a picture that is uncomfortably at odds with the popular understanding of America's war in South East Asia. As part of an imperfect alliance and in the service of a flawed state, the South Vietnamese fought for twenty-five years, at the cost of well over 200,000 military and at least 400,000 civilian dead. After the fall of Saigon, millions chose to flee to face an uncertain future abroad as refugees rather than to live under the rule of their brothers from the North. It seems, then, that many in South Vietnam fought long and hard for their own independence and were unwilling to accept defeat.

The emerging twin historical themes that the war in Vietnam was not simply an American war abroad and that South Vietnam was more than just a victim of history greatly complicate the standard intellectual framework that buttresses the American understanding of the conflict. A new generation of scholars, possessing proper language skills and lacking pre-conceived notions of those who lived through the troubled Vietnam era, must seek to unlock the history of Vietnam at war—a history that includes both North and South and all of their institutional participants and contexts.

Historians who choose to work on Vietnam at war, though, face a great disadvantage. As a defeated nation, which the victorious North has labored diligently to expunge from history, the South left behind precious few documents or collective accounts of its war. As a result, the historical playing field is heavily weighted toward the North Vietnamese view of the conflict. There does exist, though, a thriving effort within the Vietnamese expatriate community in the United States (the South Vietnamese community) to chronicle its history and to laud its heroes. Written in Vietnamese and published without the national support that undergirds the efforts of their one-time foes, the South Vietnamese documentation of their perspective on the war has remained an underground effort that has gained little popular traction.

Published primary source material is the lifeblood of history and in the case of most modern wars is readily available. World

War I historians can balance the published diary of Field Marshal Sir Douglas Haig against the *War Memoirs of David Lloyd George.* World War II historians can easily consult both the published *Memoirs of Field Marshal Montgomery* and *The Rommel Papers* in writing on the war in North Africa. However, only a very few South Vietnamese primary accounts have made their way into the historical mainstream. To reach a fuller and more complete understanding of the Vietnam War, the perspective of the South Vietnamese must be chronicled and preserved, to balance and inform the dominant American and North Vietnamese narratives of the conflict.

General Lam Quang Thi is one of the few members of the South Vietnamese community who has been able to break into the historical mainstream. His *The Twenty-Five Year Century* provided a unique look into the motivations behind the career of an officer in the Army of the Republic of Vietnam (ARVN), an institution that played a major, if almost forgotten, role in very nearly every battle in the Vietnam War. Writing the ARVN into the history of the war is critically important not only to understand how that institution eventually failed but also as a needed corrective to the existing tactical history of the conflict. From Operation Junction City, to the Tet Offensive and Operation Lam Son 719, units of the ARVN were there fighting alongside their American allies, sometimes playing distinctly subsidiary roles but on other occasions taking the lead.

As the American phase of the Vietnam War neared its end, the U.S./ARVN alliance faced one of its sternest tests of battle against the great North Vietnamese Easter Offensive of 1972. The fighting in many ways stood as a test of the entire American strategy in Vietnam, for in the wake of the increased pace of the American troop withdrawal, the ARVN stood on its own without U.S. combat forces, but with the aid of U.S. advisors and firepower, against an all-out attempt by the North Vietnamese to achieve military victory. For months, bitter fighting raged across the length and breadth of South Vietnam, from the Demilitarized Zone (DMZ) in the north through the Central Highlands, but nowhere was the struggle more brutal than at the village of An Loc, which guarded the western approaches to Saigon.

After a period of scholarly neglect, historians have now produced several major works that chronicle the events and elucidate the importance of the Easter Offensive. G. H. Turley's *The Easter Offensive*, and my own *Vietnam's Forgotten Army*, detail the history of the struggle along the DMZ. Dale Andrade's *America's Last Vietnam Battle: Halting Hanoi's Easter Offensive* takes a broader look at the ebb and flow of the Easter Offensive and includes an authoritative account of the bitter seventy-day siege of An Loc. Most recently, in his *The Battle of An Loc*, noted historian and veteran of An Loc James Willbanks has provided a thorough and impeccably researched tactical account of the hellish street fighting that took place in and around the battle's urban epicenter. All of these accounts are of great importance to understanding the latter phase of the American effort in Vietnam, and each in its own way strives to include the story of the ARVN role in the planning and prosecution of the Easter Offensive.

General Lam Quang Thi's *Hell in An Loc*, though, provides historians with something different, something more than another well-researched account of the battle. Instead, he analyzes the fighting from a fresh perspective—the perspective of the all too often voiceless South Vietnamese fighting man. Lam Quang Thi is passionate in his desire to chronicle the valor and sacrifice of the men of the ARVN in defense of their nation in what he sees as perhaps the most critical battle of the Vietnam War. Utilizing new source material, including extensive interviews with many of the South Vietnamese principals in the battle, *Hell in An Loc* provides an intimate glimpse into the inner workings of a military amid its moment of great crisis. The result is a work that not only has value as a historical monograph but also carries the considerable weight of a primary source. In *Hell in An Loc*, Lam Quang Thi provides readers with important new information, viewing the struggle from an unabashedly South Vietnamese point of view. As a result, Thi's revisionist conclusions grate against the dominant narrative of the Vietnam War. However, after years of neglect it is fitting that a South Vietnamese interpretation of events breaks into the historical mainstream to help inform future debate on a war of endless complexity.

*"Dis moi que tu reviens d'Austerlitz,
je te dirai que tu es un brave."*
(Tell me you return from Austerlitz,
I will tell you you are a brave man.)
—Napoleon

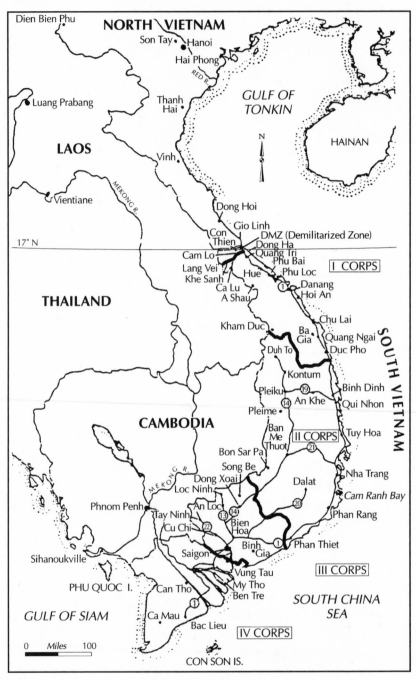

Map 1: Military Regions

Introduction

While searching for a title for this book, I was inspired by Bernard Fall's *Hell in a Very Small Place*, in which the late Vietnam historian described in dramatic detail the fifty-five-day horrors at the French *camp retranché* of Dien Bien Phu in 1954. Little did the author know that eighteen years after the French's humiliating defeat at that small place near the Laotian border, a small plantation town near the Cambodian border was to bear the brunt of a longer and more brutal onslaught and prevail.

The title to this book is also borrowed in part from the article "The Battle That Saved Saigon" by Philip C. Clarke (*Reader's Digest*, March 1973). Its introduction reads:

> Three days before Easter last spring, the North Vietnamese struck South Vietnam with a fury unknown to the Vietnam war since the Tet offensive four years earlier. They poured south across the DMZ, smashed into the central highland from Laos, crossed the border from Cambodia and, with an army of 36,000 men and 100 Russian-made tanks, raced toward Saigon, boasting that they'd be in the city by May 19, Ho Chi Minh's birthday. From one end of the country to the other, bases and villages fell before the savagery of their onslaught. By April 5, all that blocked them from Saigon was a ragtag band of 6,800 South Vietnamese regulars and militiamen and a handful of American

advisors holed up in Anloc, a once-prosperous rubber-plantation town of 15,000 astride Highway 13, which led to the capital, 60 miles to the south. Here is the story of the communists' thunderous assault on Anloc—and of the resistance that was to change the course of the war and made peace a possibility.[1]

The South Vietnamese army had indeed won a decisive victory against overwhelming odds. According to Maj. Gen. James F. Hollingsworth, Senior Advisor to ARVN III Corps, "The real credit goes to the little ARVN soldier. He is just tremendous, just magnificent. He stood in there, took all that fire and gave it back."[2]

Special credit should also be given to the American advisors who fought valiantly alongside their counterparts and, more importantly, provided effective air support and coordinated resupply and medevac operations for the beleaguered garrison. Their mere presence constituted a tremendous boost to the morale of ARVN troops because it embodied the U.S. commitment to support South Vietnam in these darkest hours of its history. Recently, a retired U.S. Army officer requested my autograph for my book *The Twenty-Five Year Century*.[3] He also said he was an advisor to an ARVN unit defending An Loc. I told that officer that, if I could borrow from Napoleon's famous address to his victorious army at Austerlitz, I would tell him he is a brave man.

An Loc, indeed, had become the symbol of the determination of the South Vietnamese Army and its people to stand at all costs in face of the enemy. A depleted army, outnumbered and outgunned, stood its ground and fought to the end and succeeded, against all expectations, in beating back furious assaults from three NVA divisions, supported by artillery and armored regiments, during three months of savage fighting.

General Paul Vanuxem, a French veteran of the Indochina War, called An Loc "the Verdun of Viet Nam." Sir Robert Thompson, special advisor to President Nixon, considered An Loc the greatest military victory of the Free World against Communism in the post-World War II era. Yet, this victory was largely unreported in the U.S. media, which had effectively lost interest in the war after the disengagement of U.S. forces following the Vietnamization of the conflict. With the exception of *Trial by Fire—The 1972 Easter Offensive—America's Last Vietnam Battle* (Hippocrene Books, 1995) by Dale Andradé and *The Battle of An Loc* (Indiana University Press, 2005) by James H. Willbanks, very little in the U.S. literature on the Vietnam conflict has been written about this epic battle. Further, while the above two books provided a wealth of details about the use of U.S. airpower and the role of the U.S. advisors, they didn't provide equal coverage to the activities and performance of ARVN units participating in the siege. This behavior may be a reflection of what an American reporter called "national narcissism," the idea that history is just about us, not the other guys.

The language barrier may be another reason many acts of heroism by South Vietnamese soldiers were ignored by the U.S. media. According to a U.S. reporter who covered the Viet Nam War in the 1960s and 1970s, few U.S. reporters tried to learn Vietnamese while the South Vietnamese were never good at explaining themselves. I believe that Americans' reluctance to learn other countries' culture and language is the reflection of their arrogance and that this situation resulted from a basic American ethnocentric attitude, which consisted of judging other people by using American customs and standards, or worse, by judging other people's customs and standards as inferior to the American ones.

Tracing a parallel between the Viet Nam War and the Iraq War, Robert G. Kaiser, an associate editor of the *Washington Post*, who covered the Viet Nam War in 1969 and 1970, recently wrote: "In truth, we are ethnocentric to a fault, certain of our superiority, convinced that others see us as we do, blithely indifferent to cultural, political and historical realities far different from our own. These failings—more than any tactical or strategic errors—help explain the U.S. catastrophes in Viet Nam and Iraq."[4] While the assertion in the second proposition is debatable, few would deny the truth as described in the first one.

This ethnocentric attitude and the resulting language barrier may explain why, for example, when Hollywood made the movie *BAT 21* in 1998 about the dramatic rescue of an American pilot shot down in Quang Tri province in 1972, it left out the key member of the rescue team: He was South Vietnamese Petty Officer Nguyen

Van Kiet, who spent eleven days behind enemy lines helping to locate the downed pilot. For his heroic action, Kiet was awarded the U.S. Navy Cross, the highest award that can be given to a foreign combatant.

In my opinion, the scarcity of information regarding the performance of ARVN troops was often due to the tendency for self-aggrandizement on the part of some American advisors. "Victory has many children, defeat is an orphan," goes a saying. In laying claims to the lion's share in the victory of a battle, such as the successful defense of An Loc, they tended—sometimes unintentionally—to minimize the contribution of the units they were advising. Even General Hollingsworth —who had given due credit to the "little ARVN soldier"—seemed, at times, to have been carried away. In his book *Reporting Viet Nam; Media and Military at War*, William M. Hammond reported that General Hollingsworth declared during an interview with *Newsweek* that he intended to "kill" all of the An Loc attackers before they returned to Cambodia. In a subsequent taped interview with CBS News, Hollingsworth said he had refused to approve the Red Cross's proposal to declare a temporary cease-fire in order to evacuate the wounded. Hammond added that: "Since it was clear that Hollingsworth considered himself the commander at An Loc even though a South Vietnamese officer was technically in charge, the remark contradicted U.S. assertions that the South Vietnamese were in total control of their own affairs. Soon after the interview appeared, indeed, an angry General Abrams instructed Hollingsworth to shut his mouth."[5] ARVN officers in III Corps held General Hollingsworth in high esteem; they appreciated his determination and invaluable contribution to the An Loc victory. Sadly, good men with the best of intentions are not immune to mistakes.

It is no secret, on the other hand, that for one reason or another, the U.S. media was biased—if not outright hostile—to the Viet Nam War. The war was presented from the most unfavorable angles with the media sensationalizing the news and distorting the truth if necessary to achieve its antiwar objectives. During the 1968 Tet Offensive, for example, in the heavily damaged Ben Tre province in the Mekong Delta, an unnamed U.S. advisor, in response to reporters' remarks about the destruction of the city, stated that "it became necessary to destroy Ben Tre in order to save it." This unfortunate remark has since been used time and again by antiwar activists and politicians. In his book *Reporting Viet Nam*, William Hammond wrote, "The *New York Times* seized upon the remark as soon as it appeared. So did *Time*. From there it passed into the lore of the war to become one of the most serviceable icons of the antiwar movement."[6] Under these conditions, reporting the victory of An Loc would contradict the U.S. media's basic premise that the war cannot be won because the ARVN was a corrupt and ineffective force.

I believe that it is time to set the record straight. Without denying the tremendous contribution of the U.S. advisors and pilots to the success of An Loc, this book is written primarily to tell the South Vietnamese side of the story and, more importantly, to render justice to the little South Vietnamese soldier who withstood ninety-four days of horror and prevailed.

One of the primary sources for this book is the ARVN/Joint General Staff's report published in 1973, titled *Tran Binh Long* (The Battle of Binh Long). This report, in particular, contains useful statistical data on the Battle of An Loc, including the rescue operations on Route Nationale 13.

In researching my book, I relied heavily on multiple Vietnamese-language writings on An Loc which were made available after 1975. In particular, Brig. Gen. Tran Van Nhut, former Binh Long province chief, provided invaluable information relative to the performance of provincial forces during the siege in his memoir *Cuoc Chien Dang Do*[7] (Unfinished War). A new book *Chien Thang An Loc*[8] (The Victory of An Loc) published in 2007 by Lt. Col. Nguyen Ngoc Anh, former Assistant for Operations, ARVN III Corps, on the other hand, provided insightful information on staff activities and decision-making process at III Corps Headquarters.

I would like to thank Brig. Gen. Mach Van Truong, former 8th Regiment commander, who has provided me with his personal account of the performance of the 5th ARVN Division units in An Loc. My deep appreciation goes to Col. Phan Van Huan, former 81st Airborne Commando Group, for having made available to me copies of old Airborne Commando editions relating the activities of this elite unit during the last stages of the siege.

I am especially indebted to numerous fellow officers who readily responded to my requests for interviews or provided me with invaluable historical documents relating to the Battle of An Loc. My special thanks to Col. Nguyen Dinh Sach, former chief of staff, 21st Division, for having provided me with a compilation of various narratives from former officers of that division, who had participated in the relief operation on Route Nationale 13.

My deepest gratitude, however, goes to my comrades-in-arms who had given their lives in the defense of the city. After the war, the grateful people of An Loc erected a special monument in honor of the fallen soldiers of the 81st Airborne Commando Group. Inscribed on the monument was the following epitaph:

"An Loc Xa Vang Danh Chien Dia
Biet Cach Du Vi Quoc Vong Than."

(In An Loc, which reverberates the fame of the Battleground,
The Airborne Commandos gave their lives for the nation.)

Although the elite airborne commandos had particularly distinguished themselves during the siege, credit should be given to all defenders of An Loc, regulars as well as territorials, who had prevailed against heavy odds. They have inspired me throughout this book and were a source of constant encouragement for me to carry out this major undertaking. To all these "unsung heroes," I dedicate this book.

One

The Sieges of the Indochina Wars

In *Valley of Decision*,[1] John Prados and Ray W. Stubbe reported that at the height of the siege of Khe Sanh, in February 1968, Gen. William C. Westmoreland asked Col. Reamer W. Argo, command historian, to make a study comparing Khe Sanh with past sieges and to recommend a course of action for the embattled garrison. Argo and his team found that of the fifteen sieges identified during the twentieth century, defenders resisted successfully only in two instances: the Russians at Leningrad (1941–1944) and the Americans at Bastogne (1944).

If asked about the successful sieges in the military history of Viet Nam, it is doubtful that the command historian would know that toward the end of the eighteenth century, at the port of Quy Nhon, 280 miles southeast of Khe Sanh, Gen. Vo Tanh, on orders from Emperor Nguyen Anh, held out for two years (from 1779 to 1801) against the Grand Army of Tay Son, preventing the latter from linking up with its navy in order to launch a coordinated attack on the cities of Phan Thiet and Gia Dinh in the south. The heroic stand of Vo Tanh also allowed Emperor Nguyen Anh's army to bypass the siege of Quy Nhon to capture Hue on February 2, 1801, and eventually unify the country under the Nguyens' rule.

Of course, Colonel Argo couldn't predict that four years after his presentation, history would record another siege where the defenders resisted successfully: the South Vietnamese at An Loc (1972).

To study the battle of An Loc it is necessary to compare it with other important sieges of the Indochina Wars. The description of the battle of Dien Bien Phu, in particular, would allow for a comparative study with An Loc, not only in terms of strength, terrain, tactics, and fire support, but also in terms of leadership traits of the respective commanders. On the other hand, the study of the siege of Khe Sanh and its subsequent abandonment amid growing concerns about a repeat of Dien Bien Phu would help explain why the NVA was able to move supplies and men into the battlefields in South Viet Nam in the late 1960s, and build up its forces in the run-up to their 1972 offensive in Binh Long province in MRIII.

A brief review of major political and military developments in 1949–1951 will help us understand French defense strategy in North Viet Nam and its decision to establish the fortified bases of Nasan and Dien Bien Phu in 1952 and 1953 respectively.

In October 1949, Mao Tse-tung took over China and since there was no controlled border between China and Viet Nam, the Viet Minh (VM) started to receive increased military aid directly from the Chinese Communist regime, which transferred to them modern, U.S.-supplied weaponry captured from Chang Kai-shek's defeated Nationalist Army, including artillery guns.

With increased military aid from the Communist bloc, the Viet Minh was able to form three regular divisions (304th, 308th, and 312th) in 1950, by incorporating their independent regiments in North Viet Nam and in the northern part of Central Viet Nam. To counter-balance the massive Chinese aid to the Viet Minh, Mr. Dean Acheson, U.S. Secretary of State, recommended military assistance to the French forces in Indochina and called for the creation of a Vietnamese National Army in early 1950; the first military equipment began to arrive in October the same year.

In October 1950, under pressure, the French decided to abandon the border garrison of Cao Bang. The French rescuing columns—consisting of four battalions of Legionnaires, paratroopers and Moroccan *Tirailleurs*—progressing on Route Coloniale (RC) 4 were ambushed by the VM 308th Division and 209th Regiment. Many units were completely wiped out and the survivors had to abandon their wounded and disperse in small units through the dense forests bordering RC4. The French suffered over 7,000 casualties during the withdrawal operation. The French also lost 13 105mm howitzers, 125 mortars, 480 military vehicles, 3 armored platoons, 940 machineguns and over 8,000 rifles (these losses included weapons that were in storage).[2]

It was estimated the above losses could be used to equip two VM divisions. Stunned by the Cao Bang disaster, the French decided to abandon Lang Son. In Lang Son, the French left 1,300 tons of ammunition and other military supplies they didn't have time to destroy.[3]

To exploit their victories at Cao Bang and Lang Son, in January 1951 the Viet Minh launched a daring attack on Vinh Yen, just twenty-five miles west of Hanoi with the 308th and 312th Divisions, but Gen. Vo Nguyen Giap's first attempt at conventional warfare was defeated by the timely reinforcement of the battlefield by Gen. Jean De Lattre de Tassigny, the new Commander-in-Chief of French forces in Indochina and the use for the first time in Viet Nam of napalm bombs supplied by the United States. The Viet Minh suffered 6,000 casualties and 500 prisoners were captured. The French losses were about half those of the Viet Minh. [4]

Nasan (November–December 1952)

In October 1952, Gen. Raoul Salan, who had replaced Gen. De Lattre de Tassigny—diagnosed with inoperable cancer the previous year—launched Operation *Lorraine* aimed at diverting Viet Minh forces from the Red River Delta and cutting the enemy rear lines of communications in the strategic Thai Highlands near the Laotian border. But Vo Nguyen Giap refused to engage the French forces and *Lorraine* was forced to withdraw without achieving its goals.

To thwart the Viet Minh's threat to the Thai Highlands and North-Laos, General Salan took advantage of *Lorraine* to establish in November 1952 a fortified base at Nasan, approximately 120 miles west of Hanoi. Salan believed that it was too dangerous to venture on narrow and tortuous roads through the forested mountains of the Thai country and that the best way to fight the Viet Minh there was to rely instead on strong bases built around an airstrip in selected strategic areas. The new concept of the "air-ground base"—a term coined by Martin Windrow,[5] an Associate of the Royal Historical Society in Great Britain—would allow the French to establish a presence in the Thai country, to reinforce and resupply the garrison by air and to destroy the attacking forces with superior artillery fire and air power.

Nasan is a two-kilometer-long and one-kilometer-wide valley surrounded by small rolling hills. It had an airstrip that could accommodate transportation aircraft in use in the French Army at the time. Salan occupied Nasan with three paratroop battalions, five infantry battalions, one engineer battalion, and one armored reconnaissance company. The defending units included the newly formed 31st VN Groupement Mobile (GM) consisting of two infantry battalions and one artillery battalion. The Nasan garrison was commanded by Colonel Gilles, the paratroop commander.

In installing the fortified Nasan base, Salan wanted to achieve three goals: a) to assemble the small garrisons located in the northwest and southeast of Nasan and to save them from being overrun by the Viet Minh; b) to thwart the enemy's attempt to take over the Thai Highlands; and c) to induce the enemy to attack and to destroy their regular forces by artillery and air power. [6]

True to Salan's expectations, the Viet Minh began to launch probing attacks on the night of November 23. During the nights of November 30 and December 1, the Viet Minh attacked in force and succeeded in capturing two outer strongpoints. The latter were retaken by counter-attacks by the units from the inner ring of defensive positions. At one point, the French had to drop paratroopers on the top of one of the hills captured by the Viet Minh to attack downhill and destroy the enemy in their bunkers. The Vietnamese artillery battalion from the 31st VN GM inflicted heavy casualties on the attackers during two days of fighting. Due to the lack of enemy artillery and anti-aircraft, the French Air force was able to maintain supply and casualty evacuation flights.

The French reported the Viet Minh suffered 5,000 losses during the battle of Nasan.[7] The French losses were modest and the "air-ground base" concept had subsequently gained acceptance within French military circles. Colonel Gilles, commander of the troops in Nasan, was elevated to brigadier-general for his successful defense of the fortified base.

Dien Bien Phu (November 1953–May 1954)

In May 1953, Gen. Henri Navarre assumed command of the French forces in Indochina. Convinced of the effectiveness of the "air-ground base"concept—which had been hailed as a great success in Nasan the previous year—Navarre decided to install a bigger *camp retranché* at Dien Bien Phu, a densely populated Thai village located near the Laotian border, approximately 300 kilometers west of Hanoi and 180 kilometers northeast of Luang Prabang, the royal capital of Laos.

Dien Bien Phu is a long valley traversed by the Nam Youm River and surrounded by a ring of mountains located at a distance of ten to twelve kilometers from the center of the *camp retranché*. The garrison itself held a perimeter of approximately sixteen by nine kilometers. General Navarre believed that the Dien Bien Phu camp would be out of range of enemy artillery if they positioned their batteries on the other side of the mountains. And if they put their batteries on the slopes facing the base, they would be easy targets for French artillery and warplanes.

According to Navarre, a fortified "air-ground base" at the heart of the Thai country would help achieve the following objectives: a) to force the Viet Minh to accept a *bataille rangée* in which the French had superiority in firepower and supply; b) to prevent the Viet Minh from reinforcing the coastal regions of Central Viet Nam that the French planned to pacify; c) to establish a barrier to interdict VM forces from attacking North-Laos; and d) to use Dien Bien Phu as a springboard to attack the enemy's rear in case the latter renewed their offensive on the Red River Delta.[8]

In November 1953, the French launched Operation *Castor* to reoccupy Dien Bien Phu, which had been lost to the Viet Minh in November the previous year. On November 11, General Gilles and three French paratroop battalions were dropped into the valley of Dien Bien Phu. They met only scattered resistance from VM local units. After the successful air drop and the occupation of Dien Bien Phu, General Gilles was replaced by Colonel De Castries, an armor officer with extensive combat experience.

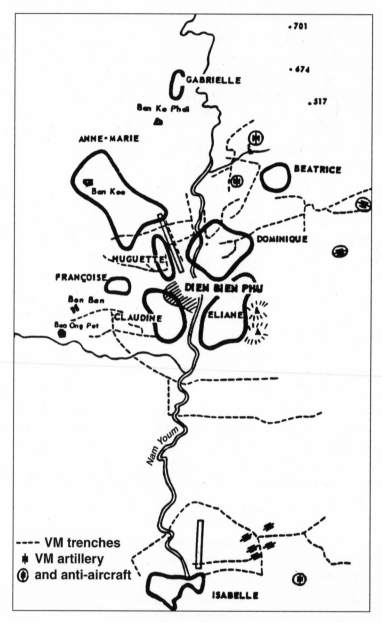

Map 2: Dien Bien Phu

Dien Bien Phu was a complex of multi-strongpoints consisting of three distinct sectors:

—The central sector with five strongpoints (Anne Marie, Huguette, Claudine, Eliane, and Dominique) surrounding the airstrip.

—The northern sector consisting of two strongpoints (Beatrice and Gabrielle) established on two hills overlooking the valley.

—Strongpoint Isabelle, located six kilometers south of the central sector; adjacent to this strongpoint was an old airstrip that was out of service.[9]

In March 1954, at the beginning of the major attack, the Dien Bien Phu camp had twelve infantry battalions (including the 5th VN Airborne Battalion). The artillery units supporting Dien Bien Phu consisted of 24 105mm howitzers, 4 155mm howitzers and 22 120mm mortars.

The French also had one armored company (-) at Dien Bien Phu with ten M-24 tanks. In addition, six Bearcat fighters and ten light observation aircraft were available at Dien Bien Phu for tactical air support and reconnaissance.[10]

To prepare for the attack, from mid-December 1953 to the end of January 1954, Giap engaged the 308th and 312th Divisions, three regiments from the 316th and 304th Divisions, and one independent regiment. The attacking forces were supported by 36 105mm howitzers, 15 75mm guns, 20 120mm mortars and 36 37mm anti-aircraft guns from the 351st Artillery Division.[11] The attacking force, including supporting units, was estimated at about 30,000 men, not counting over 30,000 civilian laborers responsible for repairing roads and carrying ammunition and supplies to the front.

The Viet Minh attacked the northern strongpoints in force on March 13. Elements of the 308th Division and 312th Divisions, supported by powerful artillery preparations, quickly overran strongpoint Beatrice with repeated human-wave assaults. Gabrielle offered furious resistance but was overrun on March 15. The French were completely taken by surprise by the effectiveness of the enemy direct artillery fire from their batteries well bunkered on the hill slopes facing Dien Bien Phu. The constant shelling of the airfield by the VM artillery and anti-aircraft fire made its use precarious from the beginning of the attack. The airfield was completely closed on March 28, limiting resupply and reinforcement by air drops into the steadily shrinking perimeter. Worse, the Thai units, frightened by the deadly enemy shelling, began to desert en masse after the first attacks, causing the French to reorganize their defense system and to reduce further the perimeter.

The Viet Minh launched a new attack during the night of March 30. Elements of the 312th Division and 316th Division succeeded in capturing parts of strongpoints Eliane and Dominique in the central sector after furious had-to-hand combat. The piecemeal reinforcement by nightly airdrops of paratroopers was used mainly to replace casualties and the lack of reserves prevented the French from mounting any significant counter-attack to recapture the lost positions.

After April 7, the situation became relatively calm and the Viet Minh took advantage of that respite to dig new trenches deep into French positions. To encourage and show support for the garrison, the French government decided to elevate all defenders to the next higher rank. De Castries was made a brigadier-general, and his new rank insignia had to be airdropped into the camp.

The final assault began on May 6. The Viet Minh overran the remaining positions on Eliane immediately east of the central sector. In the southwest, the defense of Claudine collapsed after repeated enemy human-wave assaults. On the morning of May 7, the Viet Minh attacked the last French positions around General De Castries' command post. De Castries knew the situation was hopeless; he asked Hanoi for permission to surrender to save what was left of the battered garrison. Hanoi agreed to let him act according to the circumstances. Dien Bien Phu surrendered to the enemy at 5:00 P.M. the same day.

French losses were 8,221, including 1,571 killed; 11,721 were made prisoners. According to a French document, the Viet Minh losses amounted to 9,500 killed.[12]

The Dien Bien Phu disaster marked the end of the French presence in Indochina and sparked a chain of political events leading to the involvement of the United States in this part of the world, in compliance with its post-World War II "containment" policy. Under this concept, the U.S. objective was to "contain" Communist expansion in South East Asia by supporting a non-Communist government in South Viet Nam.

General Navarre, the commander of French forces in Indochina, was relieved of his command on June 4; the French government fell on June 12. The new French Prime Minister Mendes-France promised to achieve a cease-fire within one month. Peace talks, instigated by the French government during the battle of Dien Bien Phu, had begun at Geneva on May 8. The Geneva Accords were signed in July. The agreement stipulated that Viet Nam would be partitioned at the 17th parallel and a general election would be held in two years, in 1956. Mr. Ngo Dinh Diem, back from exile in the United States, was appointed prime minister of the post-war government in the South. On October 23, 1955, Mr. Diem, having consolidated his political power, organized a national referendum, which resulted in the overthrow of Emperor Bao Dai and the formation of the First Republic. Mr. Diem, the new President of South Viet Nam, renounced the Geneva Accords.

One of the reasons—often ignored—of the French defeat in Indochina was the lack of unity of purpose among the participants. While the United States, which provided military aid to the French forces, was counting on the French to fight a proxy war to thwart Communist expansion in South East Asia, the French were pursuing their own interests in their former colonies. In the meantime, the Vietnamese, Cambodians, and Laotians—who were fighting with the French against Communist domination—also fought for the ultimate political liberation of their countries from French colonial rule. Thus, France, to the very end, had failed to spell out clearly her objectives in Indochina, and to build a consensus for the prosecution of a controversial and unpopular war.

Another cause of the failure of French policy in Indochina, in my opinion, was France's opposition to any progressive and orderly development of the States of Indochina toward true independence in concert with the emergence of genuine nationalist governments and, more importantly, the early creation of strong national armies.

The following table sums up the evolution of the Vietnamese National Army from 1949 to July 1954, the date of the signing of the Geneva Accords:[13]

Year	Regular Force	Auxiliary Force	Total
1949			45,000
1950			65,000
1951			110,000
1952	94,520	53,280	147,800
1953	151,020	47,000	198,020
1954	167,700	37,800	205,500

Please note that the numbers shown on the above table for 1949 to 1951 include the effective forces of various paramilitary units and armed religious groups in existence at the time.

The following table shows the comparative strength of the National Army and the Viet Minh regular forces at the end of 1952:[14]

National Army: 94,520, consisting of:
- 57 infantry battalions
- 5 airborne battalions
- 3 artillery battalions
- 6 reconnaissance armored squadrons
- Various combat support units

Viet Minh: 270,000, consisting of:
- 6 infantry divisions: 304, 308, 312, 316, 320, 325
- 1 artillery division
- 8 engineer battalions

In 1954, when Gen. Vo Nguyen Giap hurled his regular divisions against the embattled French forces in Dien Bien Phu, the National Army still operated mostly at battalion level. Although it was decided to create six regimental task forces or Groupements Mobiles (GM) in 1952, only four of them actually participated in combat operations before the end of the Indochina War.

Following the French disengagement from Indochina, in April 1956, the U.S. Military Assistance and Advisory Group (MAAG) was established in Saigon to take over the training of the South Vietnamese armed forces from the French. In December 1960, the Communists announced the formation of the National Liberation Front (NLF), the political arm of the Viet Cong (VC) and in May 1961, President Kennedy decided to send a contingent of Special Forces to help fight the fledging communist insurgency in South Viet Nam. In February the following year, MAAG became U.S. Military Assistance Command, Viet Nam (MACV) under Gen. Paul Harkins.

In the meantime, the Diem regime became increasingly more repressive. Diem tolerated no organized opposition; his critics were harassed or arrested and his decrees became laws. On January 2, 1963, the VC scored a psychological victory in the Mekong Delta: for the first time, a VC battalion stood up and fought against regular ARVN units at Ap Bac in Dinh Tuong province, causing moderate losses to a unit of the 7th Division. The government crackdown on the Buddhists in the fall triggered an increasingly powerful anti-Diem movement. As the political and military situation worsened, a group of generals led by Lt. Gen. Duong Van Minh staged a *coup d'etat* to overthrow the Diem regime. President Diem and his brother, Mr. Nhu, were assassinated on November 2, 1963.

Khe Sanh (January–April 1968)

In June 1964, Gen. Williams Westmoreland took over the command of MACV. By that time, Hanoi, taking advantage of the political instability in Saigon in the post-Diem era, had begun to send NVA regular units to reinforce the VC in the South.

On August 4, 1964, two U.S. destroyers on routine patrol in the Gulf of Tonkin reported torpedo attack; they returned fire and sank two North Vietnamese PT boats. On August 7, the U.S. Congress passed the Gulf of Tonkin Resolution, authorizing President Johnson to send troops to Viet Nam.

On March 8, 1965, a U.S Marine task force of 3,500 men landed in Danang. This was the beginning of a massive U.S. build-up reaching 549,000 men in 1968 at the peak of the Viet Nam War.

Parallel to this American build-up, a gradual change in military strategy took place. When the first U.S. units arrived in South Viet Nam in 1965, their mission was only to defend the airbases and protect the populated areas and logistical installations in the coastal areas under the "enclave concept." In June 1965, the American ground troops were allowed to conduct offensive operations anywhere in South Viet Nam. General Westmoreland's concept of "search and destroy"—sometimes called "big units warfare"—replaced the old concept of enclave. The objective of this new strategy was to inflict defeat on the enemy, rather than simply deny him victory.

In 1967, Westmoreland, concerned about increased enemy infiltration from Laos, ordered the U.S. III Marine Amphibious Force (III MAF)—which was responsible for tactical operations in the five northernmost provinces of South Viet Nam—to fortify and reinforce the Khe Sanh base situated on Route 9, about seven miles from the Laotian border.[15]

The village of Khe Sanh was the seat of Huong Hoa district, an area consisting mostly of Bru Montagnard villages and coffee plantations. Back in 1962, the Special Forces had built an airfield outside the village at the site of the old French fort. In 1967, Khe Sanh base was occupied by various U.S. Marine units as an outpost on the Marines' western flank.

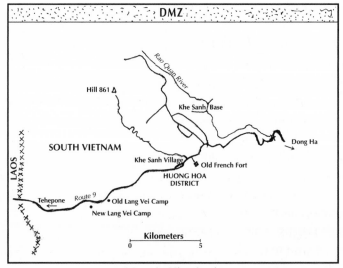

Map 3: Khe Sanh

In April 1967, two battalions from the 3rd Marine Regiment reinforced Khe Sanh and were ordered to dislodge NVA units from the strategic hills northwest of the base. The enemy was driven out of this area after heavy engagements. Enemy losses amounted to 940 casualties. The Marines suffered 165 killed and 425 wounded.[16]

In January 21, 1968, elements of the 325th NVA Division attacked Hill 861, five kilometers northwest of Khe Sanh; the enemy was beaten back after heavy close-quarters combat. At the same time, the NVA shelled Khe Sanh base with hundreds of mortar rounds and 122mm rockets. One artillery shell scored a direct hit on the main ammunition depot and set off a series of detonations. At the time of the NVA artillery attack, Khe Sanh was manned by three battalions of the 26th Marines under the command of Colonel Lownds.

Coincidental with the artillery barrage on Khe Sanh base, elements of the 304th NVA Division attacked the Huong Hoa district headquarters. The ethnic Bru members of the Civilian Irregular Defense Group (CIDG) and ARVN Regional Force held out until the next morning, when the survivors were picked up by Marine helicopters. The presence of the 304th NVA Division in the area prompted the 3rd Marine Division to reinforce Khe Sanh with one battalion from the 9th Marine Regiment on January 22. Five days later, ARVN I Corps sent the 37th ARVN Ranger Battalion to Khe Sanh to reinforce the defense of the garrison.[17]

On January 30, 1968, the second day of the new Year of the Monkey, the VC, violating the customary three-day truce on that special occasion, launched a massive attack on major urban centers in South Viet Nam, including Saigon. The situation around Khe Sanh remained calm but the Imperial City of Hue received the brunt of the VC thrust. The enemy occupied most of the city in the first few days and the 1st ARVN Infantry Division headquarters, trapped inside the Citadel, was under heavy attack.

On February 7, as if to sow confusion with regard to the enemy's main thrust, elements of the NVA 304th Division, supported by twelve PT-76 tanks (Russian-built light amphibious reconnaissance tanks equipped with a 76.2mm gun), overran the Special Forces base at Lang Vei on Road 9, ten kilometers southwest of Khe Sanh. The Special Forces team and the Bru CIDGs managed, however, to destroy some of the tanks. The next day, the Marines at Khe Sanh base sent helicopters to pick up the survivors. The CIDGs suffered 200 killed or missing and 75 wounded. The U.S Special Forces team losses amounted to ten killed and eleven wounded.[18]

The NVA launched their biggest artillery bombardment on February 23. Over 1,000 rounds of 130mm and 152mm hit Khe Sanh base during eight hours, killing ten and wounding fifty-one.[19] On February 28, elements of the 304th Division attacked the 37th ARVN Ranger Battalion on the eastern perimeter of Khe Sanh base. Supported by Marine artillery, the rangers beat back multiple enemy assaults.

The situation quieted down during the month of March. Under pressure from Washington, which was concerned about a repeat of Dien Bien Phu, General Westmoreland ordered the U.S. 1st Cavalry Division, reinforced with ARVN 3rd Airborne Brigade, to launch Operation *Pegasus* to relieve the Khe Sanh garrison. The relief operation, which began April 1, met light resistance; it ended April 8, when elements of the 7th Cavalry Brigade linked up with the Marines at Khe Sanh.[20]

General Westmoreland, however, insisted that Khe Sanh continue to be occupied, albeit by a smaller Marine unit. One week after he left Viet Nam, on June 11, his successor, Gen. Creighton W. Abrams ordered the destruction and evacuation of the Khe Sanh combat base.

In *Valley of Decision*, Prados and Stubbe reported that, over the length of the siege, "tactical aircraft delivered 39,179 tons of ordnance against 59,542 brought by B-52s. That amounts to almost 1,300 tons of bombs around Khe Sanh, the equivalent of 1.3-kiloton tactical nuclear weapon, *every day of the siege*. Allied aircraft were delivering approximately five tons of bombs for every one of 20,000 NVA soldiers initially estimated to be in the Khe Sanh area, or more than 15 tons per man measured against roughly 6,450 Marines and ARVN troops in the garrison."[21] It was estimated that NVA lost from 10,000 to 15,000 KIA during the siege of Khe Sanh versus U.S. official casualties figures of 205 KIA, 1,668 wounded, and 25 missing and presumed dead.[22] (These figures included only U.S. Marines casualties and not losses of U.S. Special Forces units in Lang Vei village and losses incurred by helicopters and air force crews.)

In February 1968, Khe Sanh was used again as a base for a new—and the last—incursion into Laos: At the instigation of the Americans, ARVN troops launched Operation *Lam Son 719* to destroy NVA's supply line to the South. The White House and the Pentagon reasoned that if successful, the attack into Cambodia and Laos would secure the safe withdrawal of the American troops in South Viet Nam. ARVN units were heavily engaged by NVA divisions on Route 9 and suffered a large number of casualties. On March 6, ARVN troops launched a successful air assault into Tchepone, the objective of the attack, and discovered many enemy bodies. However, they failed to destroy the enemy depots and logistical installations, because by then the NVA had moved their supplies South through new roads which bypassed Tchepone.

The failure of Lam Son 719 to destroy NVA supplies, the abandonment of Khe Sanh, and the subsequent drawdown of U.S. troops gave Hanoi a free hand to send materials and men to build up their forces in the South in preparation for their 1972 Easter invasion.

Two

Setting the Stage

Tay Ninh, Binh Long, Phuoc Long, Long Khanh, and Binh Tuy, the northern provinces of Military Region III (MRIII), with their dense forests, small hills, and low elevations, offer a sharp contrast to the lush and flat rice fields immediately to the south. They form a natural arc extending from Cambodia to the west and north to the South China Sea to the east. This area constitutes the southernmost foothills of the *Chaine Annamitique* and a quasi-buffer zone between the Mekong Delta and the Central Highlands.

The area known as *Dong Nai Thuong* (Upper Valley of Deer)—squeezed between the Song Be River to the east and the Saigon River to the west—contains some of the most beautiful forests consisting of a vide variety of tropical trees—including teaks and other precious species. It also contains some of the richest rubber plantations in the world. At the beginning of the twentieth century, after the situation in Indochina had been temporarily stabilized, the French colonialists began to exploit this fertile region in conjunction with large swaths of uncultivated lands in adjacent Cambodia to plant rubber trees. The soil in this area, in fact, contains a red laterite clay that is very suitable to the culture of rubber trees. Two administrative agencies were established at Hon Quan (1908) and Ba Ra (1920) to supervise the forest abatement and road construction projects. Two Routes Nationales (RN) as well as a railway linking Saigon to Loc Ninh were built. These arteries served to transport rubber from the

French plantations in Krek, Chup, Prek, Kompong Cham, Snoul, and Peanch Chang in Cambodia, and Binh Long, Phuoc Long, Binh Duong, and Bien Hoa, to Saigon, for exportation.

The various French plantations in the area formed an association called *Société Des Plantations Des Terres Rouges* (Society of the Plantations of the Red Lands). The French *colons* who owned these plantations lived in huge mansions complete with tennis courts, swimming pools, and Cambodian and Montagnard servants. (It is worth noting that the word "montagnards"—which has a distinct racial connotation—was given by the French to the tribes who lived in the *montagnes;* the Vietnamese preferred to call them *Nguoi Thuong* or Highlanders, as opposed to *Nguoi Kinh* or Lowlanders.) The luxurious life of these French *colons* was, in certain aspects, reminiscent of the life of the former American plantation owners in the South. Most of these French plantations also contained small runways of *terre battue,* which could accommodate small single-engine aircraft called *les Moranes.* (These aircraft were used as observation planes in the French Army during the Indochina War.) It was no secret that, under the French Colonial administration, some of these planteurs used these light and versatile airplanes to smuggle opium from Laos that they resold with impunity at exorbitant prices to the Chinese *fumeries* in Cho Lon.

Due to a shortage of labor in the South, the French planteurs often recruited workers from North and Central Viet Nam and also from local Montagnard tribes of Stieng, Biet, and Mnong. These workers were exploited and maltreated by the French *colons.* Many died of malaria or other tropical diseases. Not surprisingly, many of these workers were indoctrinated by the Communist cadres who professed to fight against "imperialist oppression"; they formed their own political cells and some of them later became high-ranking officials in the Communist regime. Most notorious among them was Le Duc Anh, a former plantation worker at Loc Ninh in the old Thu Dau Mot province. He was the right-hand man for one of the French planteurs, and unconfirmed reports indicated that he, at one time, had even worked for the French intelligence. Le Duc Anh later became a general and even rose to the position of President of Communist Viet Nam after the war.

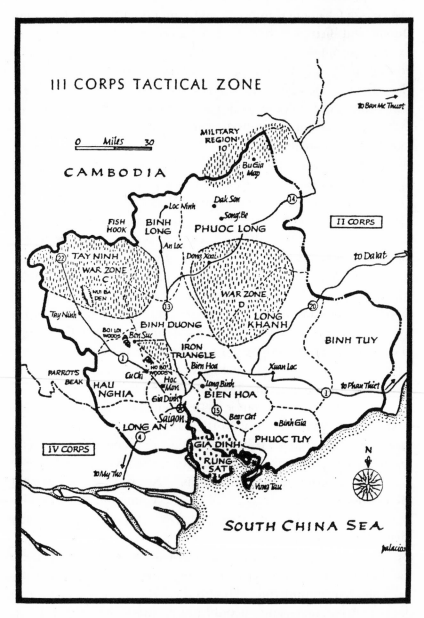

Map 4: Military Region III

Of the above five provinces, Binh Long held a special strategic importance, not only because of its proximity to Cambodia, but also because it is traversed by two important arteries: Route Nationale 13 (RN13) linking Saigon to Cambodia and Route Nationale 14 (RN14) leading to Ban Me Thuot and the Central Highlands. Binh Long was also located between two important enemy secret bases: the "War Zone C" in the west and the "War Zone D" in the east. These bases dated back to the Indochina War and were used by the Viet Minh as their safe sanctuaries.

Route Nationale 13, the natural avenue of approach to Saigon for NVA forces in Cambodia, ran the entire length of Binh Long province and bisected it into two almost equal parts. From the district town of Chon Thanh to Binh Long's capital city of An Loc—located about thirty kilometers north—Route 13 traversed successively the towns of Tau O, Tan Khai, Xa Cat, Xa Trach, and Xa Cam. It passed through the district town of Loc Ninh, eighteen kilometers north of An Loc, before reaching the Cambodian city of Snoul. Just south of Tau O was marshy and open terrain, which constituted a formidable natural barrier for attacking units moving from the south. The slightly elevated railway running a few hundred meters east of Route 13, on the other hand, provided good protection for enemy ambushing forces.

Since 1832, under the reign of Emperor Minh Mang, Hon Quan, the future capital city of Binh Long, was part of Bien Hoa province. Under the French Colonial administration, Binh Long area was annexed to Thu Dau Mot (also known as Binh Duong) province. Under President Ngo Dinh Diem, certain districts were upgraded to province status for administrative and strategic reasons. Thus, in 1956, the northern part of Binh Duong province with the districts of Loc Ninh, Hon Quan, and Chon Thanh, was integrated into the new Binh Long province and the small district town of Hon Quan on Route 13 was renamed An Loc and made its capital city. "Binh Long" in Vietnamese means peaceful and noble ("Binh" means peace and "Long" means dragon, which is also the symbol of royalty), and "An Loc" means safe and prosperous. Ironically, by a tragic twist of fate, this province of the Valley of Deer that was destined to be peaceful and noble, and its capital city that was destined to be safe and prosperous, were to be the victims of the most savage and murderous offensive of both the Indochina and Viet Nam Wars, and Route 13, with its unlucky number, was to become one of the bloodiest roads of Viet Nam, if not of the world.

With a total area of 2,240 square kilometers and a population of about 76,000, Binh Long was one of the smallest provinces of South Viet Nam. One third of the population consisted of ethnic Montagnards of different tribes, and most of them lived in small villages around Loc Ninh. In early 1970, Col. Tran Van Nhut, commander of the 48th Regiment, 18th ARVN Division in Long Khanh province, was appointed the new Binh Long province chief by Lt. Gen. Do Cao Tri, III Corps Commander. At the beginning of 1967, Gen. Nguyen Cao Ky, the then-prime minister and a political rival of General Thieu, had started to get rid of the latter's supporters in preparation for the upcoming presidential elections. As it was a common practice at that time to get rid of politically undesirable generals by sending them overseas as ambassadors, General Tri, a staunch supporter of President Thieu, was appointed ambassador to Seoul, South Korea. In September 1967, after General Thieu won the presidential election, General Tri was recalled from Seoul to take over the important III Corps whose units were responsible for the security of the capital.

Colonel Nhut, a former Marine officer, had distinguished himself in 1968, when, as a commander of the 18th Division training center, he repulsed the attack on the center by Regiment 275, 5th NVA Division, inflicting heavy losses on the enemy (over fifty bodies left on the terrain, many weapons captured). He was personally awarded the U.S. Silver Star by Gen. Creighton Abrams for this achievement. When Brig. Gen. Lam Quang Tho, the 18th Division commander, conveyed General Tri's order of transfer, he advised Nhut that it would be in his best interests to decline the new position because, in General Tho's view, the command of a regiment offers more opportunities for advancement in the army. Nhut decided, however, to accept the new offer because he wanted to come back to the area where he grew up when his father worked in the lumber industry in Loc Ninh.

Nhut, who commanded a regiment in the same Military Region, admitted, however, that his first reaction was to figure out where Binh Long province was located and what its capital city was. The city of An Loc, in fact, with a population of 15,000 people and a total area of less than two square kilometers, was an anonymous little town with no military and political significance.

As the new Binh Long province chief, Nhut lost no time reinforcing the defense of the capital city of An Loc. He conducted intensive training of the provincial Regional Force (RF), Popular Force (PF), and People's Self-Defense Force (PSDF), and aggressively implemented the pacification program within the province, including improving relations with the ethnic Montagnards. Instead of using all his provincial forces in static defense, Nhut used two-thirds of these forces for patrols and mobile operations. He also sent the Provincial Reconnaissance teams and members of the PSDF, especially the local Montagnards disguised as civilians or farmers, to gather intelligence on enemy movements or infiltration in the forests and farmlands within the province.

The above forces, known as Territorial Forces, were drawn from the local populace and were responsible for the defense of their own towns and hamlets—or as a high-ranking U.S. advisor to the pacification program put it—the establishment of "an enduring government presence in the countryside." RF battalions and RF companies were assigned to provinces and districts respectively, while PF platoons were normally controlled by hamlet and village chiefs.

For many centuries, Vietnamese villages formed the basic political structures of the country and constituted close-knit social entities with their own rules.[1] While the district and province chiefs were appointed by the central government, the village councils as well as the village chiefs were directly elected by the people. Thus, one primordial—and often ignored—role of the Territorial Forces was that, by providing the security to the local population, and in particular to the elected village and hamlet chiefs, they were instrumental in safeguarding the grassroots democratic system in South Viet Nam.

In addition to the above Territorial Forces, Vietnamese citizens of all ages—including women and old men—were recruited into the People's Self-Defense Force. Against the opposition of some of his advisors, President Thieu decided to provide the PSDF with weapons. Commented Lewis Sorley, a noted author on Viet Nam, "Thieu argued in response that the government had to rest upon the support of the people, and it had little validity if it did not dare to arm them. The self-defense forces used those weapons not against their government, but to fight against Communist domination, in the process establishing conclusively that the Thieu government did have the support of its people."[2] It was the more remarkable that, as will be seen later, the killers of one of the NVA tanks during the first enemy attack on An Loc were three young members of the People's Self-Defense Force.

In February 1971, Gen. Do Cao Tri, considered one of the best field commanders in the South Vietnamese Army, was killed in a helicopter crash while directing an operation in Cambodia. Dubbed "the Patton of Viet Nam" by a foreign reporter, Tri led III Corps' mechanized task force deep into Cambodia and succeeded in destroying many important VC logistical bases. Also killed in this accident was François Sully, a reporter for *Newsweek*. (François Sully and Bernard Fall were French journalists during the Indochina War; both had become American citizens.)

General Tri's replacement was Lt. Gen. Nguyen Van Minh, commander of the Capital District (Saigon-Cho Lon and surrounding area) and a former commander of the 21st Infantry Division in the Mekong Delta. Minh was a member of what American reporters dubbed the "Delta Clan," known for its political ties to President Thieu.

This appellation may be too broad, because only senior commanders at the 21st Division, all staunch Thieu supporters, were later rewarded with good positions in the army and in the administration. Lt. Gen. Dang Van Quang, also known as "Fat Quang," was a case in point. A former 21st Division commander, Quang was given the command of IV Corps. After he was removed from his command for corruption by Gen. Nguyen Cao Ky, the then-prime minister, he was later elevated by Thieu to the position of Assistant to the President for National Security. In this capacity, Quang transferred Minh, his protégé, to the trusted position of commander of the Special Capital District during the 1968 Tet Offensive. In that position, Minh was not only in charge of the defense of Saigon but would also be in a position to ward off a possible coup d'etat against the Thieu regime during these chaotic months.

Minh had briefly served in a parachutist battalion in North Viet Nam during the Indochina War. Rumor had it that during his first airborne operation, he was struck on the head by a peasant armed with a shovel. This incident practically put an end to his brief career as a paratrooper. Minh was also known in the army as "Minh the Musician." He got this surname, not only because he was a fairly good guitar player when he was young, but also because he was all music to the ears of his superiors, telling them what they wanted to hear.

Minh enjoyed excellent relations with his American advisors; they considered him a good soldier who—more importantly—was willing to listen to their advice. General Minh's counterpart was Maj. Gen. James F. Hollingsworth, a graduate of Texas A&M University and a veteran of both World War II and the Korean War. As the III Corps senior advisor, General Hollingsworth was also the commander of the Third Regional Assistance Command (TRAC). Whereas his predecessor, the commander of II Field Force, was responsible for controlling the tactical operations of subordinate U.S. forces in MRIII, General Hollingsworth's main focus was to provide military advice and logistical assistance to his counterpart.

Not surprisingly, one of General Minh's first decisions after assuming command of III Corps was to replace major unit commanders with his associates from the Delta. The most crucial decision, no doubt, was the appointment of Colonel (later General) Le Van Hung to the position of 5th Division commander. During an incursion into Cambodia the previous year, the 5th Division was not deemed up to task; obviously new leadership was required to face new challenges caused by increased enemy activities in this strategic region and the disengagement of American troops under President Nixon's Vietnamization program. In Minh's view, Hung, a trusted and able regiment commander in MRIV, was the man he needed for that important position.

To General Minh's credit, Hung's appointment turned out to be a good move, because under Hung's leadership, the 5th Divi-

sion was to win what many believe to be the biggest battle of the
Indochina Wars. Hung was a former commander of the 31st Regiment, 21st Division. When I served in the Mekong Delta in the
mid-1960s, I heard glowing reports about Hung. He was known
as a brave soldier, a good leader, and one of the best regiment commanders in IV Corps. Thus, I was somewhat disturbed later to read
reports from American advisors depicting Hung as weak and indecisive during the battle of An Loc. Based on statements from Col.
William H. Miller, 5th Division senior advisor, Willbanks, for example, described Hung as a "demoralized" man, "totally indecisive
and unable to handle the stress of high-intensity combat."[3] In the
same vein, Andradé reported that "Brigadier General Le Van Hung
was devastated when the North Vietnamese opened the offensive in
northern Binh Long province."[4] I thought that the problem probably arose from the fact that Hung was a rather taciturn and independent man. He liked to act on his own and was not eager to listen
to the advice of his counterparts. General Hung "disliked overbear-
ing Americans who wanted the war fought according to American
rules," wrote Andradé. "This resentment colored Hung's relations
with U.S. officers since the early 1960s, garnering him a reputation
as "anti-American."[5] It is no secret that often, in the view of some
U.S. advisors and reporters, so-called "anti-American" ARVN officers could do nothing right, even when the outcome of the battle
clearly shows otherwise. Because Hung had undeniably won the
battle of An Loc, to demonstrate his point that the 5th Division
commander was "devastated" when NVA attacked Binh Long—
and not Tay Ninh—Colonel Miller had to speculate about Hung's
reaction. "Miller thought that Hung would probably be happy as
long as he could sit and do nothing, even if the entire country
burned around him in the meantime," wrote Andradé. "But now
the chips were down and Hung's worst fears had come true. The
North Vietnamese were putting his unit on center stage. The 5th
ARVN Division had to fight and Saigon would be watching."[6]

It is common knowledge, indeed, that friction and misunderstanding often happened in the relationship between ARVN field
commanders and their U.S. counterparts and that Vietnamese unit
commanders were sometimes subjected to the rudeness of their ad-

visors. When I was an artillery officer in I Corps in the late 1950s, for example, a U.S. senior advisor to a light infantry division near the DMZ held a routine inspection of the weapons of a division's unit and noticed a dirty rifle. He wiped its grease on the division commander's hand to demonstrate his point. This might not be considered unusual or impolite as far as the U.S. advisor was concerned, but this gesture constituted a supreme insult for the Vietnamese. The Vietnamese division commander slapped his American advisor and was subsequently relieved of his command.

In the early stage of the battle of An Loc, Colonel Miller suggested to General Hung that he relinquish his command to Colonel Nhut, Binh Long province chief.[7] Relinquishing a command in combat is an unacceptable loss of face and would have adversely affected the morale of the troops fighting in An Loc. On the other hand, if Colonel Miller was convinced that a change of leadership was necessary, he could have forwarded his recommendation to General Hollingsworth, who would in turn discuss it with General Minh, the III Corps commander. Colonel Miller's in-your-face suggestion, in my opinion, exemplified the attitude of arrogance I mentioned earlier.

Frances FitzGerald, the noted American journalist in Viet Nam, offered an interesting explanation of this American "colonialist" behavior in the following terms: "Covered with righteous platitudes," she wrote,

> Theirs (the American view) was an essentially colonialist vision, borne out of the same insecurity and desire for domination that had motivated many of the French. When their counterparts did not take their instructions, these advisors treated the Vietnamese like bad pupils, accusing them of corruption and laziness, and attempted to impose authority over them.[8]

That said, one must acknowledge, however, that while there may have been friction and misunderstanding at the higher echelons, the genuine camaraderie and esprit de corps between ARVN unit commanders and their counterparts in the field were the rule rather than the exception. The majority of U.S. officers were dedicated officers who tried to bridge the gap of cultural differences and help. The presence of the U.S. advisory team in a unit considerably contributed to the morale of the troops because they knew that, in case of heavy engagements, they could rely on U.S. air support and medevac. And many victories, including the battle of An Loc, couldn't have been achieved without the dedicated officers and men of the U.S. advisory teams.

Special credit, in my opinion, should be given to province and district advisors who worked tirelessly to improve people's lives in an effort to "win the hearts and minds" of the peasantry. Col. Edward Metzner, who spent seven years as a principal advisor to district and province chiefs, expressed the feelings of these advisors in these moving terms:

> In spite of the sad outcome and the emotional scars left by our futile, costly effort, I still firmly believe that our Viet Nam cause was an honorable one and that most of those who gave of themselves in Southeast Asia and were touched by the people there feel the same way. If the stilled voices in the hamlets could speak, I believe they would testify loudly that they keenly appreciated the effort. [9]

In any event, by the time General Minh assumed command of III Corps, the Vietnamization of the war was in full swing. President Nixon's Vietnamization program called for the South Vietnamese army to take more responsibility for the conduct of the war; it also called for the phased disengagement of U.S. troops. In 1971 alone, 177,000 Americans left the country. By January 1972, only 158,000 American soldiers remained in Viet Nam. From February to April, 58,000 more U.S. troops returned to the United States.[10] And this steady drawdown of U.S. troops happened at a time when the North Vietnamese Army (NVA) was building up for the Easter Offensive.

Like other corps commanders, General Minh had to redeploy his troops to replace the departing U.S. forces operating in MRIII. "As in the rest of the country, South Vietnamese units in III Corps found themselves filling large American shoes," wrote Dale Andradé.[11] In fact, according to Andradé, at the peak of the American buildup in 1968, MRIII was the operational area of a formidable

U.S. force, consisting of the 25th Infantry Division, the 199th Infantry Brigade, the 11th Armored Regiment, two brigades of the 1st Cavalry Division, and one battalion of the 17th Air Cavalry Regiment. By December 1971, only one squadron of the 17th Armored Cavalry Regiment, the 1st Aviation Brigade, one squadron of the 11th Armored Regiment, and one battalion of combat engineers remained. By June 1972, except the 1st Aviation Brigade and the 3rd Brigade of the 1st Cavalry Division, the above-mentioned U.S. units had been withdrawn from Viet Nam.[12]

By March 1972, the three regular divisions under General Minh's command were deployed as follows: the 25th Division, headquartered at Cu Chi, was responsible for tactical operations in the provinces of Tay Ninh, Hau Nghia, and Long An; the 18th Division, headquartered at Xuan Loc, was responsible for the provinces of Bien Hoa, Long Khanh, Phuoc Tuy, and Binh Tuy; the 5th Division, headquartered at Lai Khe, was responsible for the central provinces of Binh Duong, Binh Long, and Phuoc Long.

The 5th Division was the offspring of various Nung infantry battalions that withdrew from North Viet Nam following the partition of Viet Nam under the 1954 Geneva Agreement. (The Nung were an ethnic minority living near the Chinese border.) A new Army Reorganization Plan dated July 1, 1955, called for a new effective force of 155,677 men and the creation of the following units:

- 4 field infantry divisions
- 6 light infantry divisions
- 1 Airborne brigade
- 1 Marine brigade
- 4 armored regiments
- 11 artillery battalions
- 13 regional regiments
- 6 religious sect infantry regiments

The light infantry divisions were later deactivated and were replaced by regular divisions. The 3rd Field Division became the 5th Infantry Division. (After the overthrow of President Ngo Dinh Diem in November 1963, with increased communist activities in the South, three new infantry divisions and new ranger and armored units were created. The Marine and Airborne Brigades were upgraded and became the Marine and Airborne Divisions.)

Like other infantry divisions, the 5th Division consisted of the following organic units:

- 3 regiments (7th, 8th, 9th)
- 1 armored squadron (1st Armored Squadron)
- 3 105mm artillery battalions
- 1 155mm artillery battalion
- 1 combat engineer battalion
- 1 signal battalion
- 1 logistical battalion
- 1 medical battalion
- 1 reconnaissance company
- 1 intelligence company
- 1 transportation company

Under the Vietnamization program, the 5th Division was slated to assume the tactical responsibility of the U.S. 1st Infantry Division. Its main mission consisted of controlling the three strategic corridors of infiltration toward Saigon from Cambodia: the Song Be River, the Saigon River, and RN13.

Within the 5th Division tactical area, the 9th Regiment (less one battalion located in Phuoc Long province), supported by two 105mm batteries, was positioned at Loc Ninh. The 7th Regiment, minus one battalion, and a composite battery consisting of two 155mm and four 105mm howitzers, occupied what was called "Fire Base 1," about six kilometers northwest of An Loc; one battalion was defending the Quan Loi airstrip, about six kilometers east of An Loc. The remaining regiment, the 8th, was located at Dau Tieng (Tri Tam district), about thirty kilometers northwest of Lai Khe. Dau Tieng, located on the bank of the Saigon River, was previously the base of a brigade of the 1st U.S. Infantry Division. When the above brigade withdrew from MRIII, Tri Tam subsector was unable to take over the base; it was subsequently destroyed for lack of occupants. When the 8th Regiment arrived at Dau Tieng in early 1972, the 1/8 Battalion discovered various types of ammunition and over 2,000 brand-new M-72 rocket launchers still under wraps; this cache of ammunition and weapons was stored in numerous bunkers around the base. Col. Mach Van Truong, 8th Regiment commander, distributed the M-72s to his battalions down to squad level and trained his units on the use of this important antitank weapon. He gave the excess ammunition to Tri Tam subsector.[13]

On March 1, 1972, President Thieu, himself a former 5th Division commander, and Gen. Cao Van Vien, Chairman of ARVN/ JGS, came to the headquarters of the 5th Division at Lai Khe, to preside over the ceremony marking the thirteenth anniversary of the division. On this occasion, the president awarded decorations and promotions to officers and men of the division. He also elevated Col. Le Van Hung, the 5th Division commander, to the rank of brigadier general.

In any event, for the North Vietnamese communist rulers, the spring of 1972 may be the time they had been waiting for: the overextension of the South Vietnamese Army resulting from the U.S. troop drawdown, coupled with a growing antiwar movement in the United States, seemed to offer a good opportunity for a new offensive to capture South Viet Nam by force. If there was a lesson they had learned from the 1968 Tet Offensive, it was that the traditional Communist strategy of guerilla warfare, followed by conventional warfare, and culminating in a popular uprising did not work, because the population in the South was loyal to the Saigon government. The only remaining option for North Viet Nam (NVN) was to hurl its regular divisions across the DMZ and fight a conventional war similar to the Korean War.

At the Party Central Committee meeting in March 1971, General Giap and Le Duan, First Secretary of the Party, successfully argued for their case to launch an all-out offensive in 1972. Afterward, Le Duan went to Moscow and Beijing to request military assistance. As a result, the North Vietnamese received massive quantities of modern military hardware, including missiles, tanks, trucks, long-range artillery guns, and sophisticated surface-to-air missiles and anti-aircraft weapons.

The North Vietnamese named the new offensive the "Nguyen Hue Campaign" in honor of one of Viet Nam's most celebrated heroes who soundly defeated the Chinese in the historic battle of Dong Da, near Hanoi, on the fifth day of the calendar Year of Binh Ty in 1789.[14] In planning for the Nguyen Hue Campaign, it seems, however, that Hanoi didn't expect a full victory. Although there were no credible post-war accounts of Hanoi's decision-making process —the Communists have a tendency to distort history to fit their purposes—it is reasonable to believe that the Communist rulers originally wanted to occupy as much territory as possible—preferably a few capital cities—to weaken the American and South Vietnamese position at the Paris Peace Talks.

With regard to the timing of the attack, one might ask why Hanoi didn't wait until the complete withdrawal of U.S. troops from Viet Nam. It is probable that, in the view of Hanoi's rulers, by early 1972 a military intervention was urgently needed to reverse the success of the government pacification efforts in the South and also to save the Viet Cong (VC) from possible extermination because over one-half of the VC forces had been destroyed in their ill-fated 1968 Tet Offensive. Their political and administrative infrastructure was almost entirely rooted out by the increasingly efficient government pacification program. Moreover, Hanoi considered the U.S. disengagement irreversible and a victory over the South Vietnamese army could also be claimed as a victory over the United States. A North Vietnamese victory, in Hanoi's view, would also hasten the withdrawal of the U.S. troops, upset the Vietnamization program and even influence the 1972 U.S. presidential elections.

On the other hand, new developments on the international front were causes for concern: President Nixon not only announced in the summer of 1971 that he would travel to China in early 1972, but he was also making overtures toward Moscow. The Vietnamese Communist leaders were obviously unsettled by these new geopolitical realignments and decided to act to put their patrons in a *fait accompli* situation.

To allow for strategic flexibility, Giap devised a three-pronged attack: Quang Tri and Thua Thien in MRI, Kontum in MRII, and Binh Long in MRIII. Each attack would be carried out by three to four divisions supported by artillery and armored regiments. These simultaneous assaults on three different fronts would sow confusion within the South Vietnamese JGS as to the main direction of the invasion; it would also induce it to commit prematurely all its strategic reserves (Airborne and Marine Divisions), and consequently to leave Saigon defenseless in the face of a possible *blitzkrieg* conducted by an army corps supported by an artillery division and two armored regiments massed on the other side of the Cambodian border.

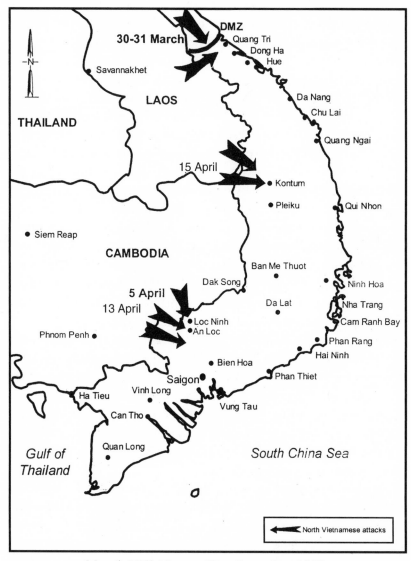

Map 5: NVA Nguyen Hue Campaign, 1972

Thus, in Hanoi's view, any successful prong would be exploited and, if possible reinforced with VC local units—such as the Binh Long VC Division in MRIII—or with units from other successful fronts, in order to capture as much territory as possible, to install a Provisional Revolutionary Government (PRG) in occupied areas, and even, in the best case scenario, to proceed toward the final conquest of South Viet Nam.

In the northern front, the fall of Quang Tri, defended by the overextended and untested South Vietnamese 3rd Division, would open the gates toward the Imperial City of Hue whose capture would constitute an irreversible blow to the morale of the South Vietnamese troops. A successful attack on the Central Highlands would entrap the southern provinces of MRI with a large pincer movement in coordination with the northern prong; or reinforce the southern prong in case of a successful NVA attack in Binh Long province. In III Corps, the capture of the weakly defended city of An Loc would allow Hanoi to install their puppet PRG in that city to influence the outcome of the Paris Peace Talks and possibly to launch a *blitzkrieg* toward the capital of South Viet Nam.

Increased NVA build-up on the other side of the Cambodian border toward the end of 1971 caused III Corps staff to believe that some kind of invasion was in the making; but as in other Military Regions, and based on past experience, they expected that it would take place during the Tet holidays. When it failed to materialize, U.S. and South Vietnamese intelligence officers increased their efforts to read the enemy intention and predict the timing and thrust of the coming attack.

In January 1972, ARVN intelligence agencies reported the presence of the NVA 5th Division at Snoul, a Cambodian city about thirty kilometers northwest of Loc Ninh on Route 13. The 7th and 9th Divisions were also reported in the vicinity of the Cambodian plantations of Dambe and Chup. Gen. Do Cao Tri, the former III Corps commander, had planned to conduct search and destroy operations in the above areas, but his death in a helicopter accident had put a stop to these planned invasions. Gen. Nguyen Van Minh, his replacement, preferred to adopt a defensive strategy along the border in lieu of offensive operations to destroy enemy secret bases within Cambodian territories.

During the months of February and March, ARVN units patrolling along the Cambodian border detected increased enemy activities in the Fishhook area. Captured documents and prisoners revealed the presence of the NVA 5th Division in the Cambodian area bordering the northern region of Binh Long province. On March 13, a III Corps mechanized task force operating in Base Area 354 (in the Parrot's Beak area) and Base Area 708 (in the Fishhook area) discovered a huge enemy depot consisting of many thousands of rifles and machine guns and a large quantity of rockets, mortar rounds, and anti-aircraft ammunition. The discovery of this important cache was compelling evidence of a major enemy offensive in MRIII, but because Tay Ninh was situated between the two subject base areas, it appeared to be the logical objective of the impending invasion.

On March 16, elements of ARVN 25th Division operating northwest of Tay Ninh near the Cambodian border captured three NVA soldiers while on a routine patrol. One of the prisoners turned out to be the executive officer of the 272nd Regiment of the NVA 9th Division. The officer carried documents indicating that the 9th Division had prepared bases east of the Saigon River and west of An Loc; these bases would be occupied by the 9th Division units on March 24.[15]

On March 27, a deserter from the reconnaissance company of the 7th Division disclosed that his unit was surveying a portion of a road between Tay Ninh and Binh Long in preparation for the division's next move.[16]

Furthermore, a document captured by the end of March during an operation in Tay Ninh province indicated that the 9th NVA Division had occupied Base Area 708 and that Regiment 272 of the 9th Division was moving to an area west of Binh Long to replace Regiment 95C/9th Division, whose destination was undisclosed. The captured document also disclosed that the 9th Division would coordinate future actions with the 7th NVA Division. More important, according to the above document, the units of the 9th Division had received training in combat in urban areas and the 272nd Regiment had been trained in the attack on a specifically chosen objective.[17] (It should be noted that the training in the technique of urban combat had been discontinued since 1969, after the failed VC Tet Offensive.)

Finally, on April 1, the 7th Regiment/5th ARVN Division, operating in an area west of An Loc, captured a number of prisoners. Some of them belonged to a signal unit whose mission was to establish telephone lines in support of a large-scale operation in the area. Among the prisoners were also members of an artillery forward observer team who were preparing preplanned fire missions along Route 13.[18]

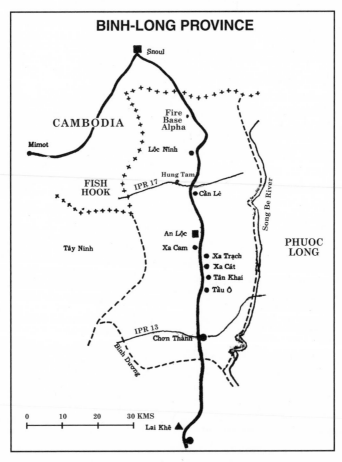

Map 6: Binh Long Province

Thus, although III Corps and U.S. intelligence agencies knew a major enemy campaign was in the making, the consensus was that Tay Ninh province, the traditional enemy invasion route, was to be again the objective of the new offensive. Indeed, Saigon, the capital city of South Viet Nam, could be attacked from three different directions: the enemy could launch an invasion from the Iron Triangle, west of Bien Hoa, using both Route 13 and the Saigon River; it could cross the Cambodian border to attack Tay Ninh and rush their mechanized units toward Saigon via Route Nationale 1; the enemy could also launch their offensive from the Parrot Beak, west of Tay Ninh, to capture Hau Nghia and Long An provinces, immediately northwest and southwest of Saigon respectively. Although the Hau Nghia-Long An route was the shortest invasion route from Cambodia, in the past, the enemy preferred to attack Tay Ninh because that city, being surrounded from three sides by the VC's secret bases of War Zone C, Iron Triangle and Parrot's Beak, was more vulnerable to an attack. And this was the reason III Corps intelligence officers predicted that the NVA would use the same traditional invasion route in their new Easter offensive.

To reinforce that perception, on April 2, the VC 24th Independent Regiment attacked ARVN Fire Support Base (FSB) Lac Long about thirty-five kilometers northwest of Tay Ninh on the Cambodian border. The base was defended by one battalion of the 49th Regiment, 25th Division. For the first time in MRIII, the enemy used tanks to support their ground assault. By noon the base was overrun and the battalion suffered moderate casualties.

In his memoir, VC Gen. Tran Van Tra, commander of the troops of the Front for the Liberation of South Viet Nam (FLSVN), described the Communist diversion in the Lac Long attack as follows: "In coordination with Quang Tri and the offensive and uprising on the entire South, on April 1, 1972, only one day after Quang Tri, the Nguyen Hue campaign of the regular forces in the East had opened an auxiliary front, which was also a diversionary front, to attract the enemy forces on Road 22 in Tay Ninh. With old enemy tanks (one operable but the gun mounted on the tank was unusable, one usable but it stopped dead in the barbed wire), but the sound of the gun and the roaring of the tanks strongly impacted the enemy morale, actively supported the powerful infantry assault causing heavy losses to the enemy's two task forces and destroying the enemy defense system along border Road 22 Tay Ninh-Cambodia. In the meantime, the Joint General Staff of the Saigon army moved two general reserve units to cope with the Tay Ninh front; on April 5, our regular troops moved on the newly opened road in secret and launched a surprise attack on Loc Ninh, a defensive base of over 500 enemies, most of them regular troops and armored units."[19]

Although all indications seemed to point toward Tay Ninh as the main objective of the enemy new offensive, to be on the safe side, General Minh, the III Corps commander, decided to occupy the Hung Tam compound, situated about ten kilometers northwest of An Loc and two kilometers west of the junction of Inter-Provincial Route (IPR)17 and Route Nationale 13, with the newly created Regimental Task Force (TF) 52. TF-52, named after Regiment 52, consisted of one battalion from the 52nd Regiment, one battalion from the 48th Regiment, one 105mm howitzer battery and one 155mm howitzer platoon. Both regiments belonged to the 18th Division, which was operating in Long Khanh province. The Hung Tam base consisted of FSB North and FSB South, located immediately north and south of IPR17. TF-52, commanded by Lt.-Col. Nguyen Ba Thinh, moved north on March 28 and was put under the operational control of the 5th Division. It would conduct operations around the Hung Tam base. It main mission was to block enemy movement toward Loc Ninh and An Loc in Binh Long province and to protect the right flank of Tay Ninh in case of an enemy attack in that direction.

Amid intelligence reports of an impending major enemy campaign, President Thieu remained optimistic. He was confident that, with the U.S.'s continued financial and military support, the South Vietnamese Army could beat back any enemy offensive and eventually win the war through the success of the pacification program. U.S. officials in Saigon, in fact, were equally upbeat about the situation in Viet Nam in the post-Tet Offensive era; they also believed that the war was almost won in the early 1972. Lewis Sorley quoted the late John Paul Vann, a former senior official in the pacification program and subsequently the U.S. senior advisor to II Corps during the Easter Offensive, as telling his friends in January 1972 that "we are now at the lowest level of fighting the war has ever seen. Today there is an air of prosperity throughout the rural areas of Viet Nam, and it cannot be denied. Today the roads are open and the bridges are up, and you run much greater risk traveling any road in Viet Nam today from the scurrying, bustling, hustling Hondas and Lambrettas than you do from the Viet Cong." And added Vann, "this program of Vietnamization has gone kind of literally beyond my wildest dreams of success."[20]

Lewis Sorley attributed the above success in part to General Abrams's "One War" concept which would integrate combat operations, pacification, and upgrading the ARVN. In place of General Westmoreland's "search and destroy" concept, Abrams applied the "clear and hold" strategy under which the pacified areas must be permanently held by allied forces. "Contrary to most people seem to believe," wrote Sorley, "the new approach during the Abrams era succeeded remarkably. And, since during these last years American forces were progressively being withdrawn, more and more it was the South Vietnamese who were achieving that success."[21]

Thus, as the waiting game continued and the thinly spread out South Vietnamese army was bracing for a new military invasion, President Thieu, seemingly undeterred, decided that, barring new dramatic developments, the government must conduct its business as usual.

Three

The Opening Salvos

Toward the end of March, President Thieu, who was actively involved in the pacification process—and for this reason was dubbed "the number one pacification officer" by William Colby, former CIA chief in Saigon—setting aside intelligence reports of an impending NVA offensive, convened the annual meeting of all corps commanders and province chiefs to review the progress of the national pacification program. The meeting took place at the Rural Development Training Center at the seaside resort city of Vung Tau. While the convention was in progress, word broke out on March 30 that NVA regular divisions, supported by artillery and armored regiments, after having conducted heavy artillery preparations on ARVN 3rd Division positions in the northern area of Quang Tri province, had crossed the Ben Hai River—which separated the two Viet Nams under the 1954 Geneva Peace Agreement. What was known as the "Easter Offensive" had begun.

The launching of this major offensive was planned to coincide with the dry season because of the difficulties in moving troops, equipment, and supplies for such large scale operations during the rainy season. The northern provinces of MRI are affected by the northeast monsoon and can expect good weather from February to September; the rest of South Viet Nam is affected by the southwest monsoon and the dry season generally lasts from October to May. Consequently, the good window for a large scale offensive in South

Viet Nam was from the month of February to the month of May. Of course it would be ideal to start the offensive in early February in order to occupy as much territory as possible before the new monsoons began. The NVA, due to delays in moving their troops and heavy equipment, chose instead the day preceding the Easter festivities as their D-day.

Meanwhile, the news from MRII was cause for concern: Coincidental with the attack on MRI, NVA forces, supported by tank units, had overrun the command post of the ARVN 22nd Division in Tan Canh, north of Kontum; Col. Le Duc Dat, the division commander, and many staff officers were reported missing.

Expecting a concurrent offensive on the Central Highlands, President Thieu ordered both Generals Hoang Xuan Lam, I Corps commander, and Ngo Dzu, II Corps commander, and all province chiefs under their command, to return immediately to their posts to cope with new developments. The province chiefs in MRIII and MRIV were asked to stay on until the completion of the pacification workshop despite a surge in enemy attacks on ARVN outposts along the Cambodian border in Tay Ninh province and the loss of the important Lac Long Base on April 2.

The attacks on Lac Long and other border outposts prompted General Minh, the III Corps commander, to pull all small isolated bases in the northern part of MRIII to more defensible areas to avoid becoming sitting ducks for superior NVA forces and also to protect more important population centers. As the ARVN unit defending Thien Ngon outpost about thirty kilometers north of Tay Ninh was pulling out, it was ambushed by Independent Regiment 274 and lost many artillery guns and vehicles. A rescuing unit from the 25th Division, which reached the ambush site the next day, was surprised to see that the lost equipment, including the 105mm and 155mm artillery guns, was not towed away by the enemy. More surprising was the fact that the enemy had left the area instead of setting ambushes to destroy the rescuing forces.[1]

Maj. Le Van Ngon, commander of the 92nd Border Ranger Battalion at Tong Le Chon, about fifteen kilometers southwest of An Loc, decided to stay and fight in his outpost, because he was convinced his unit would be ambushed if he tried to pull out. Although the enemy was determined to remove this outpost, which sat on their lifeline to War Zone C and to their secret bases in the Fish-hook area, Ngon and his men fought off many attacks and held out at the isolated base throughout the Easter Offensive and even in the post-Paris Agreement era—in which the NVA continued their attacks on isolated outposts in defiance of the agreement.

Not until April 5, after the first NVA assaults on Loc Ninh, did III Corps Staff realize that the attacks in Tay Ninh were only a diversion to cover the enemy's main thrust in Binh Long province. These attacks also helped to hide the movements of the 9th and 7th NVA Divisions into Binh Long. The 9th Division was to occupy positions around An Loc in preparation for the direct assault on the city in conjunction with the 5th Division already positioned north of Loc Ninh, while the 7th Division was to occupy blocking positions along Route 13 south of An Loc to interdict rescuing ARVN units.

Finally, at around 11:00 A.M. on April 5, Col. Tran Van Nhut, Binh Long province chief, was asked to see Lt. Gen. Cao Hao Hon, Assistant to the Prime Minister for Pacification. General Hon told Nhut that President Thieu ordered him to return immediately to An Loc because of increased enemy activity in his province.

In his book *Cuoc Chien Dang Do*[2] (Unfinished War), General[3] Nhut reported that during the pacification workshop, he regularly kept in touch with Lt. Col. Nguyen Thong Thanh, his deputy sector commander.[4] Colonel Thanh had reported sporadic contacts of RF units with the enemy north of Can Le Bridge and south of Tan Khai on Route 13. Reports from sector intelligence agencies regarding increased VC activities on Route 13 caused Colonel Thanh to order the provincial subsectors (districts) to increase night ambushes. As a result, RF and PF units had engaged the enemy during the nights of April 3 and April 4, and had killed over twenty VCs and captured an important amount of weapons. Of special importance was the fact that the enemy soldiers killed during these ambushes wore regular NVA army uniforms and didn't seem to belong to local guerilla units as had been the case in the past.[5]

Nhut also reported that Mr. E. Gaudeul, the French director of the Cexso rubber plantation in Loc Ninh, had indicated that many field telephone lines had been established by NVA forces northwest of Loc Ninh, but the 9th Regiment of the 5th Division—which was in charge of the defense of the district—was reluctant to send reconnaissance patrols into the area.

Nhut and his driver left for An Loc right after he met General Hon. When they arrived at Lai Khe around 4:00 P.M., they were stopped by Lieutenant Colonel Thanh and Lt. Col. Robert E. Corley, sector senior advisor. Colonel Thanh reported that the sector headquarters at An Loc had been hit by enemy 122mm rockets and one building was on fire. The district town of Loc Ninh was surrounded by NVA forces, and the enemy had set up *chot* (fortified blocking positions) on Route 13, at Tan Khai. Colonel Nhut left his jeep at Lai Khe and flew by helicopter with his deputy and his American advisor to Chon Thanh to meet with the district chief, Lt. Col. Pham Quang My, to inquire about the situation in the district. The three men then headed toward An Loc where Nhut met with his staff to review the friendly and enemy situation within Binh Long Sector. After the meeting, Nhut and Lieutenant Colonel Corley left for Loc Ninh to meet with Maj. Nguyen Van Thinh, Loc Ninh district chief.

When their helicopter took off, it drew anti-aircraft fire from enemy positions north of An Loc. The American pilot was unable to land at the district headquarters of Loc Ninh due to intense anti-aircraft fire. From above, Nhut saw the district town engulfed in dark smoke. The enemy artillery was bombarding the district headquarters and the headquarters of the 9th Regiment of the 5th Division without interruption.

In 1972, Loc Ninh was a dusty small district town of about 4,000. It sat on Route 13 on the edge of a small valley; its population consisted mostly of Montagnards of Stieng and Mien tribes. A small all-weather airstrip was situated about a half-mile west of the town. The district headquarters, manned by over 200 RF/PF soldiers, was located in a deep and fortified bunker in the north tip and west of the airstrip. The bunker, built by the Japanese during the Indochina War, provided good protection to the district personnel and allowed for uninterrupted radio communication with the province headquarters. The 9th Regiment occupied a former U.S. Special Forces compound located at the south end of the airstrip

and the artillery compound was located between the district headquarters and the regiment compound. To the south of the fire base
the terrain was relatively open and to the west the rubber trees and
vegetation had been bulldozed within about 300 yards.

On April 4, Col. Nguyen Cong Vinh, 9th Regiment commander, predicting an imminent attack on Loc Ninh, ordered Lt. Col.
Nguyen Huu Duong, commander of Task Force 1-5 at FSB Alpha,
ten kilometers north of Loc Ninh, to send one detachment of M-41
tanks and M-113 armored personnel carriers (APC) to Loc Ninh
to reinforce the defense of the district town. (TF 1-5 was a mechanized unit consisting of the 1st Armored Squadron, two companies
from the 2/9 Battalion, the 74th Border Ranger Battalion, and one
artillery battery. On April 2, General Hung had directed Colonel
Duong and his task force to move north to help evacuate the border ranger units manning the outposts on the Cambodian border.)
The combined mechanized detachment under Lt. Le Van Hung
left FSB Alpha during the night; it was ambushed and destroyed
by an enemy force supported by T-54 (Russian-built medium tank
equipped with a 100mm gun) and PT-76 tanks five kilometers
north of Loc Ninh.

Lieutenant Colonel Duong, TF 1-5 commander, called the 9th
Regiment to report that he had lost contact with Lieutenant Hung,
but by that time, the 9th Regiment communication center had been
damaged by enemy artillery fire. Not until the next morning was
radio communication restored. Colonel Vinh ordered Duong to
move the rest of TF 1-5 to Loc Ninh immediately to shore up the
defense of the district. TF 1-5 was again ambushed at the same spot
where Lieutenant Hung's detachment was destroyed the previous
night. Colonel Duong broke out of the ambush site with two M-
113s but was engaged by the enemy one kilometer south; Duong
escaped but was captured with fifteen soldiers on April 7.[6]

While all this transpired, around 3:00 A.M. on April 5, two
regiments from the NVA 5th Division, supported by a tank unit,
launched a coordinated attack on the 9th Regiment command post
after a powerful artillery barrage.

At first, the defenders panicked, they lay in their foxholes in
horror: never before had they been subjected to such powerful and

sustained artillery bombardment. Recovering from the initial shock and, with effective tactical air support directed by the American advisors, the defenders managed to beat back the first attack, destroying one tank. At one point, ARVN artillerymen had to lower their guns and fire directly at the attackers advancing through the rubber trees. Around noon, the enemy regrouped and launched another attack on the 9th Regiment compound but the attack was stopped by an AC-130 gunship. According to Major General Hollingsworth, III Corps Senior Advisor, the four-engine propeller-driven converted cargo aircraft armed with 7.62mm guns and one 105mm gun caught the enemy in the wire and destroyed "the better part of a regiment."[7] Another assault across the airstrip was stopped cold by well-placed CBUs (Cluster Bomb Unit). (The CBU-87/B is a 1,000-pound, air-delivered cluster weapons system, designed for attack against soft target areas with detonating bomblets; a total of 202 of the bomblets are loaded in each dispenser enabling a single payload attack on an effective area of approximately 200 meters by 400 meters.)[8] Another attempt succeeded in getting into the barbed wire of the eastern defense perimeter of the 9th Regiment command post, but was repelled by Cobra gunships. However, one gunship was hit by anti-aircraft fire and exploded on the ground. Both American pilots were killed.[9]

Although the NVA's major assaults were beaten back, the enemy kept bombarding the embattled district town with artillery and rockets. In addition, the defenders were hit by deadly recoilless rifle fire. One recoilless rifle round made a direct hit on the regiment command bunker, wounding both Lt. Col. Richard S. Schott, the senior regiment advisor, and Capt. Mark A. Smith, a member of the regiment advisory team. Captain Smith, who was proficient in the Vietnamese language, was most instrumental in the effective coordination of U.S. air support and was, for all practical purposes, the man in charge of the advisory effort during the battle of Loc Ninh.[10]

While Colonel Nhut was circling the district in his efforts to contact Major Thinh, the district chief, American observation aircraft reported that many trucks towing artillery guns were heading toward An Loc; some of them were even taking position at the district bus station at the northern outskirts of the town. The American pilots requested permission to strike these trucks. Nhut told them to hold off because he suspected these vehicles may be civilian logging trucks escaping toward Loc Ninh. Major Thinh later confirmed that these vehicles were indeed civilian trucks towing logs mounted on two-wheeled trailers, which, observed from the air, looked like artillery trucks.

Nhut continued to fly north to reconnoiter the Loc Tan area where the 1st Armored Squadron was ambushed in the early hours of April 5. Nhut was very concerned by what he saw: "The 1st Armored Squadron of the 5th Division was being shelled, assaulted, all tanks and armored vehicles were completely destroyed," Nhut wrote in his memoir, "the charred wreckages of the destroyed tanks were scattered all around the ambush site."[11] This description seems to contradict the assertion contained in both *America's Last Viet Nam Battle*[12] and *The Battle of An Loc*[13] that the 1st Armored Squadron had already surrendered to the enemy, "willingly driving their tanks and armored personnel carriers toward the Cambodian border." In fact, if Nhut's observations were accurate, then there would have been no tanks or armored personnel carriers left to drive around.

Further, according to Col. Bui Duc Diem, Assistant for Operations to the 5th Division commander, the 1st Armored Squadron was annihilated during an ambush north of Loc Ninh on its way back to the district town and Lieutenant Colonel Duong was taken prisoner during that ambush. Brig. Gen. Ly Tong Ba—whom I interviewed about the performance of the armored units during the Easter Offensive—categorically stated that not a single armored unit had surrendered to the enemy during the Viet Nam War. A recipient of both the French *Croix de Guerre* and the U.S. Silver Star, General Ba commanded the 23rd Division and distinguished himself in the Battle of Kontum during the 1972 Offensive. He assumed command of ARVN's Armor Branch right after the Easter Offensive.

In any event, Nhut was unaware that the two infantry companies from the 2nd Battalion, 9th Regiment, attached to TF 1-5, and the 74th Border Ranger Battalion, which had been put under the operational control of the task force, had broken out of the ambush and were fighting their way toward Loc Ninh. Although they ran into yet another ambush a few hundred meters north of Loc Ninh, the rangers and survivors of TF 1-5 were able to reach the district town the next day and join forces with its defenders.

Nhut also worried about the inadequacy of friendly forces defending Loc Ninh. The 3rd Battalion of the 9th Regiment had been put under the operational control of Phuoc Long province. The previous day, April 4, the 1st Battalion, 9th Regiment, operating west of Loc Ninh, was almost wiped out by enemy forces: Major Son, the battalion commander, and only about 100 men from his battalion were able to make it back to the regiment compound.[14] Two infantry companies from the 2nd Battalion, supported by two 155mm and four 105mm howitzers, were located at Can Le Bridge on Route 13, south of Loc Ninh. Thus, the 9th Regiment, supported by two artillery batteries, had only the 9th Reconnaissance Company, the Regiment Headquarters Company, and the survivors of the 1st Battalion at its disposal for the defense of its compound at Loc Ninh. Nhut ordered Major Thinh, the district chief, to maintain constant liaison with Col. Nguyen Cong Vinh, the 9th Regiment commander. He also decided to put the district under the direct command of Colonel Vinh. Nhut then contacted Colonel Vinh on the latter's radio frequency to confirm that fact.[15]

Afterward, Colonel Nhut flew back to Chon Thanh to assess the situation in this district. There he met his administrative assistant and chiefs of various provincial departments, who had just returned from the pacification seminar in Vung Tau. They told Nhut that right after he left the meeting, all province chiefs and department heads in MRIII and MRIV were also ordered to return to their posts. After he was appraised of the situation in Chon Thanh district, Nhut and his administrative assistant and provincial department chiefs boarded his helicopter and headed back to An Loc.

When he returned to his official residence, Nhut met Mr. Bui Huu Tai, the chief of the Public Works Department. Mr. Tai, known for his penchant for good French cognac, had just come back from Vung Tau—by road. As Nhut put it, "Tai drinks cognac like we drink water." As soon as he saw the province chief, Tai jumped out of his jeep and complained that ARVN soldiers had shot at him when he drove by Tan Khai. Nhut told him that the enemy had established *chot* (blocking position) at Tan Khai since that morning and that he was the only man who was brave enough to have successfully broken through the enemy road block. Nhut asked Tai whether too much French cognac had prevented him from noticing the "No Traffic" sign on Route 13. Nhut then offered Tai a glass of cognac to celebrate his daring escape.[16] In retrospect, Tai's return was no small achievement, because the entire 21st Division, moving north from Chon Thanh, was unable later to do what he single-handedly did that fateful day of April.

In the afternoon of April 6, General Hung and Colonel Miller, Senior Division Advisor, and their respective staffs moved from the 5th Division Main Headquarters at Lai Khe to the division forward command post at An Loc. On his way to An Loc, General Hung stopped at Dau Tieng to meet with Colonel Truong, 8th Regiment commander. He informed Truong that An Loc was being encircled by NVA forces and would likely be the next enemy objective after Loc Ninh, and that he was going to An Loc to personally direct the defense of the city. In Hung's view, the Saigon River was still an important avenue of approach for enemy forces to threaten the capital, and thus the 8th Regiment must temporarily stay at Dau Tieng until further order. However, after Hung arrived in An Loc, the 5th Division wouldn't be in a position to support the 8th Regiment; consequently, he had requested that the regiment be put under the tactical control of III Corps.[17]

The 5th Division combat engineer battalion had previously built a Division Forward CP with steel plates and sandbags in the eastern area of An Loc, near the railroad station. Colonel Miller, 5th Division senior advisor, told General Hung that this CP couldn't withstand 130mm artillery shells and 122mm missiles and that, due to inadequate protection, the 5th Division advisory team would leave An Loc and return to Lai Khe. General Hung invited his advisor to inspect an underground compound situated in the center of the city. This fortified structure of reinforced concrete was built by the Japanese Army to protect against Allied warplane bombardments during World War II. Named after Gen. Do Cao Tri—the former III Corps commander killed during the previous year's Cambodia invasion—this compound was located near the Binh Long hospital and was previously occupied by Sector Headquarters. When the U.S. units in An Loc withdrew in 1971, Colonel Nhut moved his headquarters to the more spacious and more comfortable U.S. compound in the south area of the city. Colonel Miller was satisfied with the new compound and agreed to stay at An Loc.[18]

In early April, when intelligence reports indicated an impending enemy attack on the district town of Loc Ninh, Colonel Miller, described by Willbanks as an "advocate of the offensive," strongly urged General Hung to seize the initiative by reinforcing Loc Ninh and to make a stand in that district town. Colonel Miller believed that if the 5th Division could mass their forces in Loc Ninh, the South Vietnamese would be in a position to defeat the NVA there and prevent a battle further south at An Loc.[19]

General Hung refused to follow Miller's recommendation and openly criticized U.S. advisors for "meddling in South Vietnamese affairs." Miller later commented that General Hung was "almost paralyzed" and couldn't make any decisions when he realized that the NVA were attacking Binh Long and not Tay Ninh province.[20] In retrospect, I believe General Hung was correct in refusing his advisor's suggestion for the following reasons: First, he didn't have time to mass his troops in Loc Ninh (the war council in Saigon didn't release the 1st Airborne Brigade and the 21st Division until the seventh of April, the day Loc Ninh fell); second, the lifeline would have been considerably extended and thus would be more difficult to secure and protect; third, even if Hung were able to bring some troops to Loc Ninh, the enemy could have massed far more superior forces to overrun the district town and then would have been home free to take the defenseless city of An Loc.

Similarly, Gen. Ly Tong Ba, former 23rd Division commander, mentioned in his memoir that when he was preparing to defend Kontum, John Paul Vann, the outspoken and aggressive II Corps Senior Advisor, strongly urged him to mount a general offensive to retake some border outposts which had been overrun by NVA forces in early April. Ba refused, arguing that, instead of embarking on risky ventures into the deep and murderous forests and mountains of the Central Highlands, he preferred to adopt the well-known strategy of "*dieu ho ly son*" (or to "lure the tiger to get out of the mountain") and to beat the enemy in one single battle. After he destroyed the NVA 320th and 10th Divisions in a well-planned *bataille rangée* in the city of Kontum, John Paul Vann acknowledged that Ba was right after all.[21]

Liddell Hart, the British military strategist who developed the theory of indirect approach, wrote:

> In strategy the longest way round is often the shortest way there; a direct approach to the subject exhausts the attacker and hardens the resistance by compression, whereas an indirect approach loosens the defender's hold by upsetting his balance.

Generals Hung and Ba, by deciding to make a stand at An Loc and Kontum respectively, while conducting delaying actions and disrupting enemy advances with airpower, had probably unknowingly adopted a corollary of Liddell Hart's strategy of indirect approach, in which the defender, facing a direct attack, can take necessary measures to exhaust the attacker and "harden the resistance by compression."

In war, the offensive is not the universal answer to all situations. According to Sun Tzu, before making a decision, a commander must carefully consider the three factors that directly impact the outcome of the battle: weather, terrain, and people. A comparative military analysis of Loc Ninh and An Loc would show that, the weather being the same for the two towns, the open terrain around An Loc with good fields of fire and observation was more favorable to the defense, and the civilian population in the Binh Long capital city was much more anti-Communist and pro-government than the Montagnards of Loc Ninh, who just wanted to be left alone. Prussian military theorist Carl Clausewitz also stressed the importance of the role of the people in war; in his view, the passion of the people is necessary to endure the sacrifices inherent in any important conflict. As will be seen later, the people of An Loc had endured tremendous sacrifices with great courage and determination.

Meanwhile, at Loc Ninh, enemy artillery, mortar shells, and rockets continued to fall on the beleaguered garrison. Late on the evening of April 5, two T-54 tanks tried to roll through the barbed wire but were engaged by ARVN 106mm recoilless fire and also by AC-130 Spectre gunships. One tank was destroyed; the other was forced to withdraw. At nightfall, things quieted down a bit, but sporadic shelling continued throughout the night. All night long, Captain Smith, although wounded, continued to coordinate air support, directing Spectre gunships on suspected enemy positions around the compound.

To reinforce the capital city of Binh Long—the true objective of the NVA's 1972 offensive in MRIII—General Hung ordered the 7th Regiment back to An Loc—which was at that time defended only by the territorial forces of Binh Long province. The 7th Regiment, minus one battalion, supported by two 155mm howitzers and four 105mm howitzers, was operating around FSB1, located six kilometers west of An Loc. The 1st Battalion, supported by a combined 105mm and 155mm battery, was operating in Quan Loi airport east of An Loc. (Quan Loi also included the rear base compound of the 9th Regiment.) The 7th Regiment had just come under attack and could be overrun by NVA's 9th Division units if left at FSB1.

On April 6, as the situation in Loc Ninh was rapidly deteriorating, General Hung ordered Lt. Col. Nguyen Ba Thinh, commander of T-52 at Hung Tam, to send one battalion to Loc Ninh to reinforce the 9th Regiment. Since April 1, TF-52 had received increasing mortar and rocket fire. Colonel Thinh ordered the 2nd Battalion of his regiment to attack in the direction of Loc Ninh and to link up with the besieged garrison. However, the battalion ran into a strong ambush near the junction of RN13 and IPR17. Because all air support was directed at Loc Ninh, the regiment used its organic artillery to support the counter-attack. Unable to break through the ambush, the battalion had to withdraw to Hung Tam Base.

Meanwhile, both fire bases at Hung Tam came under heavy artillery and rocket attacks. As the shelling continued the next day and NVA troops were on the verge of completing the encirclement of Hung Tam, General Hung, on the morning of April 7, finally ordered the immediate withdrawal of TF-52 to An Loc. General Hung also recalled the two companies from the 2nd Battalion, 9th

Regiment, at Can Le Bridge south to the capital city. These two companies were also under heavy attack and were forced to destroy all their artillery. The South Vietnamese troops also destroyed the Can Le Bridge to delay the advance of NVA tanks toward An Loc.

TF-52 left Hung Tam base around 8:00 A.M. The column was led by the 1/48 Battalion. The 2/52 Battalion continued to occupy Hung Tam base to block the NVA's efforts to pursue and destroy the retreating units.

As TF-52's column was heading toward An Loc on IPR17, it ran into a large enemy ambush only a few hundred meters from Hung Tam base. The 1/48 Battalion repulsed the enemy attack near the junction of IPR17 and RN13. In the meantime, the 2/52 Battalion, which was protecting the rear of the column, was attacked by enemy forces east of Hung Tam; the battalion was able to rejoin the T-52 column after a furious close-quarters engagement.

Three 105mm howitzers were captured by the NVA during the above ambush. General Hung ordered Colonel Thinh to destroy all equipment and to continue to move southward by foot. Because the embattled task force was unable to disable all heavy equipment during the break out, General Hollingsworth later ordered an air strike to finish the job.[22] Around 1:00 P.M., the column reached an area just north of Can Le Bridge on Route 13. By that time, both Colonel Thinh and his deputy commander, Lt. Col. Hoang Van Hien, were wounded. (Col. Hien later died from excessive bleeding while being evacuated by helicopter to An Loc.) All three U.S. advisors were also wounded, including Lt. Col. Walter Ginger, the senior task force advisor. Colonel Ginger refused to be evacuated and continued to provide effective close air support to the column. In the view of many ARVN officers, Colonel Ginger was credited for having saved TF-52 from possible annihilation.[23] In the meantime, Colonel Thinh tried to push on but the column was subjected to heavy direct fire when it attempted to cross a large open area north of Can Le.

Finally, during the morning of April 8, U.S. helicopters, supported by powerful close tactical air, succeeded in extracting the American advisors from the beleaguered TF-52. Colonel Thinh and the remainder of the beleaguered TF-52 continued to move south.

Of the original effective force of about 1,000 men, only about half reached An Loc and prepared themselves for the upcoming attack.[24]

While all this transpired, the situation in Loc Ninh continued to worsen. In the early hours of April 6, NVA infantry and tank formations began to launch probing attacks on ARVN positions. At one point, one enemy infantry company succeeded in getting inside the compound, but it was quickly dispersed by U.S. Air Force fighters and well-placed Spectre gunship fire. However, by noon, the situation in Loc Ninh became hopeless. What was left of the rapidly dwindling 9th Regiment was barely able to hold out. To prepare for new enemy assaults, the tireless and hard-working regiment surgeon sent back some of the less seriously wounded soldiers to their foxholes on the regiment perimeter of defense. By that time, however, the survivors of the two companies attached to TF 1-5 and the survivors of the 74th Border Ranger Battalion had made it into the compound of the 9th Regiment.

During the night, enemy artillery and rocket fire hit the regiment hospital bunker, killing a large number of wounded. The artillery compound, including the ammunition depot, was also hit: some gunmen were killed or wounded, a few guns were damaged, and the ammunition in storage was destroyed. An NVA unit also launched a ground attack across the airfield. The defenders repulsed the attack but, in the process, expended their last 106mm recoilless rifle ammunition.

At 7:00 A.M. on April 7, the NVA launched another assault, supported by artillery, recoilless rifles, rockets, and tanks. One tank was destroyed when it reached the barbed wire surrounding the perimeter. The situation reached a critical point and the defense began to crumble in certain sectors.

Willbanks, based on Captain Smith's account, reported that at about 8:00 A.M., Colonel Vinh, the 9th Regiment commander, and his bodyguards rushed through the compound gate to surrender to the enemy, while inside the compound, the regiment executive officer lowered the South Vietnamese flag and hoisted a white T-shirt on the flagpole as a symbol of surrender. Smith reportedly subdued the executive officer and ran the national flag up the flagpole. He also exhorted several soldiers who were ready to surrender to go back to their defensive positions.[25]

The battle raged until 9:30 A.M., when another wave of attack caused what was left of the 9th Regiment to disintegrate. However, the regiment command bunker and a few adjoining bunkers still held out, thanks to continuous AC-130 gunship and other tactical air support.

In the afternoon, NVA soldiers began to attack the command bunker by throwing satchel charges in the door. According to Captain Smith, Lieutenant Colonel Schott, who had sustained a severe head injury in earlier combat, decided to commit suicide with his .45 pistol to avoid being a burden to the other members of the regiment advisory team.[26] (By that time, Colonel Schott, Captain Smith, and Sergeant Howard B. Lull were in the command bunker, while Maj. Albert E. Carlson, Sgt. Kenneth Wallingford, and a freelance French photographer named Yves Michel Dumond, were holed up in another bunker.)

It should be noted here that, due to the lack of ARVN's records relative to the battle of Loc Ninh, most of the description of this battle comes from the two books, *America's Last Vietnam Battle* and *The Battle of An Loc*. These books in turn relied mainly on Captain Smith's account. [27] In fact, since both Colonel Schott and Sergeant Lull were reported "Killed in Action. Bodies Not Recovered," Captain Smith was the only American who survived to tell the story. Further, because Smith was located at the command center and had radio contact with the division headquarters, the Forward Air Controllers (FACs), U.S. pilots, as well as ground units, including the district headquarters, he was practically the only source available to American historians and authors who want to study or write about the last—and chaotic—hours of the battle of Loc Ninh. It should also be noted that, according to Willbanks, Captain Smith's account was not free of controversy and that "Smith and the army are at odds about what happened that day in the bunker."[28]

From the South Vietnamese side, fortunately the key player in this drama, Colonel Vinh, the former 9th Regiment commander, also survived. As a young man, in the early 1950s, Vinh, like many of his contemporaries, had joined the Viet Minh in the *maquis* to fight against the French. Disillusioned with the Viet Minh's policy of hatred and class warfare, Vinh decided to enroll at the Dalat Military Academy to serve in the newly created National Army. He rose through the ranks and commanded a regiment of the 18th Division before assuming the command of the 9th Regiment. However, in his memoir titled *Cau Chuyen Suy Tu Cua Mot Cuu Tu Nhan Chanh Tri* [29](Reflections of a Former Political Prisoner), Colonel Vinh had only this to say regarding Loc Ninh: "With the intention to seize the capital city of Binh Long province to use it as the seat for the National Front for the Liberation of South Viet Nam to improve its standing in the four-party Paris Peace Talks ...The communist troops were able only to overrun the district town of Loc Ninh after three days of attack supported by tanks, and after the 9th Infantry Regiment Task Force had disintegrated. After one day of rest and regrouping, they rushed their grand army toward the capital city of Binh Long."[30]

In a telephone interview in May 2006,[31]Colonel Vinh denied Captain Smith's allegation that he surrendered to the enemy and that his executive officer had hoisted a white flag on the regiment compound flagpole on April 7. Vinh said he was taken prisoner when he tried to escape after his compound was overrun by NVA troops.

In a subsequent letter to this author, Colonel Vinh reported that during the week prior to the attack on Loc Ninh, the 1st Battalion captured an NVA artillery captain, who was surveying artillery positions in preparation for the incoming attack. The NVA officer had lunch with Colonel Vinh and the U.S. senior advisor; he was then sent to TF 1-5 for further interrogation. Patrols from 9th Regiment also detected new traces of tracked vehicles on forest trails leading toward Viet Nam; they even reported hearing the roaring noises of tank engines. Underwater bridges built with logs were also discovered in certain upper stream locations on the Song Be River. According to Colonel Vinh, all this information had been promptly reported to the division headquarters, but 5th Division intelligence still didn't believe that the enemy had tanks. This seems to confirm Nhut's statement that upon hearing the Loc Ninh district chief's report of the possible presence of enemy tanks around Loc Ninh, he contacted General Hung and was told there was no evidence of that and that some of TF 1-5's tanks instead may have been captured by the enemy at Loc Tan.[32](In his report *The 1972 Easter Offensive*, Gen. Ngo Quang Truong disclosed that General Minh, III Corps commander, also didn't know the enemy had tanks despite the fact that intelligence reports in October 1971 indicated the presence of enemy tanks in Kratie, Dambe, and Chup in Cambodia and that in December 1971, the Cambodian Army Joint General Staff confirmed the presence of thirty enemy tanks in Base Area 363, north of Tay Ninh.)[33]

Vinh noted in his letter that four M-113s from TF 1-5 made it to Loc Ninh on April 6, but instead of reinforcing the defense of the beleaguered garrison, they continued to move south toward An Loc and it was his understanding that only one APC succeeded in reaching its final destination. In fact, one M-113 armored personnel carrier did reach An Loc on April 7. And if Vinh's statement was true, then the other three APCs must have been destroyed or captured by units from the NVA's 9th Division around Can Le Bridge, north of the city.

Colonel Vinh also reported in his letter that on April 7, the NVA unleashed a very heavy and sustained artillery barrage on his compound. Afterward, they sent four teams of T-54 tanks—with two tanks in each team—to mount a direct assault on the regimental task force headquarters. First, his soldiers thought that these tanks belonged to the TF 1-5 mechanized task force, but the tanks kept attacking, causing the defensive positions and bunkers to collapse. Colonel Vinh said he was captured by NVA troops when his command bunker was overrun. He was taken to NVA campaign headquarters in the district of Mimmot in Cambodia. The headquarters consisted of a number of underground fortified bunkers hidden inside a rubber plantation. There Vinh met Lieutenant Colonel Duong, the TF 1-5 commander. They were subsequently blindfolded and transported to a prisoner camp deep inside Cambodia on a Chinese jeep.

"I commanded a unit responsible for the defense of the border. I was defeated and feel very ashamed. If people say I am weak, I accept that, but don't blame me for what I have not done," wrote Colonel Vinh at the end of his letter.

When I asked him to put me in contact with any of his men who were with him during the last hours of Loc Ninh so they could corroborate the above facts, Vinh said he had lost contact with his former comrades-in-arm since he had come to the United States. Thus, like Captain Smith from the American side, Colonel Vinh was the only survivor to tell the story from the South Vietnamese side. On the other hand, Col. Bui Duc Diem,[34] Assistant for Operations to the 5th Division commander, reported in a telephone conversation that, to his best knowledge, Colonel Vinh didn't surrender, but was instead captured by the enemy when the NVA captured Loc Ninh. History, sadly, may never know for sure what exactly happened during these eventful hours of Loc Ninh's agony.

Colonel Vinh may not have surrendered to the enemy in his own will, but in retrospect, I believe that the rapid collapse of Loc Ninh was due in great part to his failure of leadership. Although intelligence reports indicated in mid-March that an enemy attack on MRIII was imminent, Vinh had failed to take necessary actions to reinforce the district town. He should have, for instance, secured the section of Route 13 north of Loc Ninh and recalled the mechanized Task Force 1-5 back to the district town earlier to shore up the defense of the district. He could have also sent long-range patrols to detect and destroy NVA forces with air power instead of passively waiting for the enemy attack he knew was coming.

On the other hand, Lt. Col. Nguyen Huu Duong, TF 1-5 commander, in my opinion, had failed to take appropriate precautions when he received the order to return to Loc Ninh on April 5. Instead of rolling carelessly on Route 13, he should have ordered, beforehand, the infantry to dismount and reconnoiter the area where his combined contingent was ambushed the previous day.

In any event, again according to Captain Smith's account, two bunkers inside the compound still held out until late afternoon April 7; by that time, however, the situation at the regiment command post had become hopeless. NVA troops were consolidating their positions inside the perimeter of defense and were on the verge of capturing the last two bunkers secured by walking wounded soldiers. Smith determined that it was time to escape. Smith, Sergeant Lull, and the South Vietnamese surgeon crossed the minefield to the southwest of the compound. Smith was wounded during a fire-fight with NVA soldiers. He was captured the next day, April 8, by elements of NVA 9th Division. Major Carlson, Sergeant Walling-ford, and French photographer Dumont were also captured. All were brought to a prisoner camp at Kratie in Cambodia. Lull and the regimental surgeon were never heard from again. Dumond was released on July 14 in honor of the Bastille Day. The American ad-visors were freed in Loc Ninh on February 12, 1973, in accordance with the provisions of the Paris Peace Accords.[35]

By the time the defense of the 9th Regiment headquarters collapsed, the district compound was still holding out.[36] However, by nightfall the situation rapidly deteriorated: radio contact with the regiment was lost and out of the original force of over 200 RF/PF soldiers, only a few remained. Major Thinh, the district chief, and the U.S. district advisors decided that it was time to try to break out. They rushed through the airstrip and headed toward the town, avoiding enemy patrols. Major Thinh and Maj. Thomas Davidson—who was sent to Loc Ninh to gather informa-tion on the situation in the district by Lieutenant Colonel Cor-ley, Binh Long Province senior advisor[37]—made it to An Loc on their separate ways, but Capt. George Wanat, acting senior advisor for Loc Ninh District, was captured thirty-one days after leaving the district. He later joined the American regiment advisors at the POW camp in Cambodia and was released with them after the Paris Agreement.[38]

Lt. Col. Nguyen Ngoc Anh, former Assistant for Operations to Lt. Gen. Nguyen Van Minh and spokesman for ARVN III Corps, reported the following NVA and ARVN losses in the Battle of Loc Ninh:

> Enemy: 2,150 KIA (Killed in Action)
> 2 T-54s and 1 PT-56 destroyed.
> Friendly: 600 KIA, 2,400 captured.
> 38 M-41s and M-113s destroyed or captured.
> 8 artillery howitzers destroyed or damaged.[39]

Refugees from Loc Ninh later reported that after taking the city, the NVA organized people's tribunals where militiamen, local government officials, and teachers were condemned and executed.

The rest of the "puppet civilians" were transported by trucks to an internment camp in Snoul, Cambodia.

While during the 1968 Tet Offensive—with the exception of Hue where more than 4,000 innocent people were massacred for not cooperating with the "revolution"—the VC, in the most part, tried to induce the urban population to participate in the "General Uprising" to overthrow the South Vietnamese government, in the 1972 Easter Offensive, they didn't care about "winning the hearts and minds" of the population. In fact, having failed to rally the people to their cause in 1968, this time the Communists were determined to punish the "people's enemies, reactionaries, and counter-revolutionaries."[40] During the first attack on An Loc, for example, an enemy T-54 tank rolled into a Catholic church and opened fire with its cannon and machineguns on women and children conducting prayer service, killing over 100 innocent people. The T-54 tank was later blown up by air strikes when it withdrew to the city square and put up a white flag.[41]

Four

Prelude to the Battle of An Loc

While the battle was raging in Loc Ninh, President Thieu, on April 7, convened a meeting of the corps commanders at the Independence Palace in Saigon to assess the national military crisis. Present at the meeting were Gen. Tran Thien Khiem, the prime minister, Gen. Cao Van Vien, Chairman of the JGS, Gen. Dang Van Quang, Assistant to the President for National Security Affairs, and the four corps commanders.

By that time, President Thieu and ARVN/JGS believed that the main thrust of the enemy Easter Offensive was in MRI. I Corps, in fact, was reeling from enemy multi-divisional assaults and the over-extended 3rd Division was forced to retreat behind the Cam Lo River. The 57th and 2nd Regiments, outgunned and outnumbered, had fallen back to the new defense line extending from Dong Ha to RN 9. The 56th Regiment and the 147th Marine Brigade—the latter was under the tactical control of the 3rd Division—also suffered heavy casualties and had to abandon two strategic positions on the western flank of the 3rd Division. To make matters worse, Lt. Col. Pham Van Dinh, the 56th Regiment commander, had just surrendered to the enemy at the former U.S. Camp Carroll with the remnants of his regiment. A promising young officer, Dinh had distinguished himself during the 1968 Tet Offensive and was awarded the U.S Silver Star for heroism during the fight to retake the Citadel of Hue. His betrayal dealt a heavy blow to the morale of ARVN troops at a very critical time.

In MRII, the situation was relatively quiet after the collapse of Tan Canh at the end of March and the first elements of ARVN's 23rd Division had already arrived at Kontum in an effort to stop the NVA's thrust toward Pleiku, the seat of II Corps headquarters.

President Thieu and JGS fully realized that, due to An Loc's close proximity to Saigon, the fall of this provincial capital would place the three attacking NVA divisions at a striking distance from the capital. However, the intensity of the attack in MRI, the massive use of artillery and missiles, the heavy casualties of the 3rd Division, and the fact that the attack on Quang Tri was directed by the NVA High Command itself, convinced President Thieu that the two northern provinces were the main objective of the enemy's so-called Great Offensive.

In any event, during that fateful meeting at the Independence Palace, General Minh, III Corps commander, requested additional units to help cope with the ongoing attack in Binh Long province. Minh also stressed the importance of establishing a defense line around Saigon in case An Loc was overrun and an additional division could be used for that purpose.[1] He was asked to leave the room while the war council discussed his request. Minh was later recalled into the room to be informed that the 21st Division in IV Corps will be put under his command to relieve An Loc. In addition, the 1st Airborne Brigade—which was providing security to the Independence Palace—and the 81st Airborne Commando Group, two of the few uncommitted units in the JGS general reserve, would be attached to III Corps for the defense of An Loc.

During the meeting, Gen. Dang Van Quang, Assistant to the President for Security, had convinced President Thieu that the loss of a capital city so close to Saigon would be a disastrous loss of face and a big blow to the morale of the army.[2] It should be noted that Quang was General Minh's mentor. A former commander of the 21st Division, Quang recommended Minh to succeed him at that position when he was appointed IV Corps commander in 1964. Quang, Minh, and Hung, the 5th Division commander, were members of the so-called "Delta Clan." They were all strong supporters of President Thieu who, himself, had preceded Quang as IV Corps commander. General Minh was indeed fortunate to have a mentor who had the ears of the President and thus was in a good position to help him in time of need.

At first, President Thieu had considered putting one division from IV Corps under JGS general reserve for possible deployment in MRI to help retake the lost territory north of Cam Lo River. Then, as it was decided to put the 9th Division under the disposal of III Corps to relieve An Loc, Gen. Ngo Quang Truong, IV Corps commander,[3] suggested sending the 21st Division instead because the latter had just achieved a great victory during a search and destroy operation in the U Minh Forest and had a good record in mobile operations; further, the 21st was formerly commanded by General Minh himself and that assignment would prevent any possible friction and resentment when a unit is put under a new command far away from its usual area of operation.[4]

While the NVA 5th Division was launching its final assaults on ARVN positions in Loc Ninh, elements of their 9th Division were closing in on An Loc. Workers from rubber plantations around An Loc and the civilian population reported large concentrations of enemy forces—including tank units—in the vicinity of the town. Anticipating an impending major attack on the city, Colonel Nhut recommended to General Hung to reinforce Dong Long Hill (altitude 128 meters) located one kilometer north of An Loc at the northern tip of an airstrip of the same name. From Dong Long Hill ARVN troops could observe enemy activities on the entire northern sector of the city. At that time, Dong Long Hill was manned by a RF platoon. General Hung agreed to Nhut's request and sent the 5th Reconnaissance Company to reinforce Dong Long base. This company was later replaced by the 8th Reconnaissance Company.

Furthermore, Nhut moved the 254th RF Company, which was operating in Van Hien hamlet, twelve kilometers east of the city, to Hill 169. The latter, located about four kilometers southeast of An Loc, would allow friendly forces to observe enemy movements south and east of the city. Because of Hill 169's strategic importance, Nhut recommended to General Hung to reinforce it with one company from the 3rd Ranger Group—which had received orders to be airlifted into An Loc in the next few days. Hung again acquiesced to Nhut's request.[5]

To prepare for the incoming attack, Nhut directed his provincial administrative assistant, Mr. Vo Tan Vinh, to coordinate with the An Loc district chief, and the heads of the Social and Information departments, in order to centralize the storage of rice and other basic necessities; to locate the refugees in safe centers away from military installations; to distribute food to the refugees; and to direct the population, via the public loud-speaker system, to dig trenches and foxholes in preparation for enemy artillery fire. "An Loc was going underground," wrote an American reporter. Old shelters that had been dug in the houses to protect against occasional VC mortar fire in the past were enlarged and reinforced and new ones were built.

Nhut, on the other hand, instructed Lt. Col. Nguyen Thong Thanh, the sector deputy commander, to coordinate the defense plan with friendly units, to confiscate all defense materiel, including barbed wire and sand bags from the Logistics Administration Center and even from the province's Public Works Department, and to distribute these to provincial units and also to the units of the 5th Division. In anticipation of an enemy attack by tanks, Nhut directed that M-72 antitank weapons be issued to the members of the PSDF, who would be trained immediately on their use.[6]

When General Minh ordered the 3rd Ranger Group to be heliborne into An Loc to reinforce the defense of the city on April 5, the Ranger unit was in the middle of an operation in the Parrot's Beak area west of Tay Ninh province. The objective of the Parrot's Beak operation was to identify the locations of the NVA 5th, 7th, and 9th Divisions that had suddenly disappeared from III Corps intelligence maps. During the incursion into the VC secret base, the rangers discovered in the Parrott's Beak area important weapon caches, including 82mm mortars and 57mm recoilless rifles. When they encountered the enemy, the latter just put up a cursory resistance and ran away. This indicated to intelligence officers at III Corps that these were only rear service units and that the three enemy main force divisions may have already moved into Binh Long province.[7]

The 3rd Ranger Group commander, Lt. Col. Nguyen Van Biet, was a brave officer. Because he was always friendly and cared for the welfare of his men, his staff officers affectionately called him "Anh Hai" (Elder Brother).

The 3rd Ranger Group was scheduled to be transported into An Loc by Chinook helicopters from Trang Lon airfield in Tay Ninh on April 7, but because of the rapidly deteriorating situation in Loc Ninh and the weakness of the northern sector of An Loc, General Hung asked that one ranger battalion be heliborne into the city one day earlier to occupy the high ground north of An Loc and the northern defense perimeter. Colonel Biet complied and sent the 31st Ranger Battalion to An Loc on April 6.

As the helicopters transporting Colonel Biet and his staff were approaching An Loc in the morning of April 7, the city was under enemy artillery fire. Colonel Biet was slightly wounded in the wrist after landing. Maj. Hong Khac Tran, S-3 (Operations) was also lightly wounded in the arm. The most seriously wounded were Lieutenant Tai, S-2 (Intelligence), and Captain Tho, Assistant S-3. Tai was hit in the eye by a piece of shrapnel; he eventually lost the eye entirely. Tho was hit above the ankle by shrapnel, his leg had to be amputated; he eventually recovered from his wound but was discharged from the army. All the seriously wounded were evacuated in the helicopters that brought in the last elements of the 52nd Ranger Battalion.[8]

Upon arrival, the ranger units quickly occupied their assigned positions in the northeastern sector in accordance with the defense plan that had been forwarded earlier to Colonel Biet in Tay Ninh. As the rangers moved toward their assigned sectors, they could hear announcements from the provincial Open Arms Office loudspeakers asking the residents to remain calm, and assuring them that reinforcements were arriving in An Loc. The residents were also requested to go about their business, to keep a watchful eye on possible enemy infiltration, and to report immediately to local government authorities any suspicious activities.

When Colonel Biet, accompanied by his assistant S-3 and two radiomen, reported to the 5th Division command post, he was greeted by General Hung and Colonel Vy, the 5th Division deputy commander. "You guys arrived just in the nick of time," said Hung.[9] After the short meeting, Colonel Vy briefed Biet on the friendly and enemy situation in Loc Ninh and An Loc. Before Biet left, Colonel Vy instructed him to alert the 31st Battalion about the retreating friendly infantry and armored units from Loc Ninh. The 31st Battalion must cautiously identify these units and report immediately to 5th Division Headquarters.

Back at the 3rd Ranger Group headquarters—which was established at the old U.S. Civil Defense Group base in the city, on the top of a small hill near the 5th Division command post—Colonel Biet convened a meeting of his battalion commanders to brief them on the tactical situation in An Loc and to inquire about the status of the deployment of the ranger battalions. Maj. Truong Khanh, the 31st Ranger Battalion commander, reported that he had dispatched two companies to secure the area north of An Loc. Lt. Truong Phuoc's company had occupied the section of Route 13 between Dong Long Hill and Be Moi hamlet just south of Can Le Bridge. Lt. Son Do's company was defending Dong Long Hill and the surrounding smaller hills on the east side of Route 13 north of the airfield. Maj. Tong Viet Lac, the 36th Battalion commander, reported that his unit had finished deploying along the northeastern perimeter of defense. Lastly, Maj. Le Quy Dau, the 52nd Battalion commander, reported that his unit and the 3rd Reconnaissance Company were occupying their assigned positions on the eastern sector adjacent to the 31st Battalion. One company from his battalion was defending Hill 169, southeast of An Loc, as had been requested by 5th Division.[10]

In the afternoon of April 7, Chon Thanh district came under heavy artillery fire. Lt. Col. Pham Quang My, the district chief, was slightly wounded; the deputy district chief, an army major, was killed. Colonel Nhut decided to send Maj. Nguyen Van Quoc, the sector deputy chief of staff for operations and logistics, to Chon Thanh that same night to replace the Chon Thanh deputy district chief. Major Quoc would be in charge of coordinating the efforts to support the units that had received the mission to secure Route 13 and to link up with An Loc.[11]

Also on April 7, after the fall of Loc Ninh, Maj. Vo Van Tay, commander of RF Company Group 3/25—that was operating in an area twenty-five kilometers southwest of An Loc—ordered the

987th and 989th RF Companies as well as PF and police forces in his area of responsibility to withdraw to Minh Thanh outpost, twenty kilometers west of Chon Thanh. Hundreds of administrative officials and their families also took refuge in the outpost. With a total force of 170 men, Major Tay and his deputy, Capt. Ho Ngoc Son, were determined to defend Minh Thanh at all costs. Like Tong Le Chan outpost farther north, Major Tay and his men held out during the entire battle of An Loc, beating back numerous NVA attacks. On April 8, the enemy launched the biggest ground attack so far after unleashing a powerful artillery barrage on the garrison. Because Minh Thanh outpost was an old U.S. Fire Support Base with strong defensive positions surrounded by an important system of barbed wire and minefields, the defenders were able to beat back the attack. (However, because of difficulties of supply and mounting casualties, on October 14, the outpost was ordered to withdraw after six months of heroic resistance. Although the evacuation was kept secret to the last minute, the enemy somehow discovered the garrison's intention and conducted a pursuit operation to destroy the withdrawing column. Only Lieutenant Colonel Tay—who was recently promoted—and about 50% of the garrison along with twenty women and children, made it to Chon Thanh.)[12]

In the evening of April 7, NVA units from the 9th Division overran the 1st Battalion of ARVN's 7th Regiment defending Quan Loi airstrip east of An Loc. The defenders were ordered to destroy all their equipment—including the artillery howitzers—and withdraw to the city. The battalion commander was killed during the enemy attack; only two companies made it to An Loc.[13] With the interdiction of Route 13 by elements of the NVA's 7th Division and the loss of Quan Loi airstrip, An Loc was effectively cut off from the outside world. By taking Quan Loi, the enemy also captured a great number of 2.75mm rockets left by the 1st U.S. Cavalry Division. These rockets were very effective against enemy tanks and were the main weapon of the Aerial Rocket Artillery batteries of the 1st Cavalry Division. The NVA fired these captured rockets at the garrison of An Loc from Doi Gio Hill.[14]

In the morning of April 8, Colonel Biet, 3rd Ranger Group commander, directed the 36th Ranger Battalion to execute a reconnaissance in force in the direction of Quan Loi. At a location about one kilometer east of An Loc, the rangers saw many people racing toward them from Quan Loi. They were followed by NVA units that kept shooting at them. Many were killed before reaching the 36th Ranger line. Major Lac, the battalion commander, requested the artillery batteries at An Loc to fire smoke ammunition between the fleeing population and the pursuing NVA troops. Then, as the enemy took cover on both sides of the road, he concentrated artillery fire on them. The enemy withdrew without engaging the rangers.[15]

Although the presence of the units of the 9th NVA Division around An Loc had been reported on April 5 and the shelling on the capital city had begun on that date, except for the attack on Quan Loi airport, there were no other attempts to launch ground assaults for several more days. Captured prisoners later reported that the enemy failed to mount an attack on An Loc immediately after the fall of Loc Ninh because logistical preparations were not keeping pace with the planned offensive. According to Gen. Ngo Quang Truong, the enemy's plan called for harassing and attacking ARVN's outposts along the Cambodian border during the first week of the offensive and—coincidental with these diversionary actions—moving supplies to the frontline in preparation for the attack on An Loc. However, the premature evacuation of the border outposts by ARVN III Corps had upset the enemy's plan and logistical preparations; as a consequence, the 9th NVA Division had to postpone the attack after it had occupied its forward positions.[16]

In any event, the lull after the fall of Loc Ninh allowed the South Vietnamese to quickly reinforce the garrison with—successively—the 3rd Ranger Group, the 7th Regiment (-), and the 8th Regiment. By April 8, the remnants of TF-52 also began to arrive at An Loc. It had lost about one-half of its effective force during the withdrawal.[17] All heavy equipment and artillery had been destroyed or abandoned. General Hung assigned to TF-52 the mission of defending the small central area of the city, where the 51st Artillery Battalion and one 155mm artillery battery were located.

Amidst the chaos following the collapse of Loc Ninh, Col. Truong Huu Duc, commanding the 5th Armored Squadron— which was attached to the 5th Division—was killed by enemy anti-aircraft fire while on an aerial reconnaissance mission north of Chon Thanh. The news of the death of Colonel Duc, a classmate of Colonel Nhut at the Vietnamese Military Academy, came at a time of growing concerns about the grim tactical developments in Binh Long province. When his remains were brought to Lai Khe, Vietnamese reporters misidentified him as Colonel Nhut (both were tall and grew a mustache) and the announcement of Nhut's death on Saigon newspapers the following day caused a lot of commotion for Nhut's family and friends.[18]

In the early morning of April 9, the enemy launched small ground probes on the western, eastern, and northern sectors of An Loc, obviously with the intention of identifying the perimeter of defense. These contacts lasted about four hours. ARVN forces captured four prisoners who belonged to Regiments 95C, 271st, and 272nd of the 9th Division. The next day, the enemy attacked again at 5:30 A.M. but broke off after about two hours of contact.[19]

While the An Loc garrison was bracing for an imminent enemy tank-supported assault, the defenders were encouraged by good news from Quang Tri. On April 9, the 6th Marine Battalion, using only M-72 weapons, had destroyed a dozen NVA tanks around Quang Tri city. This victory, which had been largely broadcast on the national radio, boosted the confidence of the defenders in the effectiveness of the M-72 against enemy tanks. ARVN unit commanders in An Loc also took advantage of this good news to conduct on-the-spot training in the use of this powerful weapon.

On April 10, General Minh asked Col. Mach Van Truong, 8th Regiment commander, to report to him at III Corps Headquarters at Bien Hoa immediately. General Minh told Truong he believed An Loc would be attacked in the next few days and that General Hung could not defend the city with only the 7th Regiment, the 3rd Ranger Group, and the depleted TF-52. As the JGS general reserve units had not arrived, he (General Minh) decided to commit the 8th Regiment, which would be heliborne into An Loc the following day. "The situation is very difficult and grave, try your best to bring your troops to An Loc safely. Hung is waiting for you," Minh said.[20]

In the morning of April 11, while the 8th Regiment was waiting to be picked up at Dau Tieng airstrip, Lieutenant Colonel Abramawith, the senior regiment advisor, came to tell Colonel Truong that the U.S. advisory team had received orders not to go to An Loc, and that they would return to the U.S. compound at Lai Khe.[21]

As Colonel Truong's C&C helicopter and the first lift (10 helicopters transporting 100 men) were approaching An Loc, enemy artillery was firing from all directions, interdicting the airstrip, the soccer field, and the helipads within the city. Fortunately, Truong saw a small clearing in the middle of the forest about three kilometers south of An Loc; he decided to land his troops in the clearing that had not been targeted by enemy artillery. Truong and his light headquarters landed with the first lift. During the day, two battalions landed safely. The last battalion and 400 convicted deserters, also known as *lao cong dao binh* (or LCDB)—who were assigned to the 5th Division—were brought in safely the next morning. (The LCDBs, army deserters, were assigned heavy manual labor/construction work on the frontline. Contrary to the enemy deserters who rallied to the South Vietnamese government, the ARVN's LCDBs didn't join the enemy ranks; most of them returned to their hometowns to reenlist in the local territorial forces, usually under different names.)

When Truong arrived at the 5th Division headquarters, General Hung asked him about the strength of his regiment. Truong reported that, because the 9th Regiment had been overrun in Loc Ninh and the 7th Regiment was under constant enemy attack, all division replacements had been channeled to his regiment, and as a consequence, each of his battalions had an effective strength of more than 600 men. Truong also informed General Hung that he had all his recoilless rifles, but he didn't have the rockets; he disclosed, however, that he had brought along the 2,000 or so M-72s that he had discovered at the old U.S. base of Dau Tieng. General Hung was elated; he asked Colonel Vy, his deputy, to tell all units in the garrison to contact the 8th Regiment if they had a need for these God-sent antitank weapons.

General Hung then took Truong to the division operation room. Using a grease pencil, Hung drew new boundaries in the defense plan and told his deputy: "The 8th Regiment is still fresh, well equipped and up to strength; thus, it will be assigned the northern sector. The 7th Regiment will take care of the western sector. The 3rd

Ranger Group will hold the east and Binh Long Sector will defend the south."[22]

While waiting for the operation order, Truong suggested to Colonel Vy to lay antitank mines on Route 13 because the latter obviously constituted the main avenue of approach for NVA tanks. Vy said he had discussed this matter with Colonel Nhut, but Nhut disagreed, arguing that it would hamper the traffic of the vehicles of surrounding rubber plantations.

Colonel Vy also expressed his concern about the balance of forces. The enemy had many tanks while the defenders had none. With regard to artillery, the 9th Regiment and the 52nd Regiment had lost all their artillery pieces at Loc Ninh and Hung Tam base. The 8th Regiment had been unable to bring in its own artillery. As a consequence, the only artillery units available for the defense of An Loc were the 51st Artillery Battalion—which normally provided direct support to the 7th Regiment—and one 155mm artillery battery. These artillery units had been subjected to constant enemy artillery bombardments the last few days and had suffered heavy damage. The Division was now using them in general support for the garrison with priority for those units that were in heavy contact with the enemy.

Following the new defense plan, Colonel Truong deployed two battalions on the northern perimeter. During the night, the troops dug their foxholes and bunkers and erected overheads to protect against enemy artillery. Their work was hampered by the thick layers of solid underground rocks that were characteristic of this area.

The next morning, Colonel Truong directed the newly arrived third battalion to occupy the high-rise buildings along Route 13. This battalion provided the defense in depth and also constituted the regiment reserve. Per 5th Division's request, the 8th Reconnaissance Company established an outpost on Dong Long Hill that was occupied by a ranger company from the 31st Ranger Battalion.

On April 11, while the 8th Regiment was landing south of An Loc, NVA forces supported by tanks attacked the 36th Ranger Battalion's position one kilometer east of the city from the north, east, and west. At one point, the rangers had to direct artillery fire only fifty meters in front of their frontline, where enemy assaults were pinned down by the rangers' machineguns. Lt. Dong Kim Quang,

4th Company commander, reported seeing enemy bodies jettisoned into the air under the impact of artillery fire. Then, he saw about ten enemy tanks racing toward his company from the east. He directed his men to fire their M-72 rocket launchers at the approaching tanks. One T-54 tank was destroyed and the rest of the T-54 tank column turned around and disappeared.[23]

Around noon, April 12, NVA artillery destroyed a storage facility near the airstrip. This storage and the adjacent supply depots were established by III Corps to support previous border operations. Concerned about the safety of this logistical complex, General Hung ordered all units in the garrison to get the maximum amount of ammunition from the depots so they would be able to fight many days without being resupplied.

In the meantime, the escapees from Loc Ninh were streaming back toward An Loc. During the first few days after its arrival in An Loc, the 31st Ranger Battalion, which was at that time defending the northern sector of the city, had received several soldiers from the 9th Regiment who had fought their way back into friendly lines after the collapse of the district town of Loc Ninh. The company, which was securing the portion of Route 13 from An Loc to Can Le Bridge, screened them very carefully before letting them through. On April 11, Phuoc's company received two important escapees: Maj. Nguyen Van Thinh, Loc Ninh district chief, and Maj. Thomas Davidson, along with Davidson's interpreter. The three men arrived at the same time. The rangers watched them carefully, kept them at a safe distance, and ordered them to give their name, rank, and parent unit. The rangers later recounted that the three men were so terrified that they would be shot by friendly troops when they were so close to freedom that they shouted their names, ranks, and parent units at the top of their lungs. The escapees were so happy at having reached friendly lines that they cried and effusively hugged Lieutenant Phuoc, the company commander.[24] Colonel Nhut sent a jeep to pick them up and personally thanked Phuoc for having taken care of the district chief and Major Davidson. Nhut was not only happy to know that his district chief was alive, but he was eager to debrief him on the NVA forces attacking Loc Ninh and, more importantly, on the tank formations involved in that attack.

The first few days after the fall of Loc Ninh, a unit of the 5th Medical Battalion at Dong Long had received about 200 wounded soldiers from the above district and from other units that were attacked by NVA forces around Loc Ninh. The most seriously wounded were evacuated to Lai Khe or Saigon.

A few days after the rangers arrived at An Loc, Capt. Nguyen Quoc Khue, Assistant S-3, climbed to the top of the 3rd Ranger Group Operation Center to observe the situation in the surrounding area when he heard the city's loudspeakers appealing to both sides to cease all fire to let the civilians leave the area. Then a large number of people, led by Catholic priests and Buddhist monks, appeared to the east of the Ranger Group headquarters. The column of civilians, waving white flags, walked toward Route 13 to the south. As they moved past the southern sector held by the provincial forces, Khue heard heavy artillery explosions in that direction.

"The civilians in the column, hit by one heavy artillery round after another, screamed in terror," Khue later recalled, "and the sounds of crying children echoed all the way to the place where I was standing... This time the enemy seemed to have forward observers adjusting fire, because the shells all landed right in the middle of the column of civilians, sending bodies flying in all directions. Arms and legs could be seen hanging from the trees alongside the road. Because this was an open area bordering the road leading toward the city, there was no cover the civilians could use to escape the shelling, and a number of them were forced to seek shelter behind the trunks of large trees. After the enemy stopped their artillery barrage, the civilians, and even the priests and the Buddhist monks, dispersed and returned to their homes and their former places of refuge, because the enemy shelling clearly demonstrated the enemy's vicious intentions toward them."[25]

The above-described carnage was not an isolated incident. Indeed, it had become a pattern that whenever the NVA saw people fleeing a town under siege, they brought upon them all their firepower to kill these crowds of "puppet civilians." The massacre of innocent refugees would be repeated by the carnage in MRI in May 1972, where thousands of refugees perished under artillery and missile concentrations along the section of Route Nationale 1

(RN1) south of Quang Tri, which was subsequently littered with charred corpses and burned vehicles. That section of RN1 was later known as "The Freeway of Horror."

Not only were the NVA targeting fleeing refugees, but they also sought to destroy medical centers to create additional logistical burdens for a city under siege. On May 8, for example, an enemy artillery shell hit the An Loc hospital, killing and injuring hundreds of people.

After the war, Khue was sent to re-education in North Viet Nam. One day, during a self-critique session, he mentioned the shelling of the civilians in An Loc to the Communist officials in the camp. The political cadre explained, "The revolution shelled this civilian crowd because this was a crowd of puppet civilians, filled with reactionaries and counter-revolutionaries. We could not exempt them, and we had to teach them a lesson."[26]

As the shelling increased in intensity, a large number of civilians fled their homes to seek refuge inside the troop bunkers and fortifications because the latter were larger and better built. Some ARVN units also occupied public buildings, which all had large concrete bunkers to protect government employees against occasional enemy mortar fire, even during periods of relative calm. The civilians cooked and ate with the soldiers, and the soldiers, in return, tended the civilians' wounds and provided them with medicines.

In the middle of this tense situation, the 3rd Ranger Group advisory team suddenly left. One morning, Captain Khue, the Ranger Group assistant S-3, noticed that the U.S. advisors were packing their belongings as if they were about to move out. He asked an American sergeant about it and was told that the team had received orders to be prepared to be picked up by a helicopter. Khue reported this to Colonel Biet, who in turn asked the group senior advisor. Biet received the same answer without further explanation. A few minutes later a helicopter flew in from the east at tree-top level above Quan Loi plantation. It turned toward the Ranger Group headquarters and landed on a nearby helicopter pad. The entire advisory team rushed toward the helicopter and jumped in; the helicopter took off and disappeared in the east toward Quan Loi.

The Ranger Group staff was shocked and worried that the American advisors had abandoned them to their fate and that it would be more difficult in the future to request air support in case of emergencies. Colonel Biet grabbed a telephone and called the 5th Division headquarters to inquire about the precipitate departure of his advisors, but the telephone was dead because the lines had been cut in numerous places by artillery fire. Finally, after communication had been restored, the 5th Division informed Colonel Biet in the evening that it had checked with III Corps Headquarters and was told the Ranger advisory team had completed their tour of duty and therefore had to leave. The division also informed Biet that a new team was scheduled to arrive the next day.

Sure enough, at dawn the next morning, a helicopter suddenly appeared from the direction of Quan Loi and landed on the Ranger helipad. Four American advisors leaped out and ran toward the Ranger Group Operation Center while the helicopter immediately took off and disappeared in the southeast. The new team, consisting of Lt. Col. Richard J. McManus, a first lieutenant, and two NCOs carrying radios, was warmly welcome by Colonel Biet. The new senior advisor to the 3rd Ranger Group apologized for the sudden rotation of the Ranger advisory team. He said the change was not announced in order to preserve secrecy. He also informed Colonel Biet that three NVA divisions were converging toward An Loc, but he assured Biet that the Americans would support the garrison with all strategic and tactical air resources available to defeat the enemy offensive. Everyone in the Ranger Group command post breathed a sigh of relief.

The same message of U.S. support was broadcast the next morning on the city's loudspeakers. The residents of An Loc could hear statements from the Senior Advisor to III Corps/MRIII appealing for calm and urging the people to defend the city at all costs. The American Senior Advisor also said that the U.S. Armed Forces would support An Loc with all air resources available. He introduced himself as General Hollingsworth and promised that he was ready to support An Loc.

The following day, the 3rd Ranger Group Operation Center was hit by a 122mm rocket. The rocket crashed into a corner of the bunker causing a big explosion and sending shrapnel inside the command post. Colonel Biet and his S-3, Major Tran, standing near the situation map, were lightly wounded in the arm. (This was their second wound in a period of a few days in An Loc.) Captain Nang, the assistant S-3, who was waiting for his papers to be discharged from the army, was seriously wounded in the chest. Dr. Canh, the Ranger Group surgeon, reported that Nang was in extremely critical condition and needed to be evacuated immediately because he had many pieces of shrapnel in his chest, with some very close to his heart. Several radio operators were also wounded by shrapnel.

The seriously wounded, including Captain Nang, were evacuated the next day by a U.S. medevac helicopter, which was able to land at the Ranger Group helipad between two artillery salvos. Capt. Nguyen Quoc Khue, Assistant S-3, later recalled that the senior U.S. advisor to the 3rd Ranger Group was concerned that the evacuation of Colonel Biet would adversely affect the morale of the rangers at a critical time in the defense of An Loc. He was reassured when Khue informed him that Colonel Biet and his S-3 would stay with the unit. [27]

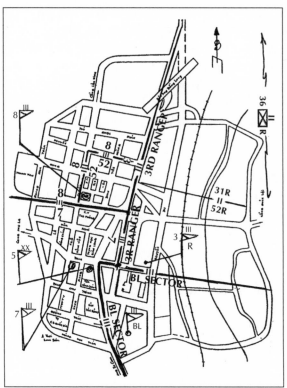

Map 7: Defense Plan

Meanwhile, with the reinforcement of the 3rd Ranger Group and the 8th Regiment, General Hung outlined the general defense plan of An Loc as follows:

- 3rd Ranger Group (1,300 men) under Lt. Col. Nguyen Van Biet, was assigned the northeastern sector. Because the defense area was relatively large, the Rangers were to adopt a "mobile defense" tactic in their area of responsibility. One company from the 52nd Battalion was dispatched to occupy Hill 169, four kilometers southeast of An Loc.
- 8th Regiment (2,100 men) under Col. Mach Van Truong was assigned the northern sector.
- 7th Regiment (2 battalions) under Lt. Col. Ly Duc Quan was assigned the southwest sector (850 men).
- 9th Regiment (-): 200 escapees from Loc Ninh and Can Le bridge.
- The remnants of TF-52 (500 men) were put in reserve and occupied a central area between the 8th Regiment and the 3rd Ranger Group.
- The Binh Long Provincial forces, supported by two 105mm howitzers and consisting of eight RF companies, PF and PSDF (about 2,000 men) were assigned the southern sector of the defense perimeter.

In addition to the two 105mm howitzers organic to Binh Long Sector, the An Loc garrison was supported by the 51st Artillery Battalion and one 155mm howitzer battery. The artillery units had about 300 men. The total effective force of the garrison, including 5th Division Headquarters and the 5th Reconnaissance Company, amounted to about 7,500 men.

On the American side, General Hollingsworth directed that non-essential advisors be evacuated. However, he was determined to avoid a repetition of the disastrous effect of the pull-out of American advisors in MRI—which was in part responsible for the collapse of the ARVN 3rd Division in Quang Tri in May 1972. Hollingsworth notified the twenty-five or so American advisors to remain with their South Vietnamese units for the duration of the siege.[28]

The enemy, on the other hand, massed three infantry divisions, supported by tanks and artillery regiments, for the attack on An Loc and the interdiction of Route 13. The NVA's order of battle, based on ARVN/JGS intelligence reports, consisted of the following units:

- 9th Division (about 7,200 men) with 271st Regiment, 272nd Regiment and 95C Regiment.
- 5th Division (5,200 men) with 274th Regiment, 275th Regiment and E6 Regiment.
- 7th Division (7,000 men) with 165th Regiment, 209th Regiment and 141st Regiment. This division was reinforced with the 11th Anti-Aircraft Regiment with 1,800 North Vietnamese soldiers. The mission of this division was to establish blocking positions at Tan Khai, about ten kilometers south of An Loc. (The 141st and 165th Regiments were later directed to reinforce the attacking units at An Loc during the second and third assaults on the capital city of Binh Long.)
- 75th Artillery Division (4,000 men) with 42nd Artillery Regiment, 208th Rocket Regiment and 271st Anti-Aircraft Regiment. In addition, NVA troops had captured a number of artillery pieces from TF-52 in the battle of Loc Ninh.
- 202nd Tank Regiment and 203rd Tank Regiment (500 men). These regiments were equipped with T-54, PT-76 tanks and BTR-50 armored personnel carriers, not counting a few M-41 tanks and M-113 armored personnel carriers from TF 1-5, which were captured north of Loc Ninh.
- 429th Sapper Group with an effective force of 1,100 men.

The total strength of the attacking forces, including independent regiments and other support units—and excluding the NVA 7th Division's blocking units on Route 13—amounted to about 21,000 men or about three times ARVN forces defending An Loc during the first phase of the siege. The NVA had many tanks and other armored vehicles while the ARVN had none. The ARVN, however, had the support of the South Vietnamese Air Force backed up by formidable U.S. airpower. The defenders, on the other hand, were determined to defeat the aggressors and to hold An Loc at all costs. President Thieu, in fact, had publicly directed senior officers and ARVN troops in An Loc to defend the city to the death and told them the nation was watching. His message had an electrifying effect on the defenders; it also constituted an open challenge to the enemy. Colonel Miller, senior advisor to the 5th Division, later commented that for President Thieu, An Loc was a "Bastogne, a place where stand or die defense would decide the fate of the enemy offensive closest to the national capital."[29] It may be more accurate, in my opinion, to compare An Loc to Verdun or, better yet, Leningrad, where the fate of the entire nation hinges on the outcome of one single battle.

Meanwhile, artillery, mortar, and rocket fire continued to increase, and ARVN patrols outside of An Loc encountered increasingly stronger enemy resistance. Refugees from surrounding hamlets reported sightings of tank units moving toward the city. Also, according to the civilian population, food displayed at local markets had all but disappeared; intelligence reports later indicated that these commodities, particularly sugar and dry foods, had been bought or taken by the enemy to supply their front-line units. ARVN soldiers who were captured at Loc Ninh, but who escaped and made their way to An Loc, reported that the enemy told them they would take the capital city of Binh Long at all costs. This intelligence and other reports indicated to General Hollingsworth that the attack on An Loc was about to begin. On April 12, Hollingsworth flew to Saigon to meet with General Abrams to request additional B-52 strikes. General Abrams agreed with Hollingsworth's assessment and directed that B-52 missions (also known as Arc Light) be diverted from I and II Corps the next day in order to support An Loc.[30]

Five

The First Attack
on An Loc

While the defenders took advantage of the lull preceding the attack to reinforce the garrison with fresh units, the NVA brought in additional anti-aircraft outfits in an effort to cut off resupply by air. At the time the attack on An Loc began, the NVA had up to nine anti-aircraft battalions positioned around the city. On the morning of April 12, a Chinook helicopter from Bien Hoa-based VNAF 237th Helicopter Squadron, piloted by Maj. Nguyen Huu Nhan, deputy squadron commander, was shot down over An Loc by enemy mortars and anti-aircraft fire while on an ammunition resupply mission. The hovering helicopter burst into a ball of flames over the LZ. All five crewmen were killed. Lt. Col. Nguyen Phu Chinh, the 237th Helicopter Squadron commander, later reported that his squadron had previously received a unit citation by III Corps for outstanding service; it also had received the Chinook pin and many letters of commendation from Boeing Company—which manufactured the Chinook helicopter—for having achieved 25,000 flying hours without accident. Alas, this safety record was shattered at An Loc where the 237th Helicopter Squadron lost ten Chinooks in a two-month period. Eleven officers and eighteen NCOs were killed; four officers and three NCOs were wounded.[1]

The same day, the provincial RF unit manning the eastern gate of An Loc reported that enemy forces were advancing toward the city behind the civilian population from Quan Loi. Not sure how to handle the situation, the RF unit commander requested the province chief's instructions. Colonel Nhut ordered the RF soldiers to fire overhead and to shoot at the civilians only if the enemy forces moved behind them to assault friendly positions. Nhut also requested U.S. gunships to shoot behind the civilians to stop NVA forces from using them as a human shield for their attack. As a result, the civilians fled in all directions. A great majority raced toward An Loc. Nhut directed the hamlet and village chiefs to identify their respective residents before directing them toward various temporary refugee camps.[2]

In the meantime, Pastor Dieu Huynh led about 500 Montagnards from neighboring villages to seek refuge at the railroad station at the eastern perimeter of the city. Families of RF and PF units as well as members of provincial territorial units, fleeing their overrun outposts, flocked to military bases to seek protection, food, and medical care. General Hung ordered all unit commanders to carefully screen these arrivals to prevent possible enemy infiltration.[3]

In anticipation of the enemy attack, III Corps provided uninterrupted tactical and B-52 support during April 11 and 12. U.S. pilots reported numerous secondary explosions. In particular, an air strike at an area five kilometers west of Phu Lo Gate at 5:00 P.M. on April 12 caused a big secondary explosion followed by series of explosions lasting until 10:00 P.M. Division intelligence officers believed that the air strike had hit an NVA advance ammunition depot.[4]

During the night of April 12, the enemy intensified the shelling of An Loc with all kinds of calibers. One round hit the provincial communication center, killing seven and wounding seven more. Civilian telephone communication with the outside world was completely cut off. The volume of the artillery barrage increased dramatically in the early hours of April 13. "Not a single square meter of An Loc was free of impacts from 82mm mortars, 122mm rockets, 130mm guns, and also from 105mm and 155mm howitzers captured by the enemy in Loc Ninh and from TF-52 at Hung Tam Base," wrote Gen. Tran Van Nhut in his memoir.[5] The original 5th Division Forward CP on the east side of the city was also destroyed. Fortunately, General Hung had decided early on to move his CP to the old Japanese underground compound. The Catholic church and the railroad station were also hit by artillery fire, causing heavy casualties to the refugees. General Hung ordered the regimental medical teams to go to these places to provide first aid to the wounded civilians.[6]

About 4:00 A.M., a reconnaissance patrol from the 7th Regiment reported hearing the sounds of tanks moving in the rubber plantations to the west. Trip flares and claymore mines laid by ARVN units in front of the perimeter of defense started to go off as the NVA tried to probe the defense line. An AC130 Spectre gunship was called; it fired on some trucks identified in the rubber trees.[7]

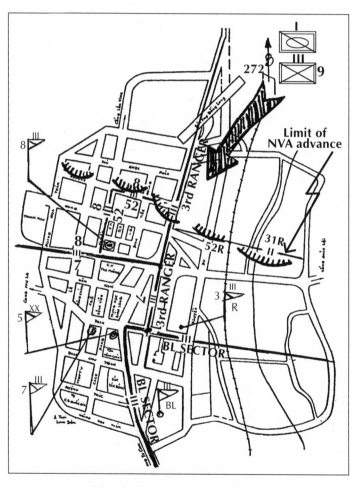

Map 8: First Attack on An Loc

The first attack on An Loc began at 5:15 A.M. The attack was launched by the 9th Division supported by elements of a tank battalion. (The 5th Division—that had suffered heavy losses during the battle of Loc Ninh—needed additional time to reorganize and re-equip before joining forces with the 9th Division.) The assault was preceded by intense artillery preparation on Dong Long airstrip and on An Loc city itself. The fuel and ammunition depot at the airstrip was hit and exploded. The RF battalion defending the airport was overrun by tank-supported enemy assaults and had to withdraw and join forces with the Binh Long territorial units in the southern sector of the garrison. At the same time, the units defending the northern sector reported a column of tanks and trucks was moving toward the city on Route 13. An AC-130 Spectre, which was covering An Loc, swung into action and destroyed one tank and four trucks.[8]

While the NVA concentrated their artillery barrage on the northern perimeter, the 8th Reconnaissance Company and the RF unit defending Dong Long Hill beat back three successive human-wave assaults and destroyed two T-54s and one PT-76.[9] Around 6:00 A.M., the 8th Reconnaissance Company reported that it was being overrun by enemy tanks. Col. Mach Van Truong, 8th Regiment commander, ordered the reconnaissance company to fall back toward Hoang Hon Boulevard and become the reserve for the regiment.[10]

The capture of the strategic Dong Long Hill provided the enemy with unrestricted fields of observation in the northern sector of An Loc. Dong Long was also an ideal site for the enemy to position its anti-aircraft weapons, mortars, and recoilless rifles to shoot with deadly accuracy at incoming aircraft and ARVN units defending the northern perimeter of defense.

Effective immediately, on order from General Hung, all units activated their AN/PRC25 radio sets, which were used only in cases of emergency and when the telephone lines were disrupted by enemy artillery fire. Day and night, every time a telephone line was cut off, the 5th Signal Battalion and the signal units of the regiments had to repair the line, and many members of the signal teams were killed in their line of duty. (After the siege, General Hung organized a special ceremony in Lai Khe to recognize the achievements of the signals personnel and award decorations to the heroes of the signal units in An Loc.)[11]

At 7:00 A.M., the enemy shifted their artillery fire toward the center of the city and their infantry began to attack. On the east and west sides, outbursts of gunfire rang out without interruption: The 3rd Ranger Group and the 7th Regiment were also under attack and were engaging the enemy in their sectors.

On the north side, the column of tanks continued to move slowly toward the city. On each side of the road, one reinforced infantry battalion progressed alongside the tank column. When the tanks reached the area that was previously targeted by ARVN artillery, just north of the defense perimeter, Maj. Hoang Trung Liem, the artillery liaison officer with the 8th Regiment, ordered a "fire for effect." At the same time, the 81mm mortars of the regiment started to fire on the accompanying infantry. The latter, taken by surprise, ran in all directions; the tanks in the rear of the column were stopped by artillery fire while the tanks in the front, unable to back up, continued to progress without infantry.[12]

However, the enemy tanks were able to regroup after the cessation of ARVN artillery interdiction fire, and a column of about fifteen M-54s started to move south on Ngo Quyen Street, which was the section of Route 13 that traversed the city of An Loc. When the tanks were about to reach Nguyen Trung Truc Street, the soldiers from the 8th Regiment positioned on the high-rise buildings on both sides of Ngo Quyen Street began to fire their M-72s and machineguns from the buildings' windows, killing or wounding many tankers, and causing the remaining enemy machine gunners to abandon their weapons, close the hatches, and hide inside their tanks. When the lead tank reached Hoang Hon Boulevard, the third tank in the column was hit by an M-72 rocket fired by a soldier of the regiment. The tank exploded and burst into flames; the burned tankers jumped out of the tank and rolled back and forth on the sidewalks in pain; they were finished off by a volley of M-16 bullets. While the lead tanks continued to roll down toward the center of the city, the tanks in the middle of the column, right behind the burned tank, had to stop and the soldiers of the 8th Regiment took this opportunity to kill three more. The tanks at the end of the column backed up and turned left and right; three tanks were destroyed by the soldiers of the 3rd Ranger Group and two by the 7th Regiment.[13]

The two lead tanks, which had escaped the 8th Regiment's ambush, accelerated and rushed southward. The first tank, approaching Phan Boi Chau Street from the north, was closing in on the 5th Division's headquarters. The soldiers guarding the gate of General Hung's underground command post panicked and ran for cover because this was the first time they had faced an enemy tank and also because they didn't believe in the effectiveness of the M-72 weapon. General Hung grabbed a hand grenade and was ready to hurl it at the enemy in case they ventured into the bunker. As the tank was turning around in an effort to identify the location of General Hung's command post, Col. Le Nguyen Vy, deputy division commander, emerged from the underground bunker, aimed his LAW at the tank and set it ablaze just in front of the division headquarters. The tank was finished off at the junction of Phan Boi Chau and Hoang Hoa Tham Streets by the soldiers of the 7th Regiment. The second tank turned back and was hit by one 105mm round from a battery of the 51st Artillery Battalion executing a direct fire in the vicinity of Tao Phung Park; the damaged tank was destroyed by soldiers from the 8th Reconnaissance Company when it tried to escape toward Hoang Hon Boulevard.[14]

Nguyen Cau, a TV reporter who stayed at An Loc during the entire siege, recalled that, when the enemy tanks were closing in on his command post, General Hung told his staff that he would not be captured alive and that in case he had to commit suicide, they must destroy the Division's signal code immediately.[15]

While all this transpired, at around 9:00 A.M., U.S. Cobras armed with 2.7-inch rockets asked the 8th Regiment to mark the tanks that had been already destroyed (with smoke grenades) so that they could chase the tanks that were still in operable condition. Mach Van Truong gave the U.S. Cobras credit for killing a total of four tanks in his area.[16]

At 10:00 A.M., elements of the NVA 9th Division renewed their assault on the northern sector. In the 8th Regiment area, despite effective close air support, the enemy succeeded in capturing the two northern blocks of lightly built houses, forcing the regiment to fall back to a new defense line running generally along Nguyen Trung Truc Street.

Meanwhile, in the northeast sector, the 31st Rangers bore the brunt of the assault conducted by the 272nd Regiment of the 9th Division supported by a tank company. Lieutenant Phuoc's company—which was securing Route 13 north of An Loc—withdrew toward the city under heavy pressure. Radio contact was lost at 6:50 A.M. with the company defending the high ground east of Dong Long airstrip. Some ARVN units who had never faced tanks before retreated in panic. Colonel Biet, the Ranger Group commander, was able to rally the 31st Rangers and to organize a new defense line about one block north of Tran Hung Dao Boulevard. Observers on the top of the 3rd Ranger Group command post reported one tank moving south on an adjacent street. The Ranger Group assistant operations officer requested an air strike. A U.S Air Force F-4 Phantom (twin-engine, long-range, all-weather, fighter-bomber) responded immediately, dropping a bomb on top of the tank and setting it afire.[17]

The 36th Battalion—which was screening the northeastern perimeter—was also under heavy attack from enemy infantry supported by a column of tanks racing from Quan Loi plantation. The Ranger Group command post requested air support. U.S. warplanes swung into action and destroyed the leading tanks, but the infantry kept attacking the 36th Battalion's defensive positions at the city's outer perimeter. The 36th Battalion suffered heavy losses, and had to withdraw toward the city. What was left of the battalion took up defensive positions on the multi-story buildings on the eastern edge of the town. In the afternoon, Colonel Biet issued an order to all units to hold the positions they were occupying, and not to withdraw any further.

While the USAF and VNAF warplanes and U.S. Army Cobra attack helicopters were chasing North Vietnamese infantry and tanks from the air, a key event on the ground galvanized the morale of the garrison and increased the confidence of the defenders in the effectiveness of the M-72. It also constituted a milestone in the fight against enemy tanks. As one of the tanks rolled down Route 13 all the way toward the southern gate, eighteen-year-old Pham Cuong Tuan, a member of the People's Self-Defense Force—with two of his comrades Tran Van Binh and Nguyen Van Giang, both sixteen—standing on the roof of the second floor of a elementary school, raised his three-pound LAW-72 rocket launcher and shot point-blank at the approaching tank. The T-54 exploded amid the cheers of his comrades. At the same time, a ranger destroyed another T-54 with his rocket launcher on the eastern sector. Word spread quickly that LAWs can stop enemy tanks and that even young members of the PSDF can do it. ARVN soldiers overcame their fear, emerged from their foxholes and started to chase and destroy tanks all over the city.[18]

"The little guy goes out to hunt a 40-ton piece of metal with a light antitank weapon on his back weighing two to three pounds," recalled a U.S. advisor with the 3rd Ranger Group. "That's beyond belief and it inspired me. How do you describe a little ARVN soldier fighting tanks? I was pretty well frightened like everyone else till it was determined we could knock them out with the weapon we had."[19] Even the LCDBs assigned to the Ranger Group also participated in the fight against enemy tanks. As a column of four T-54s coming down from Trung Vuong Street turned to Nguyen Trung Truc Street behind the Old Market, one LCDB threw a hand grenade into the auxiliary fuel tank of one of the T-54s, causing the tank to burst into flames; the North Vietnamese tankers opened the hatch and ran out in all directions. They were all killed on the spot.[20]

While the jet fighters were effective in destroying enemy formations massing for the attack outside the perimeter of defense, close support inside the city was better handled by the more versatile and maneuverable Cobra attack helicopters. The latter were credited with destroying twenty NVA tanks during the battle of An Loc, but they also had to pay a heavy price for their bravery: five Cobras were shot down during the first day of the attack and eight crewmen (out of thirty-two) were lost.[21]

The withdrawal of the 8th Regiment and the 3rd Ranger Group toward the center of the town exposed both flanks of TF-52, which occupied the central area between these two units. Depleted and lightly armed—their heavy weapons and artillery had been abandoned or destroyed at Hung Tam Base—and still in a state of shell shock from its earlier disastrous encounters with the NVA, TF-52 also fell back in disarray from enemy tank attacks. Colonel Thinh, the task force commander, finally rallied his men within Colonel Nhut's assigned area and joined his force with the province territorial units defending the southeastern sector.

In the early hours of April 13, Vo Tan Vinh, administrative deputy province chief, heard the roar of engines outside his house. Thinking that ARVN's relief forces had broken through NVA blocking positions on Route 13, he rushed to his window to greet the rescuing column. He was virtually looking down the barrel of a 100mm cannon of a forty-ton Russian-built T-54 rolling toward the center of the town. The machine gunner stood in the open hatch, whistling, while two tank men, wearing leather helmets, sat casually on the top of the tank, and three soldiers wearing slippers dangled their feet nonchalantly on the side.[22]

Around 10:00 A.M., a T-54 tank ventured aimlessly into the south sector without infantry protection. Entangled with concertina and barbed wire—which were lying all around the city blocks—the tank stopped dead like a sitting duck at a point south of the Binh Long Sector headquarters. It started, however, to use its 100mm cannon to fire at the southern watchtower. Colonel Nhut ordered Captain Khai, the sector artillery commander, to destroy the tank with a disabled 105mm howitzer located near the flagpole in front of the sector headquarters. As the howitzer's tires and sight instrument had been damaged by enemy artillery fire, Khai pointed the gun directly at the tank. He destroyed the tank with one single round. He was later promoted to major for this extraordinary exploit.[23]

One North Vietnamese soldier from the above destroyed tank was captured. He said his name was Van Mai, T-54 driver with the rank of corporal. He belonged to 226th Company, M72 battalion. His armored unit consisting of nine T-54s had arrived in Cambodia in February 1972. It moved from NVA's secret base of Kratie, Cambodia, to Snoul, then to Quan Loi. On the morning of April

13, his unit and the 272nd Regiment of NVA's 9th Division attacked An Loc. He also disclosed that his commander said that when their tanks attacked Loc Ninh, the defenders ran away in panic. This was why this time the unit commanders sent the tanks to the town first, followed by the infantry. However, the defenders at An Loc didn't run; instead, they were waiting in their foxholes to kill the tanks. Further, when the infantry from the 272nd Regiment were strafed by Air Force fighters and Cobra gunships, they fled in all directions, leaving the tanks unprotected, thus transforming them into easy targets for the defenders.

Van Mai felt tired and disappointed. He said the political officer in his unit told the tankers that when they entered An Loc, they would be warmly welcome by the populace. This was why, like other NVA troops, he had brought along a new uniform to parade in An Loc, the new capital of the Provisional Revolutionary Government (PRG) of the Liberation Front of South Viet Nam. As a matter of fact, that same day, Madame Nguyen Thi Binh, the head of the Viet Cong delegation at the Peace Talks at Paris, declared that "within the next ten days, An Loc will be proclaimed the capital of the Provisional Revolutionary Government of South Viet Nam."[24]

Van Mai was not alone in feeling tired and disappointed. The North Vietnamese soldiers, subjected to incessant earth-shaking B-52 strikes, hungry, lonesome, unwelcome by the people they were supposed to liberate, were afraid, demoralized, and hopeless. Phan Nhat Nam, an army reporter, in *Mua He Do Lua* (Red Burning Summer), recalled that on the body of NVA soldier Nguyen Dinh Nghiem from Nghe An, military ID # HT 810042 SZ7, ARVN troops found an unsent letter in which he told his parents that "the conditions of the battle are very harsh, very difficult; sometimes I can't write a letter in 2 or 3 years, therefore don't wait for my letters."[25]

On the body of Nguyen Van Huu, military ID # 271003B004, a letter from his wife read "...This Tet I will buy the standard 1.5 kilograms of sugar which are allocated by the hamlet cooperative to families of people doing military service. Mother told me to bring flour and eggs, but this would be too expensive... I will make 50 cakes and will prepare some pudding and Mother had already agreed..." This prompted Phan Nhat Nam to comment, "Nguyen

Van Huu, whom you want to liberate and for what reasons? What a pity! Three years working for liberation in exchange for 1.5 kilograms of sugar! Do you liberate your compatriots in the South to 'progress toward socialist goals' for 1.5 kilograms of sugar?"[26]

In a letter to her husband Le Van Huu, 174th Regiment, Nguyen Thi Hang, a teacher at Nghe An, wrote in part, "My only hope is that, after three years of military service, you will come back to me safe, I want to close my eyes so that time will pass by fast, faster, so that you and I, we will be able to live in a small house, to surmount obstacles together, to enjoy happiness..."[27] Le Van Huu was killed in the first attack on An Loc, six months after he crossed the *Chaine Annamitique* to go south to "liberate" his Southern compatriots.

In the meantime, the people of An Loc did everything possible to prevent the kind of "liberation" the NVA soldiers and their political commissars were talking about. In his memoir, General Nhut disclosed that before the enemy attacked An Loc, the province police and intelligence agencies within the Phoenix program[28] had preemptively arrested VC agents who had been previously identified but not apprehended because they were not deemed dangerous at the time. As the enemy relied on these VC infiltrators and sympathizers to guide them toward important objectives, such as the 5th Division and sector headquarters, or even to adjust artillery on these objectives, the detention of these agents caused NVA tanks to get lost and to roll aimlessly in the city streets. Further, when NVA troops forced the civilian population to show them the direction to their assigned objectives, people often directed them toward ARVN ambush sites.[29]

Another major problem for the NVA was that their troops had no experience with combined arms tactics and that the control of armor was centralized at the Central Office for South Viet Nam (COSVN), the People's Army of Viet Nam (PAVN) political and military headquarters. As there was no direct coordination at division and regiment level, the tanks and infantry which attacked An Loc operated under separate commands, and as a consequence, when the infantry was stopped and dispersed by tactical air and Cobra gunships, the tanks continued to roll into the city without infantry protection.

While the defenders were busy beating back enemy human-wave assaults on the northern sectors, VNAF and USAF pilots provided constant air support—including B-52 missions around An Loc—and were in great part instrumental in breaking the human wave assaults on the city. Two enemy ammunition depots to the west and northwest of the city were hit by Arc Light missions—one of them exploded for several hours. As the battle progressed, a pattern of air support developed. The B-52s usually struck the enemy logistical installations and staging areas, although in many instances, they were being diverted to close tactical support; tactical air support was used in front of the perimeter of defense; and slow-moving warplanes, such as Cobra attack helicopters, A-37 Dragonfly jet fighters (Air Force trainers converted for close air support, equipped with a 7.62mm gun) and AC-130 Spectres operated within the city in close proximity to friendly troops.

Adding to the problem of air support was that an important number of South Vietnamese warplanes also participated in the battle of An Loc and that could cause interference and increase the risk of midair collisions. To solve this problem of command and control regarding tactical air support, USAF and VNAF were assigned specific zones of responsibility: U.S. warplanes would operate in an area three kilometers north of Chon Thanh to the Cambodian border—excluding the immediate area surrounding the camp of Tong Le Chan, fifteen kilometers southwest of An Loc. VNAF would cover the area south of USAF's assigned sector.[30]

In any event, by midday of April 13, the twisted and burned-out wreckage of numerous T-54 and PT-76 tanks littered the streets of the city. Around An Loc, U.S. and South Vietnamese warplanes accounted for many more.

In the afternoon, the 5th Division received a report that an enemy unit had occupied the province's Chieu Hoi Office and was firing on friendly troops moving on an adjacent street. (Chieu Hoi was the "Open Arms" program aimed at inducing the Viet Congs to rally to the government.) Because the Chieu Hoi building was located in close proximity to both the 5th Division headquarters and the Ranger Group command post, this enemy penetration constituted a serious threat, which needed to be eliminated at all costs.

The 5th Division directed the 3rd Ranger Group to recapture the Chieu Hoi compound.

The mission to retake the building fell to a company of the 52nd Battalion. As the Chieu Hoi building was located on high ground with good fields of fire, the attackers had to cross an open area to assault the enemy position. Lt. Nguyen Van Hieu, the company commander, personally led his men in the attack; he was shot in the head and fell dead right in front of the building. His company was pinned down by all types of weapons, including heavy machine-guns and also M-79 grenade launchers that the enemy had captured from dead ARVN soldiers. By late afternoon, as the 52nd Battalion was still unable to retake the Chieu Hoi building, Colonel Biet ordered the battalion to pull its attacking company out of the range of the enemy M-79s. He then ordered the 31st Battalion to send one of its companies to do the job.[31]

This mission was assigned to Lieutenant Phuoc. Phuoc's company, which previously secured Route 13 north of An Loc, had suffered heavy casualties from enemy artillery and during the engagement against enemy tanks south of Can Le Bridge. So by the time Phuoc was ordered to take the Chieu Hoi Office, his company was down to a little more than twenty able-bodied men. Phuoc and his men, again, were pinned down in front of the Chieu Hoi building by enemy machinegun and M-79 fire. He requested air support, but the VNAF helicopter gunships, which were the first to arrive on the scene, determined that they could not fire because the target was too close to friendly troops. Thereafter, U.S. advisors with the 3rd Ranger Group requested USAF fighters. The latter requested the rangers to mark their position with white smoke, but the pilots could not see the target because strong winds caused the smoke to drift in the direction of the target and obscured it from their view.

Finally, the Ranger Group, through the advisory team, requested the support of the AC-130 Spectre that was supporting the 8th Regiment on the western sector. The advisors were informed that this aircraft was returning to its base because it had expended all of its ammunition, but that another one was on its way to An Loc and that the rangers would have the first priority. After a few moments, the American senior advisor was able to contact the FAC and to guide it toward the target, which was located a little over fifty meters southwest of the town square in the middle of Tran Hung Dao Boulevard. The FAC spotted the target immediately and fired a rocket. Lieutenant Phuoc made a few small adjustments and requested "fire for effect." A string of explosions followed and when the smoke cleared, Phuoc and his men assaulted the Chieu Hoi building. A few frightened NVA soldiers emerged from the underground concrete bunkers—typical of provincial public buildings in An Loc—to gasp for air; they were finished off by Phuoc's company. Phuoc reported that he counted more than ten bodies outside the collapsed bunkers, which were by that time heavily flooded by a torrential rain. He also captured one machinegun, two M-72s, and six AK-47s. In addition, he recovered a lot of ammunition, including M-79 ammunition; the latter was part of the pallets that had fallen into the Chieu Hoi compound, and the enemy had been using the dropped ammunition and food to resist the ranger attacks. Phuoc's company also recovered the body of Lieutenant Hieu, from the 52nd Battalion, who was killed while leading his men during the first attack on the Chieu Hoi compound.[32]

All enemy resistance at the Chieu Hoi compound was completely eliminated around 11:00 P.M. About a half-hour later, Col. Le Nguyen Vy, the 5th Division deputy commander, wearing a flak jacket and steel helmet, accompanied by a second lieutenant, visited the Ranger Group headquarters to congratulate the group for its performance. Colonel Vy and his boss, General Hung, had followed the action of Lieutenant Phuoc's company by monitoring radio conversation between Phuoc, the group headquarters, and the FAC. He said the division commander was very pleased with the rangers' performance in eliminating the enemy penetration. After he left the ranger command post, Colonel Vy went to the 31st Battalion frontline in the vicinity of the White Bridge along the road to Quan Loi. There he witnessed the bond of solidarity between the soldiers and the civilian population as the residents of this part of the city and the rangers of the 31st Battalion supported and cared for one another.

Back at the division headquarters, Colonel Vy called Colonel Biet and said he was impressed with the discipline and motivation he had observed during his visit to the 3rd Ranger Group and that this should put to rest the unfounded rumor that had been swirling around that the rangers hadn't put up a good fight during the first NVA attack on An Loc.

In late afternoon, the enemy renewed their attack on elements of the 8th Regiment on the northwest sector. Because the 5th Division artillery had been put out of combat during the day by enemy counter-battery fire, Colonel Truong, the 8th Regiment commander, had to rely on his organic 81mm mortars for close support. When one of the mortar crew was wiped out by enemy artillery, some LCDBs, who were transporting ammunition for the 8th Service Company, jumped into the mortar pit to replace the decimated crew and continued to fire until the attack was repulsed. Colonel Truong was impressed with the LCDBs' courage and professionalism.

Throughout the rest of the day, in the northern sector, the enemy was consolidating their positions around Dong Long airstrip, while small engagements at platoon and company levels and house-to-house fighting continued despite heavy air support.

The battle subsided somewhat by the evening of April 13 without a clear line of contact. NVA artillery fire, however, continued unabated. Colonel Miller summed up the situation quite well when he later commented: "We had the south side, they had the north side, and it was a no-man's land in the middle. There were mistakes on both sides that first day, plenty of them, but we must have made fewer because we were still there when it quieted down, and that means we were there from then on in my opinion."[33]

That night, Colonel Truong paid a visit to the LCDBs. While the regular soldiers were seeking cover in their foxholes or bunkers during enemy artillery bombardments, the LCDBs were assembled and kept under watch in an empty room without any protection. Colonel Truong told the LCDBs he would arm them and would request that they be restored to their old military status if they volunteered to join his battalions and fight. The LCDBs were elated; all volunteered to serve. Truong was well aware that he didn't have the authority to reenlist the LCDBs, but in a time of crisis when the very destiny of the nation was at stake, he was willing to make that decision to save the LCDBs from being annihilated by enemy artillery and at the same time to be able to replenish the ranks of his depleted battalions. Fortunately, the Department of Defense subsequently approved the 5th Division's request to restore the status of the LCDBs fighting in An Loc. Two hundred LCDBs had died during the siege and, thanks to the Department of Defense's decision, their families were able to receive pension benefits reserved for families of soldiers who fought and died for their country.[34]

According to a 5th Division post-action report, the total friendly and enemy losses for the day were as follows:

Friendly: 28 KIA (Killed in Action), 53 WIA (Wounded in Action), 6 MIA (Missing in Action).

Lost: 3 crew-served and 42 individual weapons

Enemy: 169 KIA, 2 captured.

Weapons captured: 3 crew-served and 5 individual weapons, 2 radio sets; 16 tanks destroyed.[35]

In Saigon that day, the Senate stopped its scheduled meetings to vote a resolution expressing the gratitude of the people to ARVN troops fighting in all fronts.

On April 14, the enemy continued its sporadic artillery fire, mostly in the southwestern sector of the city. As if to keep the momentum alive, a tank company with nine T-54s and two self-propelled anti-aircraft guns, supported by small groups of infantry, attacked the 8th Infantry Regiment in the western sector after an intense artillery preparation. The attack was repulsed by the defenders and Cobra gunships only a hundred meters from the 5th Division command bunker.[36]

In anticipation of renewed tank-supported attacks, General Hung ordered the immediate creation of "tank-destroying teams" at battalion level. Each battalion selected the best and most courageous soldiers in their unit to act as team leaders. Each team also consisted of members of the PSDF and even civilians who were familiar with the terrain and knew the best sites to ambush and destroy the enemy tanks without being detected. The tank-destroying teams operated only in the battalion's area of responsibility and were armed with M-72s and sometimes with B-40 and B-41 rocket launchers captured from the enemy. These teams had killed many tanks in the subsequent attacks, and many of these unsung heroes had also died chasing enemy tanks.[37]

Although An Loc had withstood the initial assault, like Dien Bien Phu after the first exploratory human wave assaults, it knew that tougher days still lay ahead.

One item of encouraging news, however: the 1st Airborne Brigade, which was moving northward from Route 13 to relieve the garrison of An Loc and which had met stiff resistance from elements of the enemy 7th Division, was heliborne directly to the vicinity of Doi Gio Hill about four kilometers southeast of An Loc. The first elements had landed at 2:30 P.M. on April 14. Also on that day, General Minh, III Corps commander, moved his forward CP to Lai Khe to directly take charge of the Binh Long campaign, including the operation to reopen Route 13.

ARVN commanders responsible for the defense of An Loc. From left: Col. Tran Van Nhat, Binh Long province chief; Col. Le Quang Luong, 1st Airborne Brigade commander; Lt. Gen. Nguyen Van Minh, III Corps commander; Brig. Gen. Le Van Hung, 5th Division commander. ARVN photo.

ARVN soldiers on a destroyed T-54 tank in An Loc. ARVN photo.

A PT-76 tank destroyed in the New Market. ARVN photo.

An ARVN defender with antitank LAWs. ARVN photo.

ARVN defenders aiming their LAWs at approaching NVA tanks. ARVN photo.

ARVN soldiers with a captured anti-aircraft weapon. ARVN photo.

81st Airborne Commando cemetery in An Loc. ARVN photo.

President Nguyen Van Thieu and Brig. Gen. Le Van Hung touring the streets of An Loc after the siege, July 7, 1972. ARVN photo.

President Thieu talking to ARVN soldiers in An Loc, July 7, 1972. ARVN photo.

Six

The Second Attack on An Loc

The landing of the paratroopers in the Doi Gio area added a new dimension to the battle of An Loc: it forced the enemy to try to capture the city before the rescuing units joined forces with the defenders. So, after only one day of recuperation and refurbishing, the enemy renewed their efforts to take An Loc. Following their usual tactics of "*tien phao hau xung*" (or first, artillery; next, assault), the enemy unleashed a devastating artillery barrage on the city on April 15 from 4:30 A.M. to 6:00 A.M. causing multiple fires. Over 1,000 artillery rounds of all calibers slammed into An Loc. The NVA gunmen were specifically targeting the 5th Division and Binh Long Sector headquarters in the southern sector.

At 6:00 A.M., the enemy's 9th Division launched a two-pronged attack with the 272nd Regiment supported by a tank company in the north and northwest, and the 271st Regiment supported by another tank company in the west.

At 7:00 A.M., the 272nd Regiment broke through the defensive positions of the 8th Regiment, which had to fall back to Hung Vuong Street, about 500 meters south of the original northern perimeter of defense. The 3rd Ranger Group also withdrew under heavy enemy pressure to establish a new defense line along Tran Hung Dao Boulevard, one block south of Hung Vuong Street.

The enemy, however, didn't seem to have learned from their past mistakes. This time, enemy tanks again penetrated deeper into

ARVN's positions without infantry protection. The first tank was destroyed on Nguyen Du Street by the 36th Ranger Battalion. The second tank was hit by an Air Force rocket and burst into flames in the vicinity of the New Market. A third tank just entering Tao Phung Park was destroyed by the artillerymen from Battery C, 51[st]Artillery Battalion, executing a direct fire with the only usable 105mm howitzer. The fourth and fifth tanks were finished off by the soldiers of the 8th Regiment near the Old Market.[1]

Also this time, learning from the experience from the first attack, the defenders emerged from their bunkers and foxholes as soon as the NVA shifted their artillery barrage, and fired at close range at the enemy attacking infantry and tanks. The defenders used not only their organic M-72s to destroy the tanks, but they also put to good use the B-40 and B-41 rocket launchers captured from the enemy.

Enemy tanks rolling in the streets without infantry protection were easy prey for the "tank-destroying teams," which were hastily created and trained on order of General Hung right after the first attack. In his memoir, Gen. Mach Van Truong had nothing but praise for these teams who knew every corner, dead end, and back alley within the city and who chose the most propitious ambush sites to destroy enemy tanks rolling aimlessly on narrow city streets.[2]

By 10:00 A.M., the enemy and ARVN forces were engaging in furious close combat along the Hung Vuong–Tran Hung Dao line. With effective support from the audacious U.S. Cobra gunships pilots—who braved intense anti-aircraft fire to provide urgently needed assistance—the stubborn defenders were able to organize new defense positions along the above line.

The attack on the west was blunted before it began. First, the enemy sent one sapper unit to open the barbed wire fence at the western gate to allow the tanks to attack ARVN positions on the defense perimeter. The sapper company was wiped out by elements of the 8th Regiment defending the northwestern sector; three prisoners were captured. Then, as the 271st Regiment and one tank company entered a plantation located four kilometers west of An Loc, and began to deploy in formations for the final assault, they were hit by a preplanned B-52 "box." (In U.S. military jargon, one B-52 "box" is usually one rectangle of one by two kilometers drawn on the intended target to be saturated with bombs from three B-52s, each B-52 carrying a 38,000-pound bomb load.) Due to heavy casualties, the 9ᵗʰ Division cancelled the 271ˢᵗ Regiment attack. A document captured afterward disclosed that at a meeting on April 17, the NVA 9ᵗʰ Division confirmed that the entire staff of the 271st Regiment and one infantry battalion had been destroyed by the B-52 strike. Because there was no available replacement for the regiment commander and other regiment staff officers, the attack on the western wing was cancelled entirely.[3]

By the afternoon of April 16, the fighting inside An Loc abated somewhat as NVA units were consolidating their newly gained territories in the northern half of the city and the defenders were busy organizing new defensive positions. In certain areas, the two opposing forces were separated only by the width of a street.

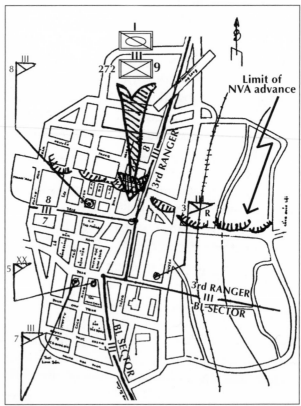

Map 9: Second Attack on An Loc

Following are the friendly and enemy losses after the second attack on An Loc on April 15:

Friendly:

18 KIA, 89 WIA, 38 MIA

An unknown number of individual weapons was lost.

Enemy:

13 KIA left on the field (an unknown number of KIA carried away); 3 prisoners were captured.

The entire headquarters and staff of 271st Regiment and one battalion destroyed.

10 tanks destroyed on the streets of An Loc.[4]

As NVA and ARVN troops—bracing for renewed fighting—were skirmishing and exchanging fire along a new demarcation line, enemy sappers detonated the field ammunition depot at Lai Khe on April 16, triggering multiple explosions. Against this embarrassing backdrop, General Minh, III Corps commander, declared to the press at his forward command post at Lai Khe that the dangerous period had passed and that he was cautiously optimistic about the situation in An Loc. He also said that his troops were prepared for the next waves of attacks by NVA forces.

As the nation was anxiously watching the progress of the enemy offensive in Binh Long and Quang Tri provinces, the NVA opened a new front on the Central Highlands: on April 15—coincidental with the second attack on An Loc—NVA's 320th Division and 10th Division, supported by T-54 tanks units, launched a two-pronged attack aimed at the 44th Regiment of the 23rd Division, which was defending the high ground northwest of Kontum, and the 45th Regiment manning the central sector, after intense artillery preparation. At the same time, the NVA 2nd Division made diversionary attacks in Binh Dinh coastal province.

The previous day, the 23rd Division had captured a secret enemy message directing the attacking units to be prepared to start the attack at 5:00 A.M. Although the exact date of the attack was not specified in the message, Col. Ly Tong Ba, 23rd Division commander, inferred from the detected movement of VC's B3 Front[5] Headquarters toward Kontum, that D-Day would be the following day. Consequently, he requested emergency B-52 strikes on suspected enemy assembly areas north of Kontum for April 15; he also ordered division artillery to prepare preplanned artillery concentrations on the enemy's likely avenues of approach.

Thus, when the NVA units deployed for the initial assault on the 44th Regiment position, the defenders were ready. Supported by close-range B-52 strikes and intense artillery interdiction fire, the South Vietnamese threw back multiple enemy assaults, inflicting heavy casualties on the attackers. A column of T-54s rolling down RN 14 toward the city was engaged by the 1/8 Tank Company. Three T-54 tanks were destroyed; the rest turned around and fled.[6]

While the NVA's western prong was beaten back by the 44th Regiment, the central sector was subjected to repeated enemy assaults supported by murderous 75mm recoilless rifle fire from the high ground to the north. Under pressure, two battalions of the 45th Regiment withdrew to a new defensive line in the vicinity of the cemetery on the northern edge of the town on April 17. The next day, Colonel Ba ordered the 1/8 Tank Company to counterattack. The 1/8 engaged the North Vietnamese units on their right flank and succeeded in crushing the enemy penetration with the help of elements of the 45th. The 1/8 Tank Company commander reported many enemy bodies were left around the cemetery. The tank company suffered eighteen KIA (including three officers), thirty WIA (including four officers); six tanks were damaged.[7]

Thus, like General Hung in An Loc, Colonel Ba in Kontum had won the first phase of the NVA's 1972 Easter offensive; but, unlike General Hung who was trapped inside An Loc, Ba was able to evacuate his wounded soldiers, get resupplies, and bring in replacements for his depleted units by helicopters despite continuous enemy artillery interdiction fire.

Meanwhile at An Loc, taking advantage of the respite after the second attack, Vietnamese and foreign journalists flocked to the city to personally assess the real situation in the garrison. General Hung, interviewed by Vietnamese reporters about the morale of his troops, declared, "As long as I am alive, An Loc will be alive."[8]

On April 17, the 5th Division sent two reporters—one American and one Frenchman—to the rangers' sector to do a battlefield report. These reporters accompanied the units from the 52nd and 36th Battalions that were battling the NVA in an effort to expand the rangers' area of responsibility. They were able to take some good pictures and footage of the battle of An Loc. They even got inside enemy tanks to search for documents and other interesting materials. In one of these tanks, the American and French journalists took pictures of dead North Vietnamese tank men chained to their tank. They also discovered on their bodies ivory-colored pills, which were later confirmed by Saigon labs to be stimulants. The pictures of dead tank men chained to their tank and the accompanying stories later appeared on the world press and constituted a good counterpropaganda to the Communists' statements that their soldiers were highly motivated fighters who were ready to sacrifice their lives for the cause of socialism. They also showed to the world that in the North Vietnamese Army, political indoctrination alone was not enough and, often, it needed to be complemented by other more draconian measures.[9]

During that time, the NVA, however, continued to tighten their grip around the besieged city. Taking advantage of their new gains in the northern half of the city, the NVA installed anti-aircraft weapons on the roof of high-rise buildings to shoot at incoming aircraft in an effort to prevent resupply and medical evacuation.

Although most of these anti-aircraft positions were quickly destroyed by U.S. warplanes, the aggressive use of anti-aircraft assets indicated that the enemy was determined to isolate An Loc at all costs. Having paid an exorbitant price in terms of human lives, the enemy was now trying to complement its military campaign by a combination of physical strangulation tactics and—and as we will see later—psychological warfare and propaganda.

On April 21, the 36th Ranger Battalion, in an effort to enlarge its area of control in the northeastern sector, directed the 4th Company to recapture the building just in front of its eastern defense line. A four-man raiding team succeeded in entering the building after having killed nine NVA soldiers in and around the building. Two rangers were wounded during the close combat inside the house. Second Lieutenant Nam, deputy company commander, took a few men to go to the rescue of the raiding team. The NCO radioman was killed by a hand grenade thrown from the roof of the building. Lieutenant Quan, the company commander, leading the company reserve, went to the rescue of Lieutenant Nam. He personally killed two NVA soldiers, but was wounded in the leg. He was evacuated four days later by a helicopter that landed on the helipad in the Airborne Brigade area. As the helicopter took off, it received two rounds of AK47 which missed Quan by a few inches. The good news was that the area of control of the 36th Battalion was expanded 200 meters eastward after the 4th Company's raid.[10]

A few days later, one night, under cover of darkness, Major Lac, the 36th Battalion commander, his assistant S-3, and a radio operator, crawled into a destroyed enemy tank stuck in a bomb crater in the middle of the street in the vicinity of the Chinese High School to search the interior of the tank. Lac was a good soldier and a multi-talented man: he knew how to repair a jeep or a truck, or a radio set. He also knew how to fly a helicopter. An officer in the 3rd Ranger Group staff reported that every time his battalion conducted a helicopter assault, Lac would personally fly the command ship to direct the landing operation.

Inside the disabled tank, Lac found important military and communication documents. He also dismantled a radio set to bring back with him. However, when the three men climbed out of the bomb crater, they were pinned down by heavy enemy fire from across the street. Lac called the Group headquarters to request air support. The 5th Division informed the rangers that the Spectre that was supporting other units had just completed its mission and had returned to its base and that the only thing available was a Stinger, which was on its way to the area. Like the AC-130 Spectre, the AC-119 Stinger gunship flew both day and night and was particularly effective at night. It flew at an operational altitude of 3,500 feet above Loc Ninh and An Loc, and its 7.62mm miniguns and 20mm cannon were very accurate.[11] The tracer bullets flashing through the night sky looked like fire gushing out from the mouth of the dragon, and for this reason, the South Vietnamese defenders called the Stinger *Rong Lua* or "Fire Dragon."

The FAC that was working above An Loc was guided to the target area by the Ranger Group staff and the American advisors, who asked it to fire white smoke twenty meters north-northeast of the tank. Following a small adjustment transmitted by Major Lac, the Stinger began firing at the identified target. After an hour of uninterrupted firing, the enemy must have been all killed because they no longer fired at Lac and his party. The three men crawled out of the bomb crater with their captured booty. Colonel Biet was shocked when he looked at the documents taken from the enemy tank: among them was the secret radio code of the 5th Division.[12]

Colonel Biet immediately reported the findings to 5th Division Headquarters. A few minutes later, Colonel Vy and two officers from the Division G-2 Section came to pick up the documents and the radio set. Immediately after that incident, the Division changed its radio code. The Ranger Group and other units also changed their internal radio codes and drew up a new list of name-codes for different prominent points inside and outside of An Loc for targeting purposes. "These measures had an immediate effect," wrote Captain Khue, 3rd Ranger Group assistant S-3, "as the enemy no longer broke into our communication channels to disrupt our communications, cursing us and inciting us to surrender or to desert... They always said to us, 'surrender and you will live; resist and you will die.'"[13]

As a matter of fact, South Vietnamese troops were constantly subjected to Communist propaganda and verbal harassment during the battles of Loc Ninh and An Loc. ARVN officers captured at Loc Ninh were forced to broadcast on Cambodia-based VC Radio stations their appeal to their former comrades to put down their arms and "join the ranks of the revolution." Madame Nguyen Thi Binh, on the other hand, declared in Paris on April 13 that An Loc would be proclaimed the seat of the Provisional Revolutionary Government of South Viet Nam within ten days. Hanoi Radio also boasted that their troops would be in Saigon on May 19, Ho Chi Minh's birthday.

A few times during the siege, NVA radiomen got into Binh Long Sector's radio frequency and talked to Colonel Nhut. They told Nhut that he had no hope and urged him to surrender. Nhut told them to come over so he could help them fulfill their wish of "*sinh Bac tu Nam*" (to be born in the North, to die in the South).

In these instances, Nhut tried to keep the conversation going but the NVA radiomen usually shut off their radio quickly because they were concerned about being detected and destroyed by artillery or air strikes.

In this regard, it is appropriate to elaborate on the enemy's and the ARVN's motivations. The VC's and the NVA soldier's behavior, indeed, was strictly conditioned by a sophisticated system of political indoctrination. The following radio debate between an RF soldier and a Viet Cong I once overheard during a sector-directed operation in the Mekong Delta, however, shows that this system was not without shortcomings.

"You, mercenary," shouted a VC, "you should be ashamed to be the lackey of the U.S. imperialists."

"You, bastard, listen to me," retorted the RF soldier, "I can say 'Down with Nguyen Van Thieu.' Can you say the same about Ho Chi Minh?"

The VC radioman must have been confused because he abruptly stopped the debate. Maybe the political cadre of his unit hadn't discussed such a thing as freedom of expression under a Communist regime. This impromptu debate, on the other hand, showed that the South Vietnamese soldiers didn't need political indoctrination to understand that they were fighting for a good cause, and this strong conviction, in my opinion, had sustained ARVN troops throughout the inferno of An Loc.

The Communist system of political indoctrination is based on the psychology of hate and the politics of control. The VC and his NVA counterpart were taught to hate the "American imperialists and their Vietnamese lackeys," the "Thieu-Ky-Khiem clique" and its "*fantoche*" government, the "reactionary" forces in the cities and the "cruel and oppressive" officials in the villages. To insure compliance with the party line, a party apparatus parallels the normal chain of command, from party cells in small units to the highest levels of command within the army structure.

However, all this can hardly be sufficient: in the battle of An Loc and also during the heavy engagements around Quang Tri in 1972, ARVN soldiers discovered bodies of tank drivers and anti-aircraft gunners chained to their tanks and weapons. One can't deny, however, that the VC and NVA soldiers, tightly controlled—mentally and physically—were able to incur hardship and generally performed well in battle.

The fighting ability of the South Vietnamese Army, on the other hand, was unequal among different units. Although some infantry divisions showed poor combat performance, the Marine and Airborne Divisions were probably the best fighting units of any army of the world. The 1st Division in Hue has been acclaimed by the U.S. news media as equal to any American infantry division. The variation of performance among ARVN units was primarily due to a difference in the quality of leadership and motivation. Although the average ARVN soldier in general fought well in most circumstances, quality leadership was often lacking and not equal to the task. Overall, I believe that ARVN units were better trained than NVA and VC forces; before 1973, when we still had adequate U.S. air support, the casualty ratio was typically one to three in our favor.

In any event, with regard to the Communist propaganda during the siege of An Loc, it was unfortunate that foreign radio broadcasting stations, by painting a gloomy picture of the situation in the city, had unintentionally helped the enemy's psychological warfare campaign. The BBC, the most popular foreign broadcasting station in Viet Nam, for example, instead of condemning Hanoi's aggression, commented day after day that the fate of An Loc had been sealed and that only a miracle could save the beleaguered garrison.

While the enemy's psychological warfare campaign had little or no impact on ARVN soldiers who were determined to defend An Loc at all costs, the strangulation tactics—consisting of cutting off ground and aerial access, tightening the stranglehold on the garrison and causing maximum casualties by continuous artillery fire—seemed to be working in the enemy's favor. The logistical situation in the city, indeed, worsened every day and would, in the long run, undermine the morale of the defenders. Small arms ammunition began to run low after one week of fighting. (Artillery ammunition was no longer needed as almost all ARVN artillery pieces in An Loc had been wiped out by enemy artillery counter-battery fire.)

The shortage of medical supplies forced Capt. Nguyen Van Quy, the An Loc Hospital surgeon, to resort to unorthodox medical practices to deal with the mounting number of wounded: Quy extracted nylon threads from sand bags, which he sanitized with quartermaster-supplied liquid soap; he then used these to perform surgeries and to stitch up the soldiers' wounds. Captain Nghi, who commanded the airborne artillery battery at Doi Gio, was the first patient. Dr. Quy used nylon thread to close Nghi's abdomen wound; Quy was happy that it worked very well. (Fortunately, in early June when the situation in An Loc had markedly improved, Maj. David Risch, former advisor to the An Loc hospital staff, returned to An Loc and brought with him the precious "cat gut" and other needed medical supplies.)

Quy was a unique son of a northern family who had emigrated to the South after the partition of Viet Nam under the 1954 Geneva Peace Agreement, and thus was entitled to a draft deferment. However, he volunteered to serve in the army. He was first assigned to the 43rd Regiment, 18th Division, under Col. Tran Van Nhut. Upon completion of a surgery course at the General Cong Hoa Military Hospital in Saigon, he followed Nhut to Binh Long.

An Loc Hospital—also known as the Binh Long Sector Hospital—was a combined military-civilian hospital. All three doctors were military and Quy was the only surgeon. A great part of the nurses and technicians were civilian, but most of them disappeared after the second attack. Fortunately, the 5th Medical Battalion, 5th Division, dispatched a small medical team that worked in tandem with the An Loc Hospital staff.

Because the hospital was located on a small hill in close proximity to the 5th Division command post, it was constantly bombarded by enemy artillery. Furthermore, Division artillery units, originally located in the soccer field, south of the city, had to move to Tao Phung Park, in the valley immediately east of the hospital, to escape devastating enemy counter-battery fire. For some, this may have caused the hospital to receive relentless artillery bombardment aimed at the above important targets. One should not forget, however, that the Communists—who were not known for their humanitarian concerns—also considered the hospital a valuable target because its destruction would help them achieve their strangulation objective sooner.

Also because the city of An Loc itself was situated on a chain of small hills, water was in short supply, even during quieter times. City electric power was also very weak. Rich residents bought their own generators. The power company that supplied electricity to the city planned to install more powerful generators. The project progressed satisfactorily when the war broke out; all four newly bought generators were totally destroyed. The two generators at the hospital were also destroyed during the first attack. In his memoir *Hoi Ky An Loc: 86 Ngay Cua Mot Bac Si Giai Phau Tai Mat Tran*[14] (Memoirs of An Loc: 86 Days of a Surgeon in Battle), Doctor Quy reported that he often had to perform surgeries a mere 300 meters from the battle, wearing a flak jacket and a steel helmet. Also because of lack of electricity, it was not unusual for him to operate under a flashlight.

Fortunately, each district of Binh Long province had a small clinic and each rubber plantation had a small infirmary to take care of its own workers. In addition, each unit participating in the defense of An Loc at battalion and regiment levels had its own medical teams who treated lightly wounded soldiers. Only the seriously wounded who needed surgery were sent to the An Loc Hospital. As the number of civilian casualties increased every day due to NVA's indiscriminate artillery fire, the hospital had to increase the original 103 beds to 160.

One effect of the war was that it rendered people callous to tragedies and calamities. Phan Nhut Nam, an army reporter at An Loc, related the tragic story of a father who, calmly and without apparent emotion, buried in a common grave his wife and five children killed by an 130mm shell by methodically collecting and assembling various body parts.[15] Captain Quy recalled that at one time, there were up to 300 bodies lying in the hospital morgue, next to his operating room, and this made everybody sick.

Toward the end of May, as the situation in An Loc had improved and some enemy units in the neighboring villages had left, about 5,000 lightly wounded civilians sought refuge in a pagoda in the village of Phu Duc, southwest of An Loc. An Loc Hospital dispatched a medical team to provide first aid and cholera shots to the refugees.

Quy later commented that in An Loc, people died not only once, but twice and sometimes three times. The shellings occasionally hit a new grave and blew up the corpses, which had to be reburied. This was the case of a female nurse killed by artillery fire. Her friends buried her near the back wall of the hospital. She had to be reburied after a shell hit her shallow grave.

Because the two operating rooms at the hospital were heavily damaged after the two attacks, in early May Colonel Nhut provided Captain Quy and hospital personnel with two big underground rooms to be used for operations and for treating wounded soldiers. These underground rooms were located in the former B15 compound of the U.S. Special Forces and were equipped with generators. Colonel Nhut had also moved the sector headquarters to the underground U.S. Special Forces bunker. Quy was stunned to see that the prefabricated houses and other structures above the ground in the compound had been flattened. One watch tower was still standing, but it was blackened by smoke. In front of the compound, right inside the twisted barbed wire, lay the hulks of two burned-out tanks. Behind the compound, another tank lay on its side with its cannon pointed skyward. Farther south, on the edge of the rubber plantations, were three other tanks and the wreckage of a helicopter.

To prevent the spread of epidemic diseases, General Hung ordered Col. Bui Duc Diem, his assistant for operations, to conduct a mass burial in the front yard of the province high school. Colonel Nhut asked to move the burial site to a vacant lot between the high school and the hospital, because he did not think a high school was an appropriate site for a mass grave. Colonel Diem ordered the division engineer company to dig the burial site, using the only available bulldozer that was provided by the province's Public Works department. The driver had just started the engine of the bulldozer when it was hit by a B40 rocket, causing light damage to its blade. Colonel Diem also used the LCDBs to perform the mass burial. Diem recalled that his men buried a total of 956 dead in one day and that after the siege had been lifted, these bodies—which included both soldiers and civilians—had never been identified. A few LCDBs, sickened by the horror of their task, tried to run away; Colonel Diem threatened to shoot them before they agreed to come back and finish the ungrateful job. Some LCDBs were also killed while at work by enemy artillery. Their bodies were thrown into the holes they had excavated; in other words, they had dug their own graves.[16]

Intense anti-aircraft fire made resupply of An Loc increasingly difficult. The logistical problem was compounded by the existence of the civilian population, which needed to be fed. It had been estimated that 200 tons of supplies daily were necessary to sustain ARVN units and the civilian population which, by that time, had swelled to over 15,000 due to the influx of refugees from surrounding villages. Water was also badly needed. Army advisors estimated that the civilian population could survive with sixty-five tons daily. This was about a third of what had been previously estimated as some brackish wells had been discovered inside the city.[17]

From the beginning of the enemy encirclement of the city on April 7, aerial resupply was the responsibility of VNAF 237th Helicopter Squadron. However, since a Chinook that attempted to bring supplies to An Loc was shot down on April 12, the resupply mission was assigned to VNAF fixed-wing aircraft. On that same day, C-123s and C-130s from the Tan Son Nhat-based 5th VNAF Air Division began dropping supplies to the city at an altitude of around 700 feet. From April 13 to April 16, a total of twenty-seven VNAF cargo planes dropped 135 tons of supplies into An Loc but only 34 tons were collected by the defenders; the rest fell into the enemy-controlled areas.[18]

In a renewed effort to cut off aerial resupply, the enemy rushed additional anti-aircraft weapons around the city. On April 17, all six VNAF C-123s and C-119s on a resupply mission were hit by enemy anti-aircraft fire; one C-123 exploded above An Loc, killing all people aboard, including Lt. Col. Nguyen The Than, the squadron commander.[19] On April 19, another C-123 carrying ammunition was hit and exploded in midair. From that point, VNAF cancelled resupply missions and the U.S. Air Force picked up the job.[20]

In actuality, the USAF was already prepared to assume the responsibility of resupplying An Loc the day the second South Vietnamese cargo plane was shot down. On April 15, two U.S. C-130s, in fact, were sent to An Loc to resupply the defenders, using a new computerized dropping system known as CARP (Computed Aerial Release Point). The pilots were instructed to follow Route 13 and as they were approaching the soccer field, the computer would take over, releasing the cargo at the prearranged point. The first C-130 dropped the pallets of food and ammunition without incident although it did receive two bullets in its fuselage. The second C-130 was hit at the cockpit compartment; the flight engineer was killed, the navigator and co-pilot were wounded. Fire broke out in the cargo hold and another one ruptured the hot air duct causing intense heat in the cargo compartment. As the pilot tried in vain to release the cargo, the loadmaster had to cut the ropes by hand. Fortunately, the crippled C-130 was able to limp back to Tan Son Nhut.[21]

On April 18, another U.S. C-130 was hit by machinegun fire on its approach to the soccer field. The pilot succeeded in dropping the supply before he was forced to perform a crash landing on an open field near Lai Khe. Miraculously, the entire crew was rescued with only minor injuries.[22]

Because this type of delivery was too costly, by April 20, the USAF used the low-altitude drops for both day and night flights. The cargo planes would approach the city at tree-top level and at a distance of three miles from the drop zone, they climbed to about 500 feet and released the supplies through the rear cargo door. This technique was relatively safe but about 70% of the supplies landed on the area controlled by the enemy.[23] An NVA lieutenant was captured by that time by ARVN troops. When his interrogators promised to give him rice and dried fish if he would inform them of the strength and identification of the attacking forces, he instead asked if he could have "fruit cocktail." Noticing the startled looks of his interrogators—who were themselves on a rather austere diet—he went on to explain that he had taken a liking to fruit cocktail after his men retrieved it from wayward drops that fell into his area.[24]

With an unacceptable accuracy rate and mounting casualties, the Air Force attempted night drops, but accuracy remained a problem. Moreover, not many soldiers volunteered to search for errant bundles at night amid relentless enemy artillery and mortar shelling.

After another C-130 was lost on the night of May 2 due possibly to pilot miscalculation, the USAF decided to adopt a new drop technique known as HALO (High Altitude Low Opening) system that had been in the experimental stages. Early in the battle of An Loc, the U.S. Air Force was forced to execute air drops at high altitudes due to numerous anti-aircraft positions, including SA-7 (Surface-Air) rocket batteries. However, parachute drift had caused many of these drops (mostly ammunition and C-ration packages) to land outside the perimeter of defense and fall into enemy hands. One ARVN officer recalled that every time there was an air drop, thousands of guns, enemy as well as friendly, were firing in unison. The enemy fire was aimed at the aircraft, while the friendly troops fired for different reasons. First, the South Vietnamese troops fired at the parachutes that were about to drift away from the perimeter of defense. (The parachutes torn out by bullets would fall straight into friendly positions.) Second, ARVN soldiers aimed directly at the packages that were about to fall into enemy territory in order to destroy them before they fell into the enemy's hands.

On May 8, the HALO technique was finally developed and adopted by the USAF. Under this new method, the parachutes were released at about 10,000 feet. A series of cords caused the parachutes to deploy only partially, thus slowing the fall rate to about 130 feet-per-second. At 500 feet above the ground, a timing mechanism allowed the parachutes to fully open. The HALO technique was a great improvement over past drops. Until June 25, when cargo aircraft could finally land in An Loc, the US Air Force flew 230 sorties delivering a total of 2,984 tons of supplies. The garrison recovered 2,735 tons, or about 90% of supplies dropped.[25]

According to a report published on August 15, 1973, by ARVN Joint General Staff, the average success rate of parachute dropping during the entire siege of An Loc was about one-third: Out of a total of 3,868 tons of supplies dropped into An Loc, only 1,138 tons had been recovered. The balance was lost to the enemy or was damaged.

Seven

Reinforcing An Loc

While the war was raging at Loc Ninh, General Minh, III Corps commander, finally realizing that Binh Long—and not Tay Ninh—was the main objective of the enemy's 1972 Easter Offensive, ordered the 43rd Regiment of the 18th Division, reinforced with the 5th Armored Squadron, to secure Route 13 north of Lai Khe. The relief column received 130mm artillery fire but met only light enemy resistance. It arrived at Chon Thanh without incident on April 7.

The next day, the column was subjected to an intense artillery barrage and engaged by a regiment-size enemy blocking force south of Tao O creek. The enemy, well protected by an intricate system of underground inter-connecting reinforced bunkers, stopped the 43rd Regiment's progression despite powerful artillery and tactical air support. The death of Col. Truong Huu Duc, the 5th Armored Squadron commander, during an aerial inspection of the battle of Tao O caused the attack to lose momentum and the 43rd. Regiment—which suffered 30% losses—to withdraw out of the enemy artillery range and reorganize.[1]

After the war council meeting in Saigon on April 7 decided to put the 21st Division and the 1st Airborne Brigade under the operational control of III Corps in order to cope with the NVA/VC offensive in Binh Long province, General Minh decided to use both of these units to attack from the south to secure the vital supply line to An Loc and to link up with the besieged city. Minh resisted the idea of transporting the 1ˢᵗ Airborne Brigade directly into An Loc to reinforce the garrison because he was concerned that NVA forces could bypass An Loc and attack the cities to the south and thus would pose a serious threat to Saigon itself.

In fact, the NVA had the capability to unleash two uncommitted independent regiments, the 24ᵗʰ and 274ᵗʰ, against elements of the ARVN 25ᵗʰ Division in Tay Ninh province. These two regiments, which had not been engaged in the battle of An Loc, could then join forces with elements of the 7ᵗʰ Division or even the 5ᵗʰ Division after the latter's victory at Loc Ninh, to attack Hau Nghia province south of Tay Ninh and to open a new front to support the enemy's planned drive toward the capital of South Viet Nam.

On the morning of April 11, the 1ˢᵗ Airborne Brigade under Col. Le Van Luong, was transported by trucks from Lai Khe to Chon Thanh in order to replace the 43ʳᵈ Regiment in the Route 13 securing mission. The paratroopers disembarked at Chon Thanh and then moved north by foot. They were stopped just six kilometers north of Chon Thanh by a well-entrenched blocking force made up of a regiment of NVA's 7ᵗʰ Division. The paratroopers were unable to destroy the enemy blocking positions due to the lack of support from attached armor units of the 5ᵗʰ Armored Squadron; the latter were reluctant to move forward after having suffered heavy losses from enemy mortar and rocket barrages.[2]

Meanwhile, the situation in An Loc became critical after the second attack. The 5ᵗʰ Division had practically given up one-third of the city to the north. The enemy had occupied the airfield and installed a powerful anti-aircraft system around the city, which had not only thwarted medical evacuation efforts, but had also taken a heavy toll on the aircraft and crews carrying out aerial resupply missions.

Faced with the possible collapse of the garrison under renewed enemy attacks, General Minh met on April 14 in Lai Khe with Lt. Gen. Duong Quoc Dong, the Airborne Division commander, and Colonel Luong, to discuss the feasibility of conducting an air assault into An Loc to reinforce the defense of the city. During that meeting, Minh informed General Dong and Colonel Luong that the NVA troops were tightening their knots around An Loc, that the friendly casualties kept mounting due to increased enemy artillery fire and that an advance base must be established in the vicinity of An Loc to provide fire support to the defenders and to allow fresh troops to link up with and reinforce the threatened garrison. According to General Minh, the 1st Airborne Brigade was the most suitable unit to carry out that difficult mission.[3]

The 1st Airborne Brigade was the offshoot of the former 1st Airborne Group. When the Airborne Division was formed in 1966 to serve as the backbone of the ARVN general reserve, the 1st Airborne Group became the 1st Airborne Brigade. It was the oldest and most experienced brigade of the Airborne Division, having participated in major operations of the Viet Nam War, including the battles to liberate Hue and Saigon during the 1968 Tet Offensive, and the invasion of Low Laos in February 1971.

Colonel Luong had graduated from the Thu Duc Reserve Officers School in 1954. He rose through the ranks and assumed command of the 1st Brigade in early 1968. Luong, who was born and raised in Binh Duong province, knew the region well, and thus was the ideal man to lead the rescue mission.

It was decided in that meeting that the 1st Airborne Brigade would be heliborne into a LZ in the vicinity of Doi Gio (Windy) Hill about four kilometers southeast of An Loc. The brigade would establish a fire support base in the Doi Gio-Hill 169 area, and the rest of the paratroopers would attack west to link up with the defenders inside An Loc. The 21st Division units that had extracted themselves without incident from their operations in An Xuyen province in the Mekong Delta, would relieve the 1st Airborne Brigade and would be responsible for securing Route 13.

General Minh, however, was concerned about the reported presence of NVA Regiment 165 in the Xa Cam-Xa Trach area, southeast of An Loc and Regiment 141 in the vicinity of Ap Soc Gon, east of An Loc. In General Minh's view, the above regiments from the NVA 7th Division—which were located within four kilometers from Doi Gio area—would pose a serious threat to the planned heliborne operation of the 1st Airborne Brigade. So, on April 13, while the NVA was launching their first attack on An Loc, Minh instructed his assistant for operations, Lt. Col. Nguyen Ngoc Anh, to attend the daily ARVN press conference—organized by the Psychological Warfare Department in Saigon to brief foreign reporters on the important military news of the day—with specific instructions aimed at disguising the planned landing of the paratroopers at Doi Gio the following day.[4]

Lieutenant Colonel Anh later reported that he began his presentation with a description of the tactical situation in An Loc at the end of the first day of the attack; then, he disclosed that one wounded North Vietnamese soldier captured by the 36th Ranger Battalion on April 11 revealed that VC Gen. Tran Van Tra, commander of the Nguyen Hue campaign in MRIII, along with his staff and key members of COSVN, had moved to Quan Loi airport to direct the attack on An Loc. Anh added that III Corps had requested ARVN/JGS to immediately drop the 81st Airborne Commando Group in an area north of Quan Loi to capture Tran Van Tra and other COSVN members. In response to a question from a foreign correspondent regarding the timing of the 81st Commando airborne operation, Colonel Anh stated that it would take place during the early morning the following day. That night, the news of the dropping of the airborne commandos behind COSVN headquarters was disseminated by the world's main broadcasting stations. Colonel Anh reported that Dr. Kissinger, who was negotiating the terms of the Peace Agreement in Paris, called to check out that news.[5]

In Colonel Anh's view, General Minh's misinformation scheme had worked because two Montagnards whom the 81st Airborne Commando Group met at the village of Soc Gon on April 16 reported that a substantial NVA force had hurriedly left the area without taking time to fill up the foxholes they had dug out a few days earlier.

Meanwhile, after the April 14 meeting at Lai Khe, Colonel Luong made an aerial reconnaissance of the Doi Gio-Hill 169 area. After carefully studying the landing zone, he decided to air-assault an area near Srok Ton Cui, a small Cambodian hamlet located approximately one kilometer east of Doi Gio and Hill 169. According to Colonel Luong's plan, the 6th Airborne Battalion would land first to clear the LZ. The following day, the fifteenth of April, the

5th and 8th Battalions with the brigade headquarters would land in the same area. Upon completion of the heliborne operation, the 5th and 8th Battalions would move toward An Loc in two columns. The 6th Battalion would establish a fire support base in the Doi Gio-Hill 169 area. In anticipation of NVA counter-attacks after landing, the 1st Airborne Brigade units had received two days before the planed heliborne operation the new rocket launcher XM-202—a modified version of the old M-72 that could fire four rockets at a maximum range of 750 meters, producing a great psychological effect, and inflicting casualties on personnel in bunkers, buildings, and covered or open foxholes.[6]

At 2:30 P.M. on April 14, the 60th Company of the 6th Airborne Battalion landed in a clearing near Community Road 245, approximately one kilometer south of Srok Ton Cui hamlet. After their landing, the men from 60th Company could see to the west An Loc burning with huge columns of black smoke. A few minutes later, Lt. Col. Nguyen Van Dinh, battalion commander, landed with his staff and the 61st Airborne Company. Colonel Dinh ordered Maj. Pham Kim Bang, battalion executive, to attack an enemy outpost on Doi Gio with 63rd Company (Lt. Vinh) and 64th Company (Lt. Tuan). The only usable 105mm howitzer in An Loc provided fire support for the attack. Lieutenants Tuan and Vinh led the respective companies in the uphill assault. Doi Gio, occupied by a small VC unit, was easily overwhelmed after thirty minutes of close-range combat.[7]

At 4:30 P.M., the enemy began massing artillery fire on the landing zone, causing moderate casualties to the 6th Battalion. On Hill 169, the 6th Airborne Battalion linked up with the 3rd Ranger Company from the 52nd Ranger Battalion, which had been occupying this high ground as an outpost for the defense of An Loc.

The news of the landing of the paratroopers at Doi Gio galvanized the spirits of the garrison and of the civilian population as well. It is noteworthy that, following the French tradition, every arm and branch of the ARVN had a patron saint: Vietnamese paratroopers adopted the Archangel Michael as their patron. Like the Archangel Michael, who was brave and who chased the evil from the heavens, the paratroopers were the bravest soldiers of the armed

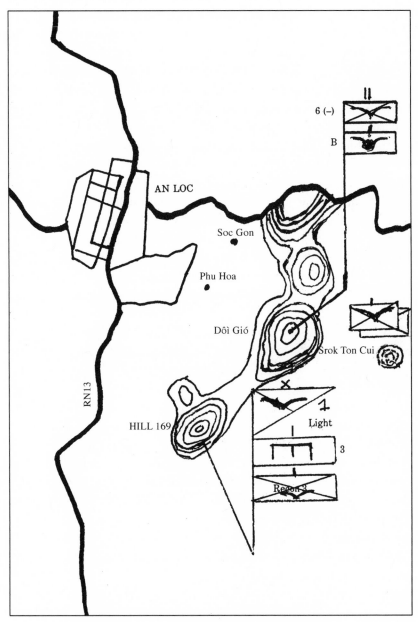

Map 10: Paratroopers Heliborne Operations

forces and were committed to chasing the VC from the Republic. Because the paratroopers descended from the sky to fight the enemy, they were dubbed "*thien than mu do*" (red-bereted angels), by an admiring civilian population.

On April 15, all units of the 1st Airborne Brigade were brought into the landing zone without incident. The landing operation was performed by the Bien Hoa-based 43rd Helicoper Squadron/3rd Air Division, under the supervision of Maj. Nguyen Van Uc, who was responsible for all landing operations and medical evacuations for the battle of An Loc. However, while the landing of the paratroopers was relatively smooth, the Chinook helicopters from VNAF 237th Squadron, which hooked eight 105mm howitzers into Doi Gio, came under enemy artillery fire and were able to bring in only the first six guns; the last two helicopters were hit by anti-aircraft fire and had to return to Lai Khe.[8] Colonel Luong decided to leave on Doi Gio and Hill 169, in addition to the artillery battery, the 6th Airborne Battalion, the 3rd Reconnaissance Company, one engineer company, and a Light Brigade headquarters under Lt. Col. Le Van Ngoc. These units were to secure the above two hills and provide artillery support to the airborne brigade in An Loc. They were also to provide an alternate command headquarters and communication center for the paratroopers.

In accordance with the operation plan, the paratroopers moved into An Loc in two columns. The column to the south, consisting of the 8th Battalion, the 3rd Ranger Company from the 52nd Ranger Battalion, and the 254th RF Company (that the paratroopers had met on Hill 169 two days earlier), under the overall command of Lt. Col. Van Ba Ninh, entered the city of An Loc at 7:00 A.M. April 17 without incident. However, the ranger company commander was seriously wounded during an engagement with NVA forces. He could not be evacuated and died a few days later in An Loc.[9]

The column to the north including the 5th Battalion (Lt. Col. Nguyen Chi Hieu) and the brigade headquarters had less success. It had to cross a dense rubber plantation to reach Soc Gon hamlet. On April 16 at 9:30 A.M., as it reached a small hill between Soc Gon and Phu Hoa hamlets, it was attacked by one regiment of the NVA 5th Division. According to a captured prisoner, the 5th Division had to move full speed from Loc Ninh to An Loc to reinforce the 9th Division, which had incurred heavy casualties during the attack on An Loc three days earlier.[10]

The 51st Company, the lead company of the 5th Battalion, was attacked by one enemy battalion; after two hours of engagement, the enemy started to deploy in a U formation in an effort to encircle and annihilate the paratroopers. Fortunately, the U.S. lieutenant from the 5th Airborne advisory team was able to contact a U.S. FAC, which directed U.S tactical air on the enemy only 200 meters in front of the paratroopers. Second Lt. Vu Van Hoi, a recent graduate of the Vietnamese Military Academy and a platoon leader in the 51st Company, reported that one bomb released by one of the U.S. jet fighters instantly transformed a portion of the rubber plantation into a soccer field-sized barren lot. Hoi was deafened by the shock and had to pinch himself in the leg to be sure he was still alive. The FAC reported the enemy battalion was totally destroyed and that twisted crew-served weapons, including mortars, were lying all around amidst charred and mangled bodies. Hoi saw in front of him about forty enemy dead with all sorts of broken and twisted weapons. In the meantime, two B-52 strikes hit a target farther west. Hoi believed they probably had hit the headquarters of an enemy regiment because after the strike, the battle suddenly became eerily silent and he could even hear the "sounds of the crickets."[11]

However, at 12:00 noon, the enemy launched a second assault, this time supported by elements of a tank company. Again, the 5th Airborne vigorously crushed the multiple human wave assaults and destroyed all the accompanying tanks.

The outcome of these two attacks reflected the intensity of the fighting. In addition to the destroyed tanks, the enemy suffered 85 KIA; 7 crew-served weapons and 20 AK-47s were captured. Friendly: 3 KIA, 13 wounded.[12]

In these engagements, the 5th Battalion was supported by tactical air requested by the U.S. advisors. After the column was resupplied and the killed and wounded evacuated by helicopters, it camped for the night on the slope of a small hill one kilometer to the north of the engagement site. That night, two enemy commandos trying to infiltrate into the paratroopers lines were shot and killed.

At 5:30 A.M. on April 17, the enemy massed artillery fire on the 5th Battalion from the north, northwest, and south. After the artillery stopped, the enemy again launched the all-too familiar human wave assaults. This time, the 5th Airborne Battalion again held out and inflicted heavy casualties on the attackers. The enemy left 30 bodies; 6 crew-served weapons (including a 12.7mm anti-aircraft machinegun) and 5 individual weapons were captured. The paratroopers suffered 5 KIA and 17 wounded, including Maj. Le Hong, the battalion executive.[13]

After the attack was repulsed, the paratroopers continued their march toward An Loc. At 10:00 A.M., when they reached the rail track near Quan Loi Gate, the paratroopers were stopped by small enemy units well entrenched in their foxholes. These foxholes were dug out by the people to protect against enemy artillery. When the NVA launched their first attacks, the people fled their hamlets to seek refuge inside the city; now the enemy was using these foxholes to stop the paratroopers from reinforcing the garrison. The paratroopers had to resort to hand grenades and close combat techniques to destroy the enemy nets of resistance one by one, despite sporadic artillery fire directed by enemy observation posts on the high ground to the north.

After two hours of bloody close-quarters combat, the paratroopers destroyed all enemy blocking positions and around noon, the first elements of the 5th Battalion entered An Loc. Lieutenant Hoi's platoon was ordered to coordinate with the 5th Reconnaissance Company, 5th Division, for the defense of the Binh Long Sector Hospital and the Health Department Office area, which was facing the enemy just across from Tran Hung Dao Boulevard. Hoi later recalled that his platoon had to fight off enemy attacks and at the same time perform mass burials of dead civilians and soldiers piling up inside the hospital.

According to Hoi, food and water were in critically short supply. All buffaloes, cows, pigs, chickens, even cats and rats, were nowhere to be found. All the wells in the city, including the ten meter-deep ones, had dried up, and his men had to scrape together whatever was left to distribute to friendly units and also to the civilians. One of his men was killed by an artillery shell while drawing water from a nearby well; his body fell into the well and had to be pulled out to be buried behind the hospital.[14] Lt. Truong Dang Si, 51st Company, 5th Airborne Battalion, was seriously wounded by shrapnel in the neck on April 17 and was evacuated to Saigon by one of the helicopters transporting the last elements of the 81st Airborne Commando into An Loc.[15] (Si was one of the three company commanders of the 5th Battalion wounded at An Loc; the battalion executive officer was also wounded during the siege.)[16]

The problem of water shortage was alleviated in early May with the first seasonal rains. Dr. Nguyen Van Quy, the surgeon at Binh Long Sector Hospital, recalled that the first rain falling on An Loc was an unusually big storm; and although the rain water was darkened by embers from smoldering buildings, the elated soldiers as well as the civilians emerged from their foxholes and hiding places to take showers and to clean up their fatigue uniforms or clothing. Dr. Quy also took advantage of this first rain to clean up his heavily damaged hospital and to get rid of the persistent stench of decomposed bodies.

Finally, at 1:00 P.M. on April 17, Colonel Luong, the airborne commander, in probably the most memorable moment of the battle of An Loc, shook hands with the man in charge of its defense: Brig. Gen. Le Van Hung. General Hung opened his last bottle of beer and gave it to the young paratroop commander; he then briefed the latter on the friendly and enemy situation in An Loc and assigned the southern sector to the 1st Airborne Brigade. After the briefing, Luong visited Colonel Nhut, the province chief. Both were former high school classmates; they were happy to meet, albeit under rather unusual circumstances.[17]

Colonel Luong decided to establish his headquarters at the sector headquarters to facilitate coordination with provincial forces in the defense of the southern area. To retain tactical flexibility and to be able to launch counter-attacks anywhere in the city, Luong decided to conduct a mobile defense outside the southern perimeter.

On April 14, the day the first elements of the 1st Airborne Brigade landed in the Doi Gio area, the 81st Airborne Commando Group, which was operating southwest of Xa Mat along the Cambodian border, was extracted to Trang Lon in Tay Ninh province. From there, it was transported by Chinook helicopters to Lai Khe on April 16. Around noon, while Lai Khe ammunition depot, attacked earlier by enemy sappers, was still exploding, the entire 81st Airborne Commando Group was ready at Lai Khe airport to be heliborne into An Loc.

The 81st Airborne Commando Group—originally named the 81st Airborne Commando Battalion—belonged to the Vietnamese Special Forces. In 1970, the Special Forces was deactivated and most of its personnel were transferred to the various ranger battalions or assigned to the Airborne Division. The 81st Airborne Commando Battalion, on the contrary, was upgraded to become the 81st Airborne Commando Group and was allowed to retain its uniform and its green beret.[18] This unit was expert in night operations and close combat techniques. It had, on various occasions, proven its effectiveness in the destruction of the enemy "*chot*" and "*kieng*" (or reinforced blocking positions) which, as we shall see later, had inflicted heavy casualties to the ARVN 21st Division during its link-up operation along Route 13. (In hindsight, the securing of Route 13 could have been more speedy and less costly, had the 81st Commando Group been assigned that task in conjunction with elements of the 21st Division.)

The Commando Group, with a combat-effective force of 550 men and consisting of one reconnaissance company and four infantry companies, was transported by a total of forty-five helicopters; it landed in two waves in a small plot of dry rice field one kilometer southwest of Doi Gio. Soon after their landing, the commandos were joined by forty-seven soldiers from the 3rd Ranger Company of the 52nd Ranger Battalion, which was defending Hill 169. The ranger company had been attacked by NVA troops five days earlier and had suffered five killed and a few wounded. The above forty-seven rangers were separated from their parent company after the enemy's attack. The wounded rangers were treated by Doctor Chau and Master Sergeant Tung from the 81st Commando medical team and were evacuated by the helicopters that had brought the commandos into the Doi Gio area. The rangers had not been supplied for many days because of heavy enemy pressure. Hungry and exhausted, they were happy to be able to join the commandos in order to return to their unit. The heliborne operation was completed by 4:00 P.M. The commandos then moved west along a small ravine located between Doi Gio and Hill 169.[19]

As the commandos were approaching An Loc, they were bombed by mistake by a jet fighter. However, due to their dispersed formations, only two commandos were wounded, including Lt. Le Dinh Chieu Thien. Captain Huggins and Master Sergeant Yerta, the two remaining American advisors, were able to request medical evacuation from the U.S. 17th Cavalry Brigade.[20]

After the medevac was completed, the commandos continued their march in a northwesterly direction. As they reached the Phu Hoa rubber plantation, they heard a heavy firefight in front of them. A reconnaissance team was sent forward to study the situation. The team met with elements of the 5th Airborne Battalion, which were engaging a regiment of the NVA 5th Division. "There are too many of them, they are like a band of ants," said Lieutenant Colonel Hieu, the 5th Airborne Battalion commander, "they stuck with me like hungry leeches."[21]

As night fell on April 16, the 81st Commando occupied what was left of Soc Gon, a Montagnard hamlet, which had been abandoned by the enemy after their early engagements with the 5th Airborne Battalion; the hamlet, partially destroyed by tactical air strikes, was deserted by the Montagnards, who had sought refuge in the city of An Loc or moved deeper into the forests to evade the Communist troops. The following day, the commandos entered An Loc without incident.

Because of interrupted shelling, the commandos had to run, each man thirty meters apart, to their assigned positions on the northern area of the city. General Hung, in fact, had asked Lt. Col. Pham Van Huan, the 81st Airborne Commando Group commander, to coordinate the defense of the northern sector with the 8th Regiment and the 3rd Ranger Group. (It is noteworthy that the airborne commando units, as their name indicates, specialize in conducting small unit long-range reconnaissance patrols deep into enemy territory, capturing prisoners, and destroying enemy rear base installations and infrastructures; they normally were not engaged in con-

ventional warfare. Their static defense mission in the battle of An
Loc was a dramatic departure from this concept.)

Sergeant Do Duc Thinh, from the 81st Commando headquarters, recalled that when the commandos entered An Loc, he saw
corpses of NVA soldiers and civilians scattered all around the streets.
And when he approached An Loc Hospital, he saw hundreds of
bodies piling up inside two big holes and the stench of these unburied corpses almost caused him to throw up. The hospital itself
was in ruins, most the roof had disappeared, the collapsed front wall
revealed a row of empty beds with bed sheets and blankets lying
around on the floor.[22]

Under the new defense plan, the 81st Commando was responsible for the central northern section between the 3rd Ranger Group
and the 8th Regiment (from Nguyen Du Street in the east to Ngo
Quyen Street in the west). Colonel Truong, 8th Regiment commander, briefed Lieutenant Colonel Huan on the tactical situation
and the terrain in the northern sector. The coordination and mutual support between these two units was made easy by the fact
that Truong and Huan, as well as their respective executive officers,
were all graduates of the Dalat Military Academy, and in ARVN—
as in most other armies—there exists a very special bond among
academy alumni.

With new reinforcements, General Hung decided to counter-
attack to regain the terrain lost to the enemy. On April 17, the 8th
Airborne Battalion was ordered to seize the rubber plantation west
of the city. The 8th Battalion moved westward along Tran Hung
Dao Boulevard, the main lateral thoroughfare of the city. After it
passed the Phu Lo Gate and reached a point about 700 meters from
the city limit, it received heavy 75mm recoilless weapon and mortar
fire. In the first few minutes, the paratroopers suffered twelve KIA
and sixty-two wounded.[23] Lieutenant Colonel Ninh, the battalion
commander, regrouped his men and launched the counter-attack.
The enemy withdrew with heavy losses. The paratroopers captured
three prisoners. The western perimeter of defense was expanded
after this bloody encounter.

In the morning of April 17, while the paratroopers were attacking west of Phu Lo Gate, the enemy unleashed a violent artil-

lery barrage on the city. Around 11:00 A.M., Colonel Truong, 8th Regiment commander, was wounded by shrapnel in the neck and became unconscious. The 5th Division surgeon reported to General Hung that the wound was very serious and they had to wait twenty-four hours to know if Truong could survive. Truong did survive despite the fact that Binh Long Hospital didn't have the technical skills nor the means to perform surgery on his neck. Because he couldn't be evacuated, Truong remained in command of the 8th Regiment until the end of the siege.[24]

Like General Hung, Truong was a product of the "Delta Clan." After graduation from the Dalat Military Academy, he served in various staff positions at the 21st Division and IV Corps. He rose to the occasion as 8th Regiment commander and was in great part instrumental in the successful defense of An Loc.

A few days later, Colonel Luong paid a visit to Col. Mach Van Truong. The latter, who had recovered from his wound, briefed Luong on the heavy pressure exerted by enemy tank-supported forces in his sector. Luong suggested that the 8th Regiment commander make improvised antitank mines by coupling two 155mm shells and inserting an explosive fuse into one of the two shells. Colonel Luong told Truong he had used this "home-made" explosive device with great success in previous battles. Sure enough, the 8th Regiment later used this improvised antitank mine to destroy a number of tanks during subsequent NVA attacks.[25]

That same night Colonel Truong was wounded, Lieutenant Colonel Huan, of the 81st Airborne Commando Group, called the 5th Division command post and asked that no illuminating flares be used that night. It was time for the airborne commandos to swing into action. Huan had earlier reconnoitered the area to be reoccupied. Most of the buildings had collapsed, many bunkers previously built by the residents were being used by the enemy, and barbed wire fences surrounded almost every house in the sector. As a result of his reconnaissance, Huan instructed his men to move slowly in small formations to avoid making noise and to use only knives and hand grenades to kill the enemy in their foxholes. From midnight to about 3:00 A.M., the commandos pushed northward and, using their traditional close combat techniques, succeeded in regaining a small enclave of 400 meters from the line of departure. "This was a short segment of the street leading toward An Loc, but it was a giant step by the 81st Airborne Commando Group toward relieving An Loc from Communist troop pressure," wrote Tran Van Nhat.[26]

Although most of the northern sector had been recaptured by the commandos during the night, the enemy still held the Field Police headquarters, whose underground bunkers were fortified with fuel barrels filled with sand, and whose roof consisted of steel plates reinforced with three layers of sandbags. The commandos from 2nd Company launched a few assaults to retake the police campus, but were pinned down by intense recoilless rifle fire from Dong Long Hill. Captain Huggins, the American advisor, requested air support. Two AC-130s responded and fired their 105mm guns on the target designated by the advisory team. Sergeant Yerta, in disregard for his own safety, stood in the middle of the street to direct the Spectre fire, which scored a few direct hits, causing the roof of the bunkers to collapse. (Yerta later received the Distinguished Service Cross for this action.)[27] After thirty minutes of uninterrupted air support, the enemy fell silent. The commandos launched their assault and recaptured the objective at 4:00 P.M., but the following day, the enemy still occupied some small pockets of resistance and, as a consequence, the positions of both sides in the northern sector were intertwined in a leopard spot pattern.

Although air support was very effective and was instrumental in the 81st Commando's early successes, the latter still needed mortar fire support in close combat situations. The problem was that the 81st Commando Group was not equipped with 81mm mortars because the commandos normally conducted long-range patrols behind enemy lines and were thus equipped only with light weapons. On the other hand, in case of engagement with the enemy, the commandos, operating out of range of friendly artillery range, usually relied on helicopter gunships and air support. Further, the ammunition pallets dropped on the soccer field south of the city contained only 81mm mortar ammunition, thus making the commandos' 60mm mortars useless.

Captain Doan had an idea. He went to the 8th Regiment and borrowed an 81mm mortar from that unit. There was one problem, however: the borrowed mortar had no sight instrument. Sergeant Yerta requested a sight through U.S. channels and obtained a brand-new M-14 sight, a sophisticated new version that was not yet available in the South Vietnamese army. Even Captain Huggins and Sergeant Yerta were not familiar with the new instrument. Fortunately, the box containing the sight also contained the instructions regarding its use. Huggins and Yerta studied the instructions and explained them to Major Lan. Lan, a graduate of the Dalat Military Academy, translated these instructions to the new 81mm crew.[28]

Sergeant Thinh, the crew chief, installed the mortar in the backyard of a deserted pharmacy surrounded by high walls. From there, Thinh provided accurate fire support to the advanced commando elements conducting house-to-house fighting. The problem of ammunition resupply was more acute than Thinh had originally thought. First, he used a three-wheeled *lambretta* abandoned by the residents to get ammunition pallets dropped by parachute at the soccer field, a two-kilometer trip undertaken under constant enemy bombardment. After the lambretta was destroyed by artillery fire, Sergeant Thinh had to use wheelbarrows to make the soccer trip under extremely hazardous conditions.

The enemy also had pinpointed the commandos' 81mm mortar site. One day, as Thinh was eating his lunch, he was called to the headquarters to take new fire instructions; a few 82mm mortar rounds landed in his mortar pit. When he returned to his mortar position, he saw a severely wounded white dog lying on the ground in pain. The dog had come to eat Thinh's ration. Tung, from the 81st Commando medical team, gave the dog the *coup de grace* because it could not be saved.

As the commandos kept moving forward, Lieutenant Colonel Huan, the 81st Airborne Commando Group commander, concerned about his exposed flanks, called the 5th Division and requested that friendly units be ordered to progress on both sides of his unit so that it could advance farther and expand its area of control; however, the 5th Division answered that it might not be able to satisfy that request because all units had suffered heavy casualties and were unable to keep pace with the commandos. Col. Mach Van Truong, 8th Regiment commander, was in particular reluctant to expose his critically depleted units to murderous direct enemy recoilless rifle fire from Dong Long Hill if he were to attack on the left side of the commandos as the lightly built houses in that area had been burnt to the ground by NVA artillery barrages and thus offered no concealment nor protection to his attacking units.[29]

When the 5th Division asked Lieutenant Colonel Biet whether he could move forward to cover the right flank of the 81st, the Ranger Group commander said he would try, because he also wanted to expand his own area of responsibility. Biet directed Major Lac, the 36th Ranger Battalion commander, to attack in the northeasterly direction with two companies. These companies were to occupy the high ground near the airfield to protect the right flank of the 81st Commando Group. One company of the 36th Battalion rapidly seized the assigned objective without difficulty, meeting only scattered resistance from enemy soldiers, who quickly fled to the jungles bordering Quan Loi plantation.

Taking advantage of the western gap, the enemy launched a two-pronged attack on the commandos: the first attack, coming directly from the north, was supported by mortars and 75mm recoilless rifle fire from Dong Long Hill; the second attack, more powerful, was directed at the left flank of the 81st Commando Group. Facing possible encirclement, the commandos retreated to the New Market area, but left a company to defend the strategic Field Police headquarters. The rangers, with their left flank exposed, withdrew also toward the center of the town.

The failure of the 81st Commandos to expand northward was obviously due to the lack of coordination with and support from the 8th Regiment. Although the open terrain to the left of the commandos would not provide protection to the attacking troops, the 8th Regiment, in retrospect, could have helped the attack of the commandos by establishing blocking positions to ward off the enemy's counter-attacks on the latter's left flank.

During the night, the commandos started to dig graves in a vacant lot near the city bus station to bury their dead. The commandos took pride in the fact that they braved artillery fire and took time during the battle to provide their fallen comrades with a decent burial. It had become a routine for the commandos to fight during the day and to bury their dead at night. "Some nights, when torrential rains and artillery shells were falling in unison on the city, we had to fumble in the dark to dig small foxholes to avoid artillery fire, then to dig big graves to bury the bodies of our friends," recalled a commando.[30] Soon, a well-kept cemetery emerged amid the ruins of a besieged city. Old ladies often came to the cemetery to burn incense at the graves and to offer prayers during quieter times.

In the meantime, a new document captured on April 18 by the ever-resilient 92nd Border Ranger Battalion at the lonely outpost of Tong Le Chan, west of An Loc, not only confirmed that the NVA was ready for yet another assault, but also revealed the exact date of that assault. A company of the 92nd Rangers patrolling in an area west of the outpost, and inside the province of Tay Ninh, killed a number of VCs. In the pocket of one of the bodies, the rangers found a hand-written paper, which turned out to be a letter from the 9th Division senior political commissioner to COSVN. The letter detailed the plans for a new assault to be launched the next day, April 19. The letter attributed the failure of the 9th Division to take An Loc to the effectiveness of tactical air and B-52 strikes, but was also highly critical of the performance of the 9th Division and the coordination between armor and infantry.[31]

In any event, the enemy was so confident of the success of the next attack that they announced on the National Liberation Radio that effective April 20, An Loc would become the seat of the Provisional Revolutionary Government of South Viet Nam. As planned, after unleashing a heavy pre-assault artillery barrage in the early morning of April 19, the NVA launched a powerful attack on the northern sector. Once again, the assault was stopped by effective close air support.

As the enemy regrouped to renew the attack, the 81st Airborne Commando Group received the order to counter-attack. The commandos were specifically directed to cross Tran Hung Dao Boulevard and seize the New Market, the bus station, and Thanh Mau hamlet to regain the northwestern area that had been abandoned earlier by the retreating 8th Regiment. While advancing toward their assigned objectives, the commandos had to dig holes in the city walls to avoid being observed by enemy snipers. (These holes, later enlarged to about one meter high and one-half-meter wide, allowed the commandos to move speedily and safely from house to house.) During their advance, the commandos used hand grenades and M-72 rocket launchers to destroy enemy bunkers, forcing enemy units to withdraw to the north. But when the commandos were about to reach the pagoda and the Field Police headquarters, the enemy began to counter-attack by unleashing a barrage of all kinds of calibers and assaulting the left flank of the 81st Commando Group. Tactical air support temporarily blunted the assault. The 5th Division had to request that a B-52 mission be diverted from its preplanned objective and that its ordnance be unloaded instead on the enemy attackers only 200 to 300 meters from the commandos to prevent the latter from being overrun.[32] The commandos regrouped and engaged in hand-to-hand combat to dislodge the last enemy pockets of resistance; at the end of the day, they had regained most of the lost territory.

In the south, an element of the 9th Division launched a probing attack on the 5th Airborne Battalion's positions southeast of Xa Cam Gate. The 5th Battalion suffered six KIA and twenty-one wounded. The enemy left thirty-five bodies. The 5th Battalion captured six crew-served and six individual weapons.[33]

While the situation in An Loc was temporarily under control, the paratroopers at Doi Gio Hill and Hill 169 were fighting for their lives. Concurrent with the attacks on An Loc by elements of the 9th Division, on April 19 the 275th Regiment of the 5th Division and the 141st Regiment of the 7th Division were unleashed against the paratroopers defending the strategic high ground southeast of the city. Because all artillery pieces inside An Loc and at Quan Loi airport had been damaged or destroyed by NVA's attacks and counter-battery barrages, the airborne battery on Doi Gio Hill was the only one available for close fire support to the besieged city; and the enemy was determined to knock out this last ARVN artillery outfit around An Loc.

Again, following their usual tactic of *tien phao hau xung*, the attack was preceded by an intense artillery preparation on Doi Gio Hill. The 105mm artillery battery on Doi Gio was completely neutralized; the artillery ammunition depot containing over 1,000 shells was hit and exploded. Around 9:00 P.M., Colonel Luong, the 1st Airborne Brigade commander, gave complete authority to Lt. Col. Le Van Ngoc, his deputy in charge of the Light Brigade headquarters, to take appropriate decisions to deal with the situation around Doi Gio. Ngoc ordered the 6th Battalion headquarters and the 62nd Company to reinforce the 61st Company at Srok Ton Cui hamlet. The 63rd and 64th Companies, under Maj. Pham Kim Bang, executive officer, were assigned the task of defending Doi Gio.

After the NVA had lifted their artillery preparation, an enemy unit supported by tanks attacked Doi Gio from the north and northeast. Second Lt. Tran Dai Chien, a recent graduate of the Vietnamese Military Academy, opened fire when the enemy tanks were within a fifty-meter range The first two tanks were hit and exploded; the enemy infantry ran down the hill in panic. The enemy resumed artillery fire on Doi Gio, then assaulted the paratroopers' positions with a new infantry unit supported by two remaining tanks. The paratroopers destroyed these last two tanks but had to disperse under heavy enemy pressure. Chien, severely wounded by an artillery shell and unable to move, decided to stay at his position; he ordered his platoon to withdraw without him. When the enemy overran Doi Gio, Chien threw his last grenade toward them; he died under a hail of enemy bullets. Chien's father had served in the 1st Division; his older brother, a battalion commander, also in the 1st Division, was killed in Quang Tri. Although he was entitled to a draft deferment, Chien enrolled in the Vietnamese Military Academy and like many top graduates, he chose to serve in the Airborne Division upon graduation in December 1971.[34]

The survivors of 63rd and 64th Companies withdrew to Hill 169, which was occupied by the 1st Airborne Light Brigade headquarters and the 3rd Reconnaissance Company. The enemy started to shift their artillery fire to Hill 169. Judging the situation on Hill 169 untenable, Colonel Luong ordered Ngoc to withdraw to An Loc with the remnant units of the brigade. The reconnaissance and engineer companies and the 63rd Company from the 6th Battalion, in conjunction with individual soldiers from other units, followed the previous itinerary of the 8th Battalion and arrived at An Loc on the morning of April 21.

The situation of the 6th Battalion was more critical. The battalion headquarters and what remained of the 60th, 61st, 62nd, and 64th companies, ran out of food and ammunition. Burdened with sixty wounded soldiers, they were still trapped in Srok Ton Cui hamlet. During the night of April 20, they withdrew toward Song Be to the southeast to be extracted by helicopters. Three B-52 missions were executed in support of the extraction operation. The paratroopers were attacked by the enemy many times during their withdrawal and also at the preplanned extraction point. Only 106 men, including Lt. Col. Nguyen Van Dinh, the battalion commander, and 14 artillerymen were picked up by helicopters and transported to Lai Khe.[35] Later, small groups of survivors and stragglers were able to stream back for several days into friendly lines at An Loc and further south at Chon Thanh and Lai Khe. The 6th Battalion, minus the 63rd Company, was reorganized and replenished at Lai Khe pending further deployment.

The fall of Doi Gio and Hill 169, which secured the landing zone, dealt a heavy blow to the morale of the troops in An Loc. The last link to the outside world was effectively removed and from then on the city was completely sealed off. The only artillery unit available for close support had been destroyed. The NVA now controlled all the high ground to the southeast and from there they were able to direct deadly artillery fire into An Loc.

On the other hand, however, the arrival of the 1st Airborne Brigade and the 81st Airborne Commando Group, the two elite units of the South Vietnamese army, had galvanized the garrison as well as the civilian population and reinforced their confidence in the final outcome of the battle of An Loc. Colonel Miller, who had the highest praise for the above units, later commented that "we were home free; with the 81st inside and the airborne outside, there was no way we would go down."[36] Captured NVA prisoners admitted that they were mostly afraid of three things: B-52 strikes, "Commandos number 81," and paratroopers. Unfortunately for them, all these three things were present at An Loc.

Due to mounting civilian casualties caused by uninterrupted shelling, the International Red Cross, on April 20, asked for a twenty-four-hour cease-fire so that the wounded could be evacuated, but the Communists, intent to take the city at all costs, refused the Red Cross' request. Madame Nguyen Thi Binh, chief VC negotiator in Paris, declared that no truce was possible and that the offensive must go on. In fact, the enemy hoped that the rapidly mounting death toll combined with the critical shortage of basic needs would sap the morale of the defenders and force the surrender of the garrison in accordance with their strangulation tactic.

In the early morning of April 21, the enemy intensified their shelling of An Loc, focusing in particular on the southern sector held by the 1st Airborne Brigade. During the night of April 22, NVA troops assaulted the position of the 8th Airborne Battalion in the vicinity of the Southern Gate. The attacking troops were supported by two T-54 and two PT-76 tanks. This time, the paratroopers were ready. Armed with the new antitank weapon XM-202, the soldiers of the 8th Airborne Battalion destroyed all four enemy tanks. The paratroopers were also able to guide a C-130 Spectre to a column of five enemy tanks approaching from the south. All the tanks were destroyed.[37]

In the meantime, a column of three tanks attacked the position of the 5th Battalion in the southwestern sector. Second Lieutenant Hoi from the 51st Company, recalled that three T-54 tanks rolled directly into his position without infantry protection. Hoi directed his men to take position in the trenches behind the barbed wire and to aim their M-72s at the approaching tanks. (His 32-man platoon was equipped with 16 M-72 LAWs, one XM-202 antitank weapon, and 16 claymore mines.) Hoi fired his XM-202 weapon and set the lead T-54 afire; the two remaining tanks were finished off by his men.[38]

During the night of April 30, the NVA renewed the offensive in an effort to take the capital city of Binh Long to celebrate the May 1 Labor Day. NVA troops launched violent assaults on ARVN positions on the northern and western sectors after a powerful artillery and 122mm rocket preparation. The fighting lasted the entire morning of May 1. Around 11:00 A.M., the enemy withdrew, but the front-line battalions reported heavy concentrations of NVA troops on the edge of the rubber plantations about two kilometers west of the defense perimeter. Colonel Truong, 8th Regiment commander, called General Hung and requested tactical air support. General Hung told him six A-37 sorties were on the way to An Loc and he should contact the orbiting FAC to identify the targets. The air strikes were accurate but they didn't stop the enemy. Truong called General Hung again and reported that the enemy was preparing to launch a human wave assault; he also requested napalm bombs on Hill 100 northwest of An Loc. Lt. Col. Ly Duc Quan, 7th Regiment commander, also requested air strikes on a target west of Phu Lo Gate.

At that time, the two battalion commanders of the 8th Regiment on the frontline called on the telephone and reported that their 81mm mortars were unable to stop the advancing NVA troops. They urgently requested napalm bombs. Suddenly, Colonel Truong noticed an eerie silence in the sky; even the FAC that was orbiting over An Loc had disappeared. A few seconds later, Truong heard the frightening whistles of the big bombs falling from high above, followed by a chain of earth-shaking explosions on the targets requested by the 7th and 8th Regiments, only one kilometer from ARVN positions. A big cloud of red dust rose up and covered the entire northwestern sky.

General Hung called and asked Truong to observe the targets and report the results of the B-52 strikes. After the dust had settled, Truong scrutinized the western horizon and saw no enemy standing. Hung later told Colonel Truong—who was wondering how on earth an Arc Light strike could be requested in just thirty minutes—that his regiment had just been saved by three God-sent B-52 missions. He went on to explain that these missions had been requested by II Corps, but when the B-52 bombers were approaching the Vietnamese coast, II Corps cancelled the missions. MACV asked III Corps if it had any good targets for these B-52s. As the 5th Division was requesting urgent tactical air, it was decided to divert these Arc Light missions to support the defenders of An Loc.[39]

While the An Loc garrison had thwarted the enemy attempt to take the city to celebrate the Labor Day, the Quang Tri garrison was not so lucky. Despite a heroic defense by the 3rd Division and attached units, casualties began to mount and on May 1, NVA divisions, spearheaded by armored units, crossed the Thach Han River and encircled the 3rd Division inside the Citadel. Under pressure and unable to control all his organic and attached units, General Giai, judging the situation hopeless, ordered the evacuation of the Citadel and withdrew his troops to the next defense line south of My Chanh River, which was defended by the Airborne Division (-) and one Marine brigade.

The fall of Quang Tri jolted the country and was a harbinger for somber days ahead, but in An Loc, General Hung and his unit commanders were grappling with more pressing problems: not only had they to prepare for anticipated enemy renewed attacks, but they also had to cope with the daunting challenge of an orderly collection and distribution of the scarce supplies that were air dropped daily into the encircled garrison: with the increasing influx of refugees from surrounding areas seeking "safe haven" in the city, food, water and medical supplies became alarmingly in short supply. Every time there was an air drop at the city soccer field, soldiers from various units fought for the few recoverable packages. Food was also in short supply at An Loc Hospital and Colonel Miller reported that he saw hospital patients, including amputees, struggling with soldiers to recover food for themselves.[40]

To deal with this chaotic situation, the 5th Division directed Col. Bui Duc Diem, Assistant for Operations, in coordination with Maj. Nguyen Dinh The, Sector Chief of Staff, and Maj.Nguyen Kim Diem, Sector S4, to assume the responsibility for the recovering, processing and distribution of the supplies to various units in the garrison as well as to the civilian population.[41] However, as the enemy was shelling the soccer field after each drop to destroy the supplies, and as the recovering team was waiting for the cessation of the shelling, many soldiers braved the artillery fire to grab the dropped packages. Colonel Diem reported that one day as he was "escorting" Colonel Miller to watch parachute drops under the new HALO technique, enemy artillery started to fire on the soccer field. Colonel Diem pushed Colonel Miller into a nearby bunker while he stayed outside to supervise the recovery operation. His radioman carrying a PCR-25 radio set was killed by shrapnel from an artillery shell and a soldier was crushed to death by an errant pallet.[42]The Ranger Group also reported two casualties from the air drops: A warrant officer from the 36th Battalion was also crushed to death by a pallet and an American sergeant in the advisory team was wounded in the head by another.[43]

General Hung finally asked Colonel Luong, the airborne brigade commander, to take charge of the recovery and distribution operations. Luong and his no-nonsense paratroopers quickly reestablished order and the supply operation proceeded without incident. The improved accuracy of parachute drops and the more efficient distribution of supplies greatly improved the logistical situation within the garrison. A U.S. advisor with the 5th Division recalled that the successful drops "had almost an indefinable impact in raising the ARVN defenders' morale, giving them hope and raising them from a total situation of frustration to one of confidence."[44]

Special credit should be given to the officers and men of the USAF who braved intense anti-aircraft fire to resupply An Loc. From mid-April to mid-May, 5 C-130s were shot down, 56 aircraft were hit, 17 crew members were killed or missing in action, and another 10 were wounded.[45]

In the beginning of May, the situation in An Loc had greatly improved. The enemy continued to shell An Loc, but most of the fire was from mortars. This lull in the shelling had allowed a few helicopters to land and pick up the most seriously wounded. The normalization of the aerial resupply operations, the limited success of medical evacuation, and the ability of the defenders to hold their ground in face of two major attacks had bolstered the confidence of the garrison. The defenders also took advantage of the break after the failed second attack to consolidate and reinforce their positions.

Although the constant flow of refugees added to the logistical problems for the city, they provided, on the other hand, invaluable information on the enemy. The ethnic Montagnards, in particular, were an excellent source of information: because they didn't attract the attention of the North Vietnamese, the Montagnards were able to move around more freely and thus provided reliable details on enemy activities. Some members of the Provincial Reconnaissance teams, disguised as Montagnards wandering by mistake into enemy lines or pretending to be pursued by South Vietnamese soldiers, later came back and reported what they had observed or heard. Capt. Nguyen Van Thiet, Sector S2, and Capt. Le Van Dao from the province's Phoenix committee, skillfully exploited the above sources of information to determine the locations of the enemy assembly areas, logistical installations, artillery sites, and tank formations.[46] The destruction of identified enemy targets by B-52 strikes and tactical air undoubtedly impacted the enemy offensive capabilities as they were preparing for yet another assault on An Loc.

Eight

The Third Attack on An Loc

In early May, intelligence reports confirmed that two regiments of the NVA 5th Division, the E6 and the 174th, had moved from their location south of Loc Ninh to the Doi Gio-Hill 169 area southeast of An Loc. This area was abandoned by the 1st Airborne Brigade after the 6th Battalion was overrun by superior NVA forces on April 20. There were also reports that elements of the 9th Division were occupying new positions southwest of the city and the 141st and 165th Regiments of the 7th Division had moved from their blocking positions in the vicinity of Tau O on Route 13 to an area just three kilometers south of An Loc.

During the night of May 5, the enemy launched a probing attack on the 81st Commando Group positions. The fighting lasted until dawn. The enemy left many dead on the barbed wire on the defense perimeter. In the pocket of each dead body the commandos found a small piece of paper inscribed with the following words: "At all costs, capture the 5th Division commander alive, raise the flag of victory."[1]

The night of May 6, the 212th Binh Long RF Company captured a North Vietnamese warrant officer during an ambush near Quan Loi Gate on the eastern perimeter of An Loc. His name was Nguyen The Hoa. His unit was the 228th Sapper Battalion of the NVA 5th Division. Hoa's mission was to reconnoiter the above area in preparation for the upcoming attack. He didn't know the exact date of the new attack, but guessed it would be within a week. The prisoner also disclosed that on April 20 and 21, COSVN officials had made an assessment of their failure to take An Loc. During the above critique session, the NVA leaders had castigated the 9th Division for its poor showing. They also decided that the leading role for the next attack would be assigned to the 5th Division, which would be reinforced by elements of the 9th Division and tank units.[2] The NVA 5th Division commander promised he would replicate what he did in Loc Ninh and take An Loc in two days.[3]

Based on these new indicators, General Minh and his advisor, General Hollingsworth, agreed that a new NVA assault was in the making and that increased Arc Light missions were needed to thwart the enemy plan. At General Hollingsworth's request, General Abrams agreed to allocate to III Corps a full twenty-four hours of B-52 strikes. Since a total of twenty-five B-52 strikes had been made available to him on April 10, General Hollingsworth called General Abrams and told him he wanted one B-52 strike every fifty-five minutes for the next twenty-five hours, effective 5:30 A.M. on May 11, the expected date of the new NVA offensive.[4]

During the battle of An Loc, General Hollingsworth frequently flew over the besieged city to boost the morale of the defenders by talking to the American advisors and also to senior ARVN commanders and assuring them of the full support of U.S. airpower. On one of these occasions, General Hollingsworth, using his code name "Danger 79," called Colonel Nhut to inquire about the situation in his sector. Nhut—code name "M-72" (the LAW antitank rocket launcher was obviously a popular weapon in An Loc)—invited General Hollingsworth to drop by for a drink and to see for himself what was going on on the ground. General Hollingsworth politely declined; he told Nhut he would do that at another time.[5]

As it was apparent that the NVA were preparing for another push to take the city, General Hollingsworth had reason to be concerned because the American advisors had reported that the morale of the defenders had rapidly deteriorated, that symptoms of battle fatigue were evident everywhere, and that the troops, understandably, were physically and mentally exhausted. They had beaten back two major assaults, tenaciously held to this small piece of property since early April despite constant artillery bombardments and probing attacks; their wounded had not been evacuated and their effectives had critically dwindled.

On the national front, May 10 was a somber day for the country. In MRI, NVA forces, after their victory at Quang Tri on May 1, were preparing to attack the friendly positions on My Chanh River, the last defense line before the Imperial City. In MRII, ARVN's 23rd Division in Kontum was under imminent renewed attacks from two NVA divisions, which were regrouping after their failed offensive on April 15. In An Loc, the enemy was determined to take the city before May 19 to celebrate Ho Chi Minh's birthday. So on May 10, President Thieu declared the nation in danger and imposed a night curfew on all South Vietnamese cities effective the following day.[6]

The shortage of troops was also a major concern for General Minh. In fact, only about 4,000 ARVN soldiers, including regulars as well as territorial forces, were about to face two NVA divisions supported by tanks and artillery. An attempt was made to bring reinforcement to the garrison by air, but by that time, the NVA had moved their anti-aircraft batteries closer to the city. On May 9, a VNAF Chinook helicopter transporting fresh troops into An Loc was hit by enemy anti-aircraft fire. Maj. Nguyen Tan Trong, chief pilot, tried to land in an area just south of An Loc, but the helicopter burst into flames, killing three crewmen. Maj. Nguyen Tan Trong and Lt. Nguyen Van Thanh, co-pilot, were captured by the enemy; they were released in 1973 after the Paris Peace Agreement.[7] The destruction of Major Trong's helicopter over An Loc put an end to any effort to reinforce the garrison.

This, however, didn't stop Col. Walter Ulmer from flying in to relieve Colonel Miller, who was near exhaustion after over one month of uninterrupted fighting. General Hollingsworth believed it was time to replace him and to inject new blood in the division advisory team before the upcoming attack. On May 10, a Huey helicopter flown by the commander of the 12th U.S. Aviation Group, escorted by Cobra gunships, touched down briefly on the helipad at the southern area of the city; as Colonel Ulmer leaped out, Colonel Miller jumped in and the helicopter lifted up in a hurry before the inevitable arrival of the enemy artillery. Colonel Miller was slated to command a brigade of the 101st Airborne Division in Fort Campbell, Kentucky.[8] Colonel Ulmer, a West Point graduate, had previously served as an advisor to the 40th Regiment of the ARVN 22nd Division in the Central Highlands.[9]

Hell broke out half an hour past midnight on May 11. "North Vietnamese artillery rained down with such intensity that the sound of exploding rounds melted together in a single rolling roar," wrote Dale Andradé.[10] An estimated 8,300 rounds of artillery and mortars of all calibers hit the city without interruption. As the area held by ARVN troops was reduced to about one square kilometer after the first two attacks, this means that, in the average, every 120 square meters (or a square of 11 meters each side) of South Vietnamese positions received one round of enemy artillery. This was by far the biggest offensive launched on the city of An Loc. The NVA this time decided to launch a four-pronged assault aimed at cutting An Loc into four different zones and to destroy these one by one. The NVA 5th Division conducted the main attack directed to the north and northeast, while the 9th Division's secondary attack was aimed at the western and southern sections of the city.

The four attacking columns approached from four different directions, as follows:

- 174th Regiment/5th Division in the north.
- Regiment E6/5th Division in the northeast.
- 271st Regiment /9th Division in the south (through the Xa Cam Gate).
- 272nd Regiment/9th Division in the west (through the Phu Lo Gate).

The 275th Regiment of the 5th Division was held in reserve. Each attacking column was supported by six to eight tanks.

Around 4:30 A.M., the enemy lifted their artillery fire and their infantry and tanks started the assault. However, when they approached the ARVN defense line, their tanks bypassed their infantry, because they were afraid to be sitting ducks and be hit by M-72 LAWs if they progressed at infantry pace. As a consequence, a number of these tanks were destroyed as soon as they penetrated the perimeter of defense.

In the north, the 174th Regiment/5th NVA Division launched repeated assaults on the positions of the 8th Regiment and the 3rd and 4th Companies of the 81st Airborne Commando Group. The 8th Regiment withdrew under pressure toward the city but some units were able to cling to the high-rise buildings and stop the attacking forces along Nguyen Trung Truc Street. A few tanks that penetrated deep into the defenses of the commandos to the east were destroyed by soldiers of the 8th Regiment. Also under heavy enemy pressure, the 81st Commandos had to give up some of the terrain regained three weeks earlier. At one point, the commandos were on the verge of being overrun by ferocious enemy assaults. The 5th Division command post, in close coordination with the U.S. advisors, again, had to divert one preplanned B-52 strike to drop its payload on top of the attackers, just a mere 600 yards from the commandos. This last-minute change saved the 81st Commando from possible annihilation while inflicting heavy casualties on the attackers. (It was estimated that 90% of all Arc Light strikes in support of An Loc were diverted from their original targets to drop on more urgent ones.)[11]

"The close explosions shook the houses," as a commando later described the effects of the B-52 air strikes. "The earth vibrated violently, the compressed air caused me to have difficulty breathing, I didn't know if the two sorties were finished because I had not recovered my consciousness. The city darkened as the cloud of dust had risen and covered the sun light. The civilians in my sector had been given instructions regarding personal safety in case of close B-52 strikes but many children still had bleeding in their ears and nose."[12]

The well-placed Arc Light strike allowed the commandos to reorganize and during the day, they succeeded in recapturing some of their positions after launching violent counter-attacks, sometimes leading to hand-to-hand combat.

In the northeast, the E6 Regiment of the NVA's 5th Division launched a two-pronged assault on the 3rd Ranger Group positions. One PT-76 tank was destroyed, but the 36th and 31st Battalions in the north and eastern sector were under heavy attack. Supported by effective air strikes and protected by heavily fortified positions inside public buildings, the 36th Battalion beat back wave after wave of enemy assaults in the vicinity of the Chinese School; however the battalion lost contact with some of the outposts south of the airport, which were driven back or overrun by superior enemy forces.

In the 31st Battalion's sector, the situation was more critical. Around 2:00 A.M., the enemy launched human wave assaults against the battalion positions in the eastern side of the city, driving back the forward outposts in the western edge of Quan Loi plantation and threatening to overrun the battalion units in the vicinity of the White Bridge. Colonel Biet requested an urgent B-52 strike one kilometer from the defense perimeter to stop the enemy from breaking through the line of the 31st Battalion. The request was approved and the American advisor told the air support officer in the S-3 section that when the FAC arrived over the target area and called the group call-sign on the radio, all he had to do was to squeeze the speaker button on the radio handset twice to confirm that he knew the B-52s were about to bomb the requested target. A few minutes later, the air support officer heard the FAC calling on the air support frequency. He squeezed the speaker button twice and five minutes later, a string of tremendous explosions shook the entire northeastern sector. Major Khanh, the 31st Battalion commander, immediately yelled and cursed on the radio; he protested the fact that the Ranger Group did not alert him ahead of time so his men could take cover. His men were shaken in their bunkers, but fortunately nobody was hurt.

Khanh later called back to report that the enemy must have been all destroyed because everything was quiet after the B-52 strike. Early the next morning, Khanh sent patrols out in the direction of Quan Loi plantation. They found a large number of dead, charred enemy corpses with all sorts of light and heavy weapons in the southwestern edge of Quan Loi.[13]

Corp. Nguyen Van Xuan from the 3rd Ranger Group recalled that in the morning of May 11, a seventy-year-old man named *Ong Sau* (or Mr. Sau), noticed a T-54 tank was stuck in a drainage ditch under the balcony of his two-story house, while the tankers were busy trying to get the tank out of the ditch. Mr. Sau went inside and asked the rangers—who were taking up position in his house—to give him a hand grenade and teach him how to use it. The rangers wanted to go out to take a look, but Mr. Sau told them to stay put; he went back to the balcony, removed the safety pin of the grenade and dropped it into the open hatchet of the T-54. Mr. Sau rushed inside the house and escaped by the rear door. There was a big explosion followed by several smaller explosions, then a column of black smoke rose up in front of the house. When the firing died down outside, Mr. Sau furtively came back; he saw a few charred bodies inside the blackened carcass of the tank while the façade of his house was partially burned and covered with black smoke.[14] Obviously, this was not the type of welcome the North Vietnamese tankers were told they would receive in An Loc.

While the situation on the northeast and east of the city was temporarily stabilized, elements of the NVA E6 Regiment supported by tanks, launched a furious assault on the weakly defended area in the northern sector between the 81st Commando Group and the 3rd Ranger Group. The attacking force succeeded in driving a wedge between the above two units; it broke through the 52nd Ranger Battalion—which fell back in disorder—and advanced toward the center of the city. Lt. Col. Richard J. McManus, the senior advisor to the 3rd Ranger Group, later blamed Major Dau, the 52nd Ranger Battalion commander, for failure of leadership in combat.[15] However, during the siege of An Loc, the 52nd Ranger Battalion lost about half of its effective force while the remaining fighting men were wounded at least once.[16] A battalion that did not fight would not have incurred such exorbitant losses.

In the western sector, the 272nd Regiment of the 9th NVA Division attacked through the Phu Lo Gate. Two leading PT-76 tanks were knocked out by the 7th Regiment, but the enemy succeeded in capturing the city's prison and the Public Works Department building at 9:15 A.M., despite a furious resistance from South Vietnamese defenders. In particular, the American advisors had nothing but praise for Lt. Col. Ly Duc Quan, the 7th Regiment commander: three times wounded in the battle of An Loc, Quan kept commanding his troops while being propped up in his cot.[17] Colonel Quan was a Nung officer. As we have seen earlier, the ARVN's 5th Division was the offspring of the 3rd Field Division, which consisted of former Nung battalions; the above battalions—which fought the Indochina War in North Viet Nam under the French—resettled in the South and were integrated into the National Army after the partition of Viet Nam under the 1954 Geneva Accords. Like the North American Indians, the Nung—an ethnic minority living near the Chinese border—were exceptionally brave warriors and Colonel Quan had upheld that tradition in the Battle of An Loc.

An enemy post-action report indicated that the attacking force in 7th Regiment sector made a major tactical mistake by not pressing southeastward to capture the command post of the 5th Division, the nerve center of the defense of An Loc, instead of capturing the Public Works campus, "an objective of no tactical value."[18] At 9:30, the 3rd Battalion of the 7th Regiment, under relentless enemy attacks, withdrew toward the center of the city, in close proximity to the 5th Division command post. The enemy started to consolidate their positions in the newly gained salient on the western sector.

In the south and southeastern sector, the enemy committed the 275th Regiment of the 5th NVA Division—which was held in reserve—to launch a two-pronged attack. The first thrust was aimed at the Sector Psychological Warfare Company headquarters. As one PT-76 tank emerged in front of the perimeter of defense, Sgt. La Trong Thang destroyed it with an M-72 rocket,[19] but the enemy was able to establish a foothold in Binh Long Sector area. The second thrust was aimed at the Xa Cam Gate, which was defended by the 1st Battalion of the 48th Regiment. (The 1st Battalion was part of TF-52 from ARVN 18th Division. After its withdrawal from Hung Tam Base on April 7, TF-52 was assigned a central area between the 3rd Ranger Group and the 8th Regiment. After the second attack, the 1st Battalion of the 48th Regiment was attached to the 1st Airborne Brigade.) The NVA pushed back the 1/48 Battalion and captured the area around Xa Cam Gate.[20]

Because the USAF had been alerted about the impending attack, it was ready to provide uninterrupted air support starting at 4:00 A.M. Jet fighters, Cobra gunships, and B-52s strafed enemy formations around the perimeter of defense and sometimes within the city itself. During the day, 350 tactical air sorties and 26 B-52 missions had been accomplished in support of the garrison.[21] The American pilots reported that many enemy assaults were completely neutralized by CBU bombs which proved very deadly on exposed targets. However, stopping the enemy offense with massive air support was not without its price: One U.S. A-37, two Cobra gunships, two FAC O-2 aircraft, and one VNAF A-1 were shot down during the course of the day's action.[22]These heavy losses were due in part to the introduction to the battle of An Loc of the SA-7 Strela, a new surface-to-air missile that had been used by the enemy earlier in MRI. A Soviet-made shoulder-fired heat-seeking missile, the Strela was very effective against low-flying Cobra gunships. The introduction of this new weapon reflected the NVA's attempt to neutralize, or at least to minimize, the air support in An Loc in an all-out effort to take the city.

Despite heavy air support, the situation became critical by 10:00 A.M. In the north, the enemy broke though the friendly line in certain areas and seized the Field Police headquarters and the New Market. In the northeast, the office of the "Open Arms" program fell and the enemy reached a point only 500 meters from the 5th Division headquarters. In the west, elements of the NVA 9th Division occupied the Public Works building and were stopped a mere 300 meters from the 5th Division command post. The Binh Long sector in the south was broken through. In the southeastern sector—except for the area in the vicinity of Xa Cam Gate which was occupied by the enemy—the paratroopers held their line and inflicted heavy casualties on the attackers. It was clear that the enemy's plan was to cut An Loc in half with a pincer movement of two main attacks in the northeastern and western sectors. Linking up these two penetrations would indeed separate the defenders into enclaves that could be defeated in detail.

Around 10:00 A.M., Colonel Luong, 1st Airborne Brigade commander, ordered the 8th Airborne Battalion to counter-attack to recapture the Xa Cam Gate area. U.S. warplanes supporting the paratroopers' counter-attack destroyed six enemy tanks, including a BTR-50 amphibious armored vehicle.[23] After the Xa Cam Gate had been recaptured, Colonel Luong replaced the 8th Battalion with the 63rd Company of the 6th Airborne Battalion, which had earlier withdrawn from Doi Gio Hill with heavy losses. The 8th Battalion, in coordination with Binh Long provincial forces, again launched a new counter-attack to recapture the portion of the south and southwestern sectors that had been broken through by elements of the NVA 275th Regiment. After the defensive line of Binh Long Sector had been restored, Lieutenant Colonel Ninh, 8th Battalion commander, reinforced the defense of the southern sector with the 82nd Airborne Company.

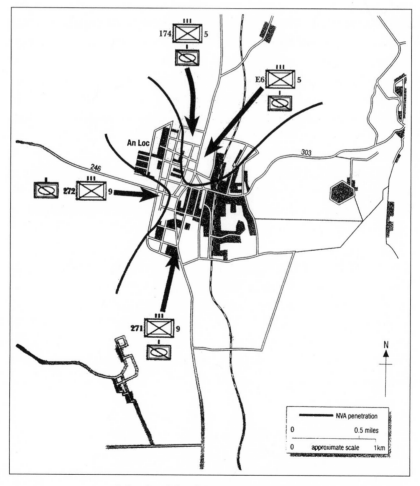

Map 11: Third Attack on An Loc

While the situation in the southern sector had been temporarily stabilized, the enemy tried to widen their northeastern and western penetrations. At around 10:30 A.M., General Hung ordered the 1st Airborne Brigade to counter-attack to destroy the enemy's two prongs, which threatened to seize his command post.

Around 11:00 A.M., General Hung called Colonel Truong, the 8th Regiment commander, to inquire about the situation in the latter's sector. Truong assured his division commander that his men had been able to regroup and stop the enemy roughly along the Nguyen Trung Truc line. Hung then informed Colonel Truong that the 7th Regiment had been overrun despite round-the-clock support from the 155mm guns at Tong Le Chan outpost. Hung also said that elements of the 7th were now taking positions near his command post, that the enemy was firing B-40s at his bunker, and that he had ordered Colonel Luong to send one airborne battalion to his rescue. "If the paratroopers arrive after the enemy overrun the 5th Division headquarters, I would commit suicide instead of being taken prisoner," said Hung. "After I die, take your regiment and try to move to Chon Thanh with the 81st Airborne Commando." Truong told General Hung not to give up and let him know he would immediately dispatch the 8th Reconnaissance Company to reinforce the protection of the 5th Division headquarters pending the arrival of the paratroopers.[24]

In the meantime, Colonel Luong ordered the 5th Battalion—which had been screening the terrain to the south of the city—to enter An Loc and to attack in two divergent directions to stop and destroy the enemy's two converging columns that were dangerously closing in on General Hung's command post. The left column of the 5th Battalion stopped the enemy in the vicinity of the Public Works building; the column to the right battled the enemy around the Montagnard elementary school. In the afternoon, Colonel Luong dispatched the 3rd Airborne Reconnaissance Company to protect the 5th Division headquarters. To provide close fire support to the 5th Battalion's counter-attack, Colonel Luong used the four organic 81mm mortars serviced by the artillerymen from the battery that was overrun earlier at Doi Gio. The street combat raged all day long and by nightfall the outcome of this seesaw battle remained uncertain.

Andradé had a more optimistic assessment of the situation on May 11 when he wrote: "By noon on 11 May it was over. The North Vietnamese had failed to take An Loc. Panicked enemy soldiers fled from air strikes, trying to disperse in the forests to the west. . . On at least one occasion fleeing North Vietnamese soldiers were caught in the open and torn to pieces by tactical air strikes. Not a single enemy tank was reported moving anywhere near An Loc during the rest of the day, although many abandoned and destroyed hulks were counted. All forty tanks involved in the morning attack were dead on the battlefield. Some were smoking carcasses, others undamaged though abandoned. Some had been left with engines still running."[25]

Despite the severe beating they had received, the enemy, in fact, was determined to press on and expand their penetration. During the night of May 11, the NVA consolidated their newly gained territories while ARVN forces sent small units behind their lines to cut their supply routes and force them to withdraw. On May 12, despite their staggering losses, the enemy tried to widen their gaps by launching a new pincer attack, employing the 272nd Regiment of the 9th Division in the west and the 174th Regiment of the 5th Division in the northeast. Both of these columns were supported by elements of a tank company. With efficient tactical air support, the garrison held out and beat back the enemy attack.

In the 81st Commando sector, the enemy effort to exploit their penetration was spoiled by a lack of communication between their forward observer and the supporting artillery unit. One commando from the 3rd Company later reported that as the enemy was preparing to launch their tank-supported assault, the first elements were hit by their own artillery fire, which obviously failed to stop or to hit deeper targets in accordance with their *tien phao, hau xung* tactic. The battalion commander, the forward observer, and his radioman were killed. One NVA officer grabbed the radio and ordered the artillery to stop; but, as he was unable to provide the artillery internal radio code, the artillery unit continued to fire because it suspected the call came from ARVN troops who had been hit by their fire.[26]

By night fall it became apparent that the enemy offensive had lost its momentum and that, like the first two attacks, this one had also failed. The next morning, a dozen NVA soldiers, whose unit was hit by a B-52 strike the previous night, got lost and wandered into the 5th Airborne Battalion positions. A master sergeant in the battalion headquarters and his men killed all the intruders but the sergeant was fatally hit by a stray bullet.[27]

Following are the results of the two days' fighting:

> Friendly: 51 KIA, 137 WIA, 136 MIA, 142 weapons lost.
> Enemy: 218 KIA, 2 captured, 13 crew-served and 23 individual weapons captured, 23 tanks destroyed.[28]

After this last attempt to take An Loc, COSVN decided to withdraw the 5th Division from the battlefield and to continue the siege of An Loc with their 9th Division. Intelligence information indicated that the 5th Division had withdrawn to Cambodia to reorganize; its presence at the border of Kien Tuong province in MRIV was reported on June 6. A COSVN document captured by ARVN/JGS intelligence bureau also indicated that NVA forces suffered extremely heavy casualties; each combat battalion had only about ninety fighting men (as compared to the original average effective force of 350), and the morale of the troops was very low; but the Politburo in Hanoi had decided that the campaign would be continued for three additional months to strengthen the Communist position at the Paris Talks.[29] This was asking too much, however, and in the weeks following that third failed attempt to take An Loc, the enemy could not muster any significant attack, but instead maintained the siege with only sporadic artillery fire and small-unit actions.

For the defenders, the situation was not much better. Although they had repulsed three major attacks, the battle fatigue caused by uninterrupted fighting, lack of sleep, hunger, the unbearable stench of unburied dead, and the mounting number of unevacuated casualties began to set in; the morale of the troops had almost reached the breaking point. "If it were not an army with a high degree of discipline, a war with a good cause and a high spirit of sacrifice for the national cause, then no human being would have the energy to endure this tense life for many consecutive months," wrote Mach Van Truong in his memoir.[30]

On May 13, taking advantage of the period of relative quiet after the third attack, some religious leaders and political organizations requested permission to go to Chon Thanh despite the fact that the section of Route 13 between Tan Khai and Chon Thanh was still under enemy control. Colonel Nhut agreed to let them go in spite of the objections from Lieutenant Colonel Corley, the provincial senior advisor, who was concerned about their safety. Nhut ordered the provincial Administration and Logistics Agency to allocate rice rations to thousands of evacuees. He also allowed some public employees, whose presence was not necessary at An Loc, to leave the city to avoid being wounded or killed by continuing enemy artillery fire. Nhut asked Colonel Corley to request U.S. Cobra gunships to escort the column of evacuees to Tan Khai, because some sections of Route 13 north of the town were still occupied by NVA blocking forces. Later, Colonel Nhut was informed that the enemy stopped the evacuees in order to screen them. Some residents were allowed to proceed to Chon Thanh, but high-ranking provincial administration officials were detained and sent to prisoner camps inside Cambodia; they were released only after the signing of the Paris Agreement in January 1973. Nhut was particularly proud that no members of the province RF and PF units had joined the columns of refugees.[31]

While the situation in An Loc became relatively calm after the third attack, the VC's B3 Front on the Central Highlands resumed the long-awaited offensive to take Kontum on May 18 in order to celebrate Ho Chi Minh's birthday the following day. This time, instead of launching frontal attacks on the northern perimeter, their infantry units, taking advantage of the persistent fog in the Highlands, infiltrated behind ARVN positions to occupy strategic key points within the city and to use these salients as springboards to capture the rest of the city.

This tactic had been used with great success by the Viet Minh in North Viet Nam during the Indochina War. It consisted of infiltrating behind the defenders' lines or attacking a weak point of the defense, normally an area between two units, then once inside the defensive positions, one element would destroy the command headquarters while the rest of the attacking forces would spread out to attack the front-line units from the rear. The Viet Minh called this type of attack the "blossoming flower" tactic.

True to this tactic, in addition to infantry units from the 320th and 10th Divisions, the NVA also sent their last T-54 tanks to infiltrate between the front-line defensive positions to launch a direct attack on the 23rd Division headquarters, hoping to achieve a repeat of their much celebrated victory against ARVN's 22nd Division in Tan Canh in March. However, as the T-54 column progressed to within fifty meters from the 44th Regiment command bunker, one soldier from the 44th Reconnaissance Company fired his XM-202 rocket and destroyed the leading tank, causing all tank crews to get out of their tanks and escape in great panic.[32] In the meantime, however, the enemy units that had infiltrated behind the 23rd Division front-line positions quickly spread out to occupy strategic key points in the city, including the airport, the Logistical Center and the Armored Regiment's rear base.

The next day, Colonel Ba launched a counter-attack spearheaded by the 45th Regiment—which had replaced the 44th Regiment on the high ground northwest of the city—and the 53rd Regiment, which defended the northeastern sector. These two units were ordered to attack toward the city to eliminate the enemy penetrations while the 1/8 Tank Company, reinforced with an infantry unit, was directed to eliminate NVA *chot* in strategic areas within the city. Supported by division artillery and tactical air support provided by AD-6 Skyraiders from the VNAF 6th Air Division in Pleiku, the counter-attacking forces succeeded in eliminating the enemy enclaves one by one.

Capt. Le Quang Vinh, 1/8 Tank Company commander, later reported that, during the battle of Kontum—including the encounter with the enemy *chot* at the Chu Pao Pass north of Pleiku on April 26—his unit suffered sixty-eight KIA (including eighteen officers), over 300 WIA; two M-41 tanks were destroyed, ten were damaged. The enemy losses included ten T-54s destroyed, one T-54 captured; over 1,000 North Vietnamese soldiers were killed.[33] Gen. Ly Tong Ba reported in his memoir that the NVA left 1,000 dead after the second attack on Kontum and he had to use bulldozers to dig a common grave for a mass burial.[34]

After the failed offensive of May 18, the NVA gave up their ambition to take the Central Highlands in order to cut South Viet Nam in half and to eventually reinforce the successful prongs in MRI or MRIII.

Despite their failure to take An Loc, the Communists were not ready to give up. A secret COSVN message captured by the ARVN/JGS intelligence bureau after the third attack on An Loc directed the NVA attacking forces to withdraw, reorganize, get replacements and celebrate Ho Chi Minh's birthday three days ahead so that they could try one more time to take An Loc on May 19, Ho Chi Minh's birthday. One ARVN commando team was inserted into the suspect area and reported the coordinates of the identified enemy assembly location. Six B-52 sorties dropped their bombs on the targeted area the day of the birthday celebration. Unconfirmed reports indicated that 60% of the enemy forces were destroyed.[35]

Despite these severe setbacks, on May 19, Uncle Ho's official birthday, an NVA force, supported by tanks, attacked the 1st Airborne Brigade through the rubber plantations south of An Loc. Instead of achieving tactical surprise, the North Vietnamese tanks, on the contrary, had difficulty maneuvering at night in a dense plantation with limited vision and restricted fields of fire. The attacking forces were ambushed and annihilated by the paratroopers before daylight. The paratroopers jumped on the tanks and threw grenades through the hatches, destroying many T-54s and PT76s. A few M-113s, captured by the NVA in Loc Ninh the previous month, were also destroyed.[36]

Toward the end of May, most of the enemy anti-aircraft defense system had been suppressed by air power and by early June helicopters were able to land at An Loc for resupply and medevac. The lull in the fighting allowed the 81st Commando Group to improve and decorate its cemetery. (By the time of the liberation of An Loc in mid-June 1972, the commando cemetery contained 67 graves, or 12% of the strength of the Commando Group.) A small brick wall painted in white was built around the cemetery. In the middle of the cemetery was erected a memorial monument on which were inscribed the two famous verses that had been quoted earlier in the introduction to this book. These two verses were composed by

Ms. Pha, an elementary class teacher who was wounded by NVA artillery fire and was treated and saved by the commandos' medical team. Ms. Pha, as one story had it, fell in love with a soldier from the 81st Commando Group, but her lover was killed during a close combat engagement.

Because the commando cemetery was the biggest military cemetery erected in An Loc during the siege—the paratroopers had two small cemeteries, one near the Binh Long Sector Hospital, and one in the vicinity of the helicopter pad in the southern area of the city—it was a testimony to the sacrifice of all fallen soldiers. And these verses expressed the gratitude of the city toward not only the commandos, but also toward all soldiers who had given their lives in the defense of a small and innocent border town with a peaceful and noble name. It was also an expression of love, pride, and sorrow of a beautiful girl toward her fallen hero.

In front of the cemetery, one commando had painted two verses from the famous Chinese poet Vuong Han:

> *"Tuy ngoa sa truong quan mac van,*
> *Co lai chinh chien ky nhan hoi"*

(Awake or drunk after a battle, no one cares to ask.
From ancient times, how many had returned from a distant military campaign.)

Nine

Securing Route Nationale 13

As mentioned in an earlier chapter, General Minh, III Corps commander, was concerned about an attack on the cities immediately north of Saigon by elements of NVA's 7th Division in conjunction with two independent VC regiments and other local units. The latter constituted what was known as the Binh Long Division. An attack on these cities would not only threaten the capital of South Viet Nam, but may also cost Minh his command. Thus, to defeat the enemy attempt to bypass An Loc and to race toward Saigon, Minh used the entire 21st Division, reinforced with one armored squadron, to secure Route 13 and link up with the besieged garrison of An Loc from the south.

In General Minh's view, blocking a possible enemy advance toward Saigon, in fact, was as important as securing Route 13, at least during the initial stage of the 21st Division deployment in MRIII. The U.S. advisors with the 21st Division seemed to agree: in response to complaints by Saigon correspondents about the lack of progress of the 21st Division, Col. J. Ross Franklin, senior advisor to the 21st Division, angrily told one journalist: "You people write that the 21st is not clearing the highway to An Loc. That's not our job. We are here to find and engage the NVA 7th Division, which is the only big enemy outfit not committed to this Hanoi offensive. We're fighting the 7th, engaging it and keeping it at bay. So you guys in Saigon can sleep tonight."[1]

159

Maj. Gen. Nguyen Vinh Nghi, the commander of the 21st—like the former commanders of that division—was himself a member of the famous "Delta Clan." When General Minh, who commanded the 21st Division, was offered the job of commander of the important Capital Special Military District in the middle of the 1968 Tet Offensive, Nghi, a *protégé* of President Thieu with little combat experience, was picked to replace Minh.

Nghi's division, which operated in the Mekong Delta under IV Corps, was put under the operational control of III Corps by the war council meeting in Saigon on April 7. The 32nd Regiment arrived in Chon Thanh by vehicle on April 11 without incident. By April 12, the remaining units of the 21st, including division artillery, had been airlifted to Bien Hoa airport and transported by trucks to the Lai Khe area. From April 12 to April 23, the 21st Division consolidated its operational base in Lai Khe and organized its logistical system in preparation for its relief mission. The troops that operated in the flooded rice fields, swamps, and canals in the Mekong Delta against lightly armed VC units, needed also to adapt to the new battlefield—consisting mostly of small hills covered with dense forests and rubber plantations—where they were expected to face well-armed NVA regular divisions supported by tanks and artillery regiments.

The deployment of the 21st Division to Binh Long province was a welcome change in the static mentality that prevailed within ARVN before 1972. Previously, there existed a fierce competition between division commanders; their respective tactical areas were considered inviolable and the incursion of outside units into their jealously guarded fiefdoms was unthinkable. This static mentality fortunately changed during the North Vietnamese 1972 and 1975 offensives, when it was necessary to deploy units from different corps and divisions into areas under attack.

In the interim, the 21st Division's initial inactivity allowed the enemy to quickly shift forces to deal with the new front to the south in an effort to defeat ARVN's attempt to link up with An Loc. The NVA 7th Division immediately dispatched the 101st Regiment and a sapper battalion to occupy blocking positions about ten miles north of Lai Khe. On April 22, NVA troops fired B-40 rockets on a civilian bus at Bau Bang, six kilometers south of Chon Thanh, killing four and wounding twenty civilians.[2]

Finally, on April 23, General Nghi was ready to act. He directed the 32nd and 33rd Regiments to attack from Chon Thanh and Lai Khe, respectively, in an effort to destroy the enemy blocking forces in a coordinated pincer movement. The southern column, supported by a tank unit from the 5th Armored Squadron, ran into heavy resistance fifteen kilometers north of Lai Khe. It took the 21st Division five days of tough fighting to annihilate the enemy blocking force and by April 29, the South Vietnamese controlled the portion of Route 13 between Lai Khe and Chon Thanh. A 21st Division after-action report indicated that the 101st NVA Independent Regiment and the attached sapper battalion left around 600 bodies on a four-kilometer stretch of the railway running parallel to Route 13. The 32nd and 33rd Regiments suffered over 300 casualties.[3]

During that time, the ARVN Joint General Staff, realizing the seriousness of the NVA's threat to the capital city of South Viet Nam, decided to reinforce III Corps with the 3rd Airborne Brigade. On April 24, while the 21st Division units were battling the NVA 101st Regiment and a sapper battalion north of Lai Khe, the Light Headquarters of the Airborne Division under the command of Colonel Ho Trung Hau was heliborne into Chon Thanh to coordinate the operations of the 1st and 3rd Airborne Brigades.

III Corps assigned to the Airborne Division (-) the mission of clearing the section of Route 13 from Tau O creek to Xa Cam, just south of An Loc. The 21st Division would be responsible for the territory south of Tau O, including Binh Duong province, and must be ready to provide assistance to any area under attack within its area of responsibility.[4]

Only one day after its arrival to Lai Khe, the 3rd Airborne Brigade swung into action. On April 25, the 2nd Airborne Battalion air assaulted into an area northeast of Tau O and another area about one kilometer east of Tan Khai. The first elements immediately received artillery fire upon landing. After regrouping, the battalion established a fire support base named Anh Dung. A 105mm artillery battery was transported by VNAF Chinook helicopters into Anh Dung base to provide fire support to friendly units participating in the road opening operation and also to the garrison of An Loc. On April 26, the 1ˢᵗ Airborne Battalion was heliborne into the Duc Vinh area, about four kilometers north of Tan Khai. Like the 2ⁿᵈ Battalion, the 1ˢᵗ came under artillery fire upon landing but made only light contact with the enemy. However, the next day, NVA troops fired recoilless rifles directly at the artillery battery at Anh Dung base, heavily damaging three howitzers.

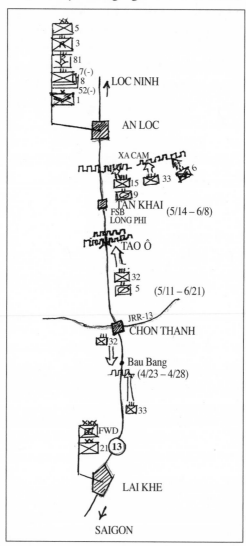

Map 12: Route Nationale 13 Securing Operations

On May 2, Colonel Hau, in charge of the Airborne Division Light Headquarters, committed the 3rd Battalion, which was heliborne into an area east of Route 13, between Tan Khai and Tau O. The mission of this battalion was to widen the ARVN's control area westward and to link up with the two airborne battalions to the north. From May 5 to May 7, the 3rd Battalion engaged in heavy combat with the NVA forces at battalion level. Both sides incurred heavy losses. On May 5, the enemy directed artillery fire on the 2nd Battalion operating south of Tao O, wounding the battalion commander. Lt. Col. Ngo Le Tinh, deputy brigade commander, was directed to take over the command of the battalion. The 21st Division also reinforced the depleted 2nd Airborne Battalion with the 21st Reconnaissance Company.[5] It was increasingly clear that the enemy had developed a new tactic with regard to the 3rd Airborne Brigade: They tried, if possible, to avoid engaging directly the paratroopers; instead, they kept shadowing them and at times, they closed in on the airborne units in order to harass them or to direct artillery fire on them to cause maximum casualties.

The situation of the 3rd Battalion operating west of Route 13 was particularly critical. It was ceaselessly pursued by the enemy and heavily bombarded by enemy artillery. From May 12 to May 14, the battalion was harassed or attacked without respite. It was also bombed by mistake by a friendly warplane, killing the battalion executive officer and a number of paratroopers. On May 14, the battalion was ambushed by an NVA force when crossing an open rice field about 500 meters south of Tau O. Despite massive air support, the 3rd Battalion suffered heavy losses. The 3rd Company commander and a great number of paratroopers were killed in this ambush. The battalion had to destroy all heavy equipment in order to carry their wounded and dead soldiers. On April 15, after the battalion had been resupplied and the medevac operation accomplished, it was again harassed and targeted by enemy artillery and incurred additional casualties when moving east of Route 13.[6] In the meantime, the 1st Battalion operating in the Duc Vinh area was unable to move north because of the inability of the other two battalions to secure Route 13 north of Tau O and to link up with it.

Because of the deteriorating situation in MRI, ARVN/JGS decided to pull the 3rd Airborne Brigade out of Binh Long in order to reinforce the Airborne Division (minus two brigades), which was defending the My Chanh River, the last ARVN line before Hue. The 3rd Airborne Brigade would be replaced by the 15th Regiment, 9th Division, which was operating in the Mekong Delta. The 15th Regiment was commanded by Lt. Col. Ho Ngoc Can, a fearless man and one of the most decorated officers in the South Vietnamese Army. Can had graduated from *Vung Tau Thieu Sinh Quan School*, a school reserved for children of military personnel who chose to follow their fathers' footsteps. The students were subjected to a strict military discipline and were imbued with a high sense of duty and service to the country. Those who graduated from the school were sent to officer schools while those who didn't graduate served as non-commissioned officers. Many graduates had become high-ranking generals in the South Vietnamese Army.

Following are the losses during the bloody fighting between the 3rd Airborne Brigade and NVA blocking forces south of An Loc:

Enemy: 254 KIA, 1 captured
 12 crew-served and 19 individual weapons captured.
Friendly: 60 KIA, 340 WIA, 24 MIA
 21 crew-served and 38 individual weapons lost.[7]

While the 3rd Airborne Brigade was heavily engaged north of Tau O and was unable to effectuate a link-up with the 1st Airborne Brigade just south of An Loc, the 21st Division encountered heavy enemy resistance north of Chon Thanh. On May 1, the 31st Regiment air assaulted an area seven kilometers north of that town. The regiment was attacked by elements of the 165th Regiment, 7th Division, right after landing. During the course of the battle north of Chon Thanh, the 165th Regiment was reinforced with the 209th Regiment, also from the NVA's 7th Division. As the 31st Regiment was still unable to advance, the 21st Division ordered two battalions of the 32nd Regiment to conduct an envelopment east of the enemy positions on May 6. On May 8, the 3rd Battalion, 31st Regiment, launched a vertical envelopment by air assaulting an area north of the line of contact. Despite massive fire power, consisting of eight B-52 strikes, 142 sorties of tactical air support and some 20,000 rounds of artillery,[8] the 31st Regiment was unable to remove the enemy blocking positions south of Tao O. During the battle north of Chon Thanh, the enemy left many bodies on the terrain, but the 21st Division also paid a heavy price in that encounter: the commander of the 31st Regiment, Col. Nguyen Huu Kiem, was seriously wounded, two battalion commanders (Captains Hoi and Nhuong) from the 31st Regiment, as well as the executive officer of the 2nd Battalion, 32nd Regiment, were killed; over 300 soldiers were also killed.[9]

The 21st Division incurred heavy losses on Route 13 because, during the 1972 offensive, the Communists had devised a new blocking tactic consisting of what they called *chot* and *kieng*. *Chot* in Vietnamese means bolt, pin, or a fastening devise to close a door. A *chot* usually consisted of an A-shaped six-meter-deep trench with reinforcement overhead, constructed in a horseshoe configuration on a key terrain feature, that allowed for effective enfilade fire on likely avenues of approach. The *chot* were categorized as "A" (squad size), "B" (platoon size), and "C" (company size). "*Kieng*" in Vietnamese means chain, or shackle. *Kieng* in Communist military parlance means a system of inter-connected *chot* which provided for mutual support and a solid defense in depth. With this system of *chot* and *kieng*, the enemy was able to use a relatively small force to effectively block a much bigger force for a long period of time. The *chot-kieng* system south of An Loc was established generally along the railway running parallel to Route 13 and was concentrated behind the deep marshes in Tao O creek area. It was linked to the rubber plantations west of Route 13 by an elaborate network of trenches that allowed for resupply and medical evacuation.

While the NVA's 5th and 9th Divisions were launching the third attack on An Loc on May 11, the 32nd Regiment, reinforced with an element of the 5th Armored Squadron, and the 6th, 73rd and 84th Ranger Battalions, began a new offensive to dislodge the enemy blocking positions south of Tao O. The attackers met strong resistance from the NVA 209th Regiment, reinforced with the Reconnaissance Company of the 7th Division, the 94th Sapper Company, and the C 41 Anti-Tank Company.[10] The enemy forces were deployed over a three-kilometer front in the middle of hilly terrain covered with dense vegetation, which constituted formidable obstacles to the attacking forces. It took three days of extremely heavy fighting for ARVN attacking forces to defeat the NVA blocking units about eight kilometers north of Chon Thanh. On May 13, both the NVA 165th and 209th Regiments, severely beaten, withdrew to new defensive positions south of Tau O creek where they took advantage of a strong connecting network of underground blocking positions to stop the advance of the ARVN's 32nd Regiment.

Despite massive artillery and air support, including B-52 strikes, for the next forty days, from May 11 to June 21, the 32nd Regiment was unable to destroy well-entrenched NVA forces. The casualties for both sides during that period reflected the viciousness of the battle to secure Tao O—known as the battle of Tau O Bridge—probably the most ferocious fighting during the rescuing operation:

32nd Regiment: 95 KIA (including a battalion commander), 455 WIA, 4 MIA, 4 M-113s damaged.
Enemy: 503 KIA, 37 crew-served and 71 individual weapons captured.[11]

The 209th Regiment of the 7th Division alone lost over 250 killed and most of its crew-served weapons. Despite these staggering casualties, Hanoi's English-language propaganda publications considered the stalled South Vietnamese drive a victory for the "people's forces." "Nguyen Van Thieu had sworn to relieve Route 13 before June 19, 1972—the ARVN Day—but now he still remains helpless," bragged the propaganda. "Thus, Route 13 is not only the 'Road of Thunder,' but also a 'Road of Death' for Nixon's strategy of 'Vietnamization' of the war."[12]

The enemy messages captured at that time showed, however, that after two months of fierce engagements with South Vietnamese attackers, the NVA blocking units, constantly bombarded by U.S. and V.N. warplanes, suffering heavy losses in terms of human lives and weapons, and fighting under the sweltering summer heat of the inland *plateaux*, had become hopeless and demoralized. They urgently requested supplies, rice, and water, and openly cursed on their radios without bothering to camouflage their messages.[13]

However, despite mounting casualties and lack of supplies, the enemy blocking forces, well-protected by their reinforced *chot-kieng* system and regularly replaced by fresh troops, were able to resist the advance of the South Vietnamese attackers. Explaining ARVN units' failure to secure Route 13, Colonel Franklin, 21st Division senior advisor, commented that, "it doesn't take a lot of guys in bunkers to stop an uncoordinated attack,"[14] implying that the attacks were not well orchestrated and powerful enough to overwhelm the enemy.

In reality, to remove the well-bunkered *chot*, mass and fire power were not the answer. Attacking en masse in this case may have caused unnecessary losses of lives. As the experience in MRI indicated, what was needed instead were initiative, exploitation of the terrain features, and close combat technique. In his book *Memoirs of An Loc*, Dr. Nguyen Van Quy, the An Loc surgeon, related an interesting story in this regard. In 1972, Dr. Quy was recognized as one of the most outstanding soldiers of the year and, along with other nominees, was awarded a one-week vacation in Taiwan. During the trip, Quy befriended Cuong, a young corporal from the Airborne Division, who told him how he was selected.

In June 1972, the Airborne Division's counter-attack to recapture Quang Tri ran into stiff resistance from NVA's blocking positions from the high ground west of Route Nationale 1. Corporal Cuong and two volunteers from his squad climbed to the top of the hill behind the enemy *chot* in an area covered with high grass. Hearing the noise behind them, three NVA soldiers left their bunker to reconnoiter the suspect area; the paratroopers discharged their M-16s and killed them all. Cuong dispatched one man to report their action to his platoon leader and asked for reinforcement in case of enemy counter-attack. The remaining paratroopers then occupied the enemy *chot* after having set up a claymore mine on a small trail behind their position they expected the enemy would use for supply or replacement. Sure enough, about ten minutes later, three NVA soldiers appeared on the trail. As they were about ten meters from the claymore mine, Cuong detonated the mine, and when the smoke cleared, all that was left were some charred body parts and a lot of blood. Afterward, Cuong and the reinforcing platoon destroyed the other *chot* downhill without difficulty.

When asked about his exploit, Cuong said he was very proud of his achievement, but he also felt somewhat uneasy because the NVA soldiers he killed were very young, maybe eighteen or nineteen years old. He had a young cousin about that age who stayed in Hanoi after the partition of Viet Nam in 1954, and the thought that he may have killed his own cousin made him feel very uncomfortable.[15]

While the Route 13 securing operations had just begun, the fall of the city of Quang Tri in MRI on May 1 caused an important change in the command structure of the South Vietnamese army. Lt. Gen. Ngo Quang Truong, IV Corps commander, was appointed the new I Corps commander, and was put in charge of the counter-attack to recapture Quang Tri. Truong had a remarkable military career, to say the least. Back in 1964, Truong was a captain commanding an airborne battalion. Seven years later, he was a lieutenant general and corps commander.

Maj. Gen. Nguyen Vinh Nghi, the commander of the 21st Division—which was haltingly fighting its way toward An Loc—was appointed IV Corps commander to replace General Truong. Col. Ho Trung Hau, in charge of the Airborne Division Light Headquarters at Lai Khe, was elevated to brigadier general and took over the command of the 21st Division.

The corps commanders constituted the most exclusive club in Viet Nam. Foreign anti-war correspondents called them "warlords"; the Vietnamese press called them the four "pillars" of the Thieu regime. They were selected from the most trusted officers who were members of the President's inner circle. Many of them were Thieu's cadets when he was instructor at the military academy in Dalat in the mid-1950s, because, according to Confucian tradition, the students must respect and be loyal to the teacher. General Nghi was one of these cadets.

Immediately after he assumed command of the 21st Division, General Hau tried to create a diversion by ordering division engineer units to repair the western portion of Inter-Provincial Route 13 east of Chon Thanh and moving his mechanized units as if to launch an attack on the enemy's rear in Dong Xoai area. Hau hoped that this feigned attack would force the enemy to release the pressure on the relief column, but this stratagem apparently hadn't worked as the enemy resistance on Route 13 had not lessened.[16]

On May 11, as the 32nd Regiment of the 21st Division was launching a new offensive north of Chon Thanh, the 9th Division's 15th Regiment, reinforced with the 9th Armored Squadron, arrived in the district town. On May 14, the 15th was ordered to send one company from the 2nd Battalion into An Loc to reinforce the garrison. However, due to heavy anti-aircraft fire, the helicopters were unable to land and had to return to Lai Khe. That afternoon, by order of the 21st Division, the 15th Regiment became Task Force 15 (TF-15) consisting of 1/15, 2/15, 3/15 Battalions, 15th Reconnaissance Company, 9th Armored Squadron, one 105mm battery and one 155mm platoon.

The next day, May 15, 1/15 Battalion, reinforced with the 9th Armored Squadron and Battery 95C, launched an eastern envelopment by seizing Ngoc Lau, east of Route 13, and reached Tan Khai without incident. The following day, 2/15 Battalion air assaulted into Bau Nat village, 1,500 meters east of Tan Khai, then linked up with the 1/15 at the above location. Afterward, TF-15 headquarters, plus one combined 105mm and 155mm battery, were heliborne into Tan Khai to establish FSB Long Phi.[17]

On May 17, the 15th Reconnaissance Company and the 3/15 Battalion air assaulted an area northwest and west of Tan Khai, respectively. At the same time, one battalion from 33rd Regiment/21st Division, was heliborne into FSB Long Phi to replace the 2/15 Battalion; the latter was ordered to link up with the 3/15 Battalion. The remaining units of the 33rd Regiment also were instructed to move to Tan Khai through the forested areas east of RN13 in order to participate in the much anticipated thrust toward An Loc. The 33rd Regiment column was repeatedly engaged by the enemy forces and sustained heavy casualties. In a period of only fifteen days, the regiment suffered 50 KIA and 300 WIA.[18]

The next day, TF-15, reinforced with the 9th Armored Squadron on the west and the 33rd Regiment(-)/21st Division, on the east, using Tan Khai as the line of departure, began to move northward in an effort to link up with the besieged capital city of Binh Long. On the same day, NVA started shelling FSB Long Phi. On May 19, TF-15 made contact with the enemy as it was about to enter Duc Vinh 2 hamlet. In the next few days, the enemy tried to close in on the units of TF-15, staying within fifty meters of ARVN positions, while pounding the latter with mortars and rockets (the Communists called this the "grab the belts" tactic). At the same time, NVA forces started to surround and bombard FSB Long Phi with increasing intensity. Faced with this new threat to its rear, Colonel Can, TF-15 commander, dispatched 1/15 Battalion to reinforce the defense of the strategic Long Phi base, which not only provided fire support to the attacking forces, but also served as the logistical and medical evacuation base for the defenders at An Loc.

During the night of May 20, while TF-15 was silently crossing Xa Cat creek to move toward Duc Vinh 2 hamlet, the advance elements reported hearing the roars of tank engines in front of them. The next day, the task force continued to move northward, but it was stalked by the enemy reconnaissance elements and received sporadic shelling. Small contacts with the enemy were also reported. Lt. Col. Ho Ngoc Can, task force commander, ordered his units to "progress in echelons": the first unit that reached a designated point stopped and dug in to support the second echelon elements; when the latter reached another objective forward, they again dug in to cover the advance of the first echelon units, and so on. This formation provided effective mutual support when progressing into enemy-held territories.[19]

Due to strong anti-aircraft fire, TF-15 had to be supplied by parachute drops. On May 22, when the task force reached an area about one kilometer south of Thanh Binh hamlet, it was surrounded and attacked by NVA forces. The situation became very critical as the number of wounded and dead kept mounting. The lightly wounded soldiers stayed at their positions to fight off the enemy assaults while the dead had to be buried on the spot.

As a result of mounting casualties on both sides, a tacit agreement was reached during that period; it called for a cease-fire at the end of each day to allow for the dead to be buried and the wounded to be evacuated to the rear.

On May 23, the enemy mounted another tank-supported assault. At 6:00 A.M., enemy tanks broke through the friendly lines. The lead PT-76 was destroyed but other tanks continued to advance. The defenders held their line and destroyed another tank. The enemy finally broke off, leaving behind twenty-four bodies and eighteen assorted weapons. TF-15 had twelve KIA and twenty-five WIA.[20] To support TF-15's defense, B-52 strikes hit enemy supporting elements in Thanh Binh hamlet.

During this period, medical evacuation and resupply missions couldn't be carried out by helicopters or parachute drops because friendly and enemy positions were only about 100 meters apart. Thirsty soldiers from TF-15 couldn't even get water from nearby Xa Cat creek because the enemy would shoot at them from the other side of the creek. As a result, TF-15 had to stop its progress northward, and to use the APCs from the 9th Armored Squadron to escort medical evacuation and resupply convoys from Duc Vinh to Tan Khai and vice versa. The medevac and resupply operation was carried out without incident.

On May 24, however, the 9th Armored was ambushed on the above itinerary by NVA 141st Regiment, 7th Division, which used all kinds of antitank weapons such as B-40s, B-41s, recoilless rifles, and even AT-3 Saggers. In particular, the B-41 rocket with an effective range of 400 meters was very deadly against lightly armored M-113s. The 9th Armored Squadron incurred heavy losses (8 KIA, 77 WIA, 8 MIA, 22 APCs damaged) and had to return to Long Phi Base to be reequipped and reorganized. The enemy left twenty bodies and fourteen individual weapons were captured.[21]

The next day, after having consolidated a new base about one kilometer south of Thanh Binh hamlet, TF-15 continued its northward progression. It was attacked by the enemy and had to stop and defend in place. In the meantime, the 33rd Regiment (-), moving from Dong Phat hamlet toward An Loc, was stopped by furious resistance from NVA blocking forces.

According to Lt. Col. Nguyen Ngoc Anh, Assistant for Operations/ III Corps, radio intercepts confirmed the presence of NVA 7th Division headquarters in an area seven kilometers southwest of An Loc and the 165th Regiment of the 7th Division in the middle of

Xa Cam plantation four kilometers south of An Loc. The regiment headquarters occupied a large reinforced underground bunker built under the railway; it was protected by a dense system of *chot-kieng*, which had been able to stop the progression of Regiment 33/21st Division and TF-15, causing heavy losses to these two units. General Minh had requested B-52 strikes on this formidable defense structure—the last obstacle to the liberation of An Loc—but Minh's request had been denied by the III Corps U.S. advisory team for unspecified reasons.[22]

As a consequence, General Minh turned to the VNAF for assistance. At a meeting at III Corps Headquarters in early June with Brig. Gen. Huynh Ba Tinh, commander of the Bien Hoa-based 3rd Air Division and his deputy, Col. Nguyen Van Tuong, Minh wanted to know if the 3rd Air Division had any CBU bombs or other bombs capable of destroying the enemy *chot* system at Xa Cam, and the kind of aircraft that can deliver these bombs. Minh added that the issue of infringement on the USAF's assigned zone of responsibility also needed to be addressed.

After a brief consultation with Colonel Tuong—who was both 3rd Air Division deputy commander and commander of the division's fighter squadron—General Tinh answered that it was his understanding that the U.S. warplanes usually returned to their bases or aircraft carriers after 6:00 P.M., and as a consequence, AD-6 Skyraiders from his division could drop CBU bombs on enemy positions at Xa Cam after 6:00 P.M.

At that point, General Tinh introduced Colonel Tuong, his deputy, to elaborate on the availability and delivery of CBU bombs. Tuong reported that he had five or seven small-size CBU bombs given to him by the Americans and that the best means to deliver these bombs would be by slow-flying (maximum speed 320 mph) AD-6 Skyraiders; these single-seat attack bombers could drop the bombs with more accuracy on the intended targets than the A-37 jet fighters.

General Minh concluded the meeting by ordering the destruction of the enemy *chot* at Xa Cam by CBU bombs dropped by the 3rd Air Division's Skyraiders.[23]

One piece of good news, finally, that boosted the morale of the relief forces: The 6th Airborne Battalion, which had been severely defeated in the Doi Gio-Hill 169 area southeast of An Loc on April 21, had been refurbished and reorganized, and was ready to act. On June 4, the 6th, with an effective force of 600 men, was heliborne into Long Phi FSB, bringing with it a 2,200-man replacement contingent for TF-15 and 33rd Regiment/21st Division in Tan Khai, and other units in An Loc; the latter had not received replacements since April 13, the date of the beginning of the attacks on the city. [24]

On June 6, the 6th Airborne Battalion—reinforced with the remaining 1,000 replacements for the units defending An Loc—was heavily engaged by the enemy just north of Duc Vinh 2 hamlet. Although most of the men were new recruits, the battalion fought valiantly because the original officers had remained with the unit and also because Lt. Col. Nguyen Van Dinh, the battalion commander, had vowed to return to An Loc to avenge his earlier defeat. The 6th Airborne succeeded in destroying the enemy blocking positions with relatively limited casualties: one KIA, sixty-four WIA. The enemy left thirty-one dead; two crew-served and twelve individual weapons were captured.[25]

On June 7, the 33rd Regiment (-), 21st Division, and TF-15 were able to evacuate some wounded soldiers. After the completion of the medevac operation and after having been replenished and resupplied, TF-15 on the left, the 33rd Regiment in the middle, and the 6th Airborne Battalion on the right, renewed their progression toward An Loc.

The same day, at 6:30 P.M., two VNAF A-37s strafed the enemy positions in Xa Cam in preparation for the CBU bombing run; they were followed by four Skyraiders that dropped successively four CBU bombs on the 165th Regiment's *chot* system, causing four big explosions and flattening an area one kilometer around the target.

After the VNAF airplanes had left the area, General Minh—who was circling the Xa Cam hamlet in his C&C helicopter—ordered the 6th Airborne Battalion to attack northward to destroy the remnants of this last enemy blocking position south of An Loc. The paratroopers quickly overran Xa Cam and discovered about 200 intact bodies in a 300-square-meter bunker built three meters underneath the railway; the North Vietnamese troops were obviously killed by the tremendous pressure exerted by the CBU bombs. Among the dead was an officer with a senior colonel rank insignia.[26]

On June 8, when moving toward the eastern part of Thanh Binh hamlet, the 6th Airborne engaged again with the enemy. Exploiting its apparently irresistible momentum, the paratroopers overwhelmed the enemy resistance, killing seventy-three North Vietnamese soldiers and capturing two crew-served and thirty-three individual weapons. The 6th Airborne suffered eleven KIA and thirty-one WIA.[27] In probably the most spectacular action of the rescuing operation, the 6th Airborne Battalion cleared the remaining two kilometers to Thanh Binh hamlet in a forty-five-minute battle. An Loc was finally linked up when the 62nd Company of the 6th Battalion shook hands with the 81st Company of the 8th Battalion at 5:45 P.M. on June 8, 1972.[28] That historic handshake marked the beginning of the end of the siege of An Loc.

Lt. Col. Nguyen Van Dinh, 6th Airborne Battalion commander, and Lt. Col. Tran Thien Tuyen, exective officer, 8th Airborne Battalion, both graduates of the Vietnamese Military Academy, heartily embraced amid the wild cheers of the paratroopers.

Phan Nhat Nam, an army reporter and former officer in the Airborne Division, who visited the 6th Airborne Battalion after the above described link-up at an area about 1,700 meters south of An Loc, recalled that from his vantage point, he could only see one red-roofed, multi-story building still standing in the city. Next to where he stood, fifty-six North Vietnamese bodies from C7, C8 (7th and 8th Companies), 2nd Battalion, 275th Regiment, 5th Division, piled up inside defensive fortifications. Nearby lay two dead T-54s and three charred tanks of an unidentified model with their heads buried in bomb craters and their engines blown up by hand grenades.[29]

As Nam was ready to leave the 6th Battalion to head toward the 5th Battalion located 800 meters further north, Lieutenant Colonel Dinh, the 6th Battalion commander, told him to be careful and to watch for the direction of enemy artillery fire. "If the fire comes from the southeast, don't worry; if it comes from the northwest, you must lean your back against a rubber tree or jump into a foxhole right away."[30]

When Phan Nhat Nam arrived at the 5th Airborne Battalion's location thirty minutes later, he was surprised to see no soldiers on the surface of the earth. Apparently, the paratroopers had gone underground. When he started to call Lieutenant Colonel Hieu, the battalion commander, he saw a few steel helmets emerging from the earth like "tiny graves." At the sound of the ensuing departing enemy artillery fire, the paratroopers plunged into their foxholes like "small creatures burying themselves in the beach sand at the noise of approaching passers-by."[31] Finally, after a few minutes, Colonel Hieu emerged from his bunker to greet him. The battalion commander invited Nam to his underground bunker and offered him a can of hot beer.

"It has been a while. I haven't seen the sun," said Hieu, "the enemy still targets this area, and if I get killed, the morale of the unit would suffer."[32]

TF-15 finally linked up with elements of the 1st Airborne Brigade near Thanh Binh hamlet. Colonel Nhut, province chief, went out to personally greet Lt. Col. Ho Ngoc Can, task force commander, and his advisor, Maj. Mandela Craig. Nhut presented them with a bottle of cognac, the last bottle in the entire city. It was a fitting reward for an embattled unit that had paid a heavy price for having successfully carried out its difficult mission after uninterrupted murderous combat with the enemy 7th Division: During the Route 13 reopening operation, TF-15 had 153 KIA, 592 WIA, 27 MIA; one M-60 machinegun and three M-16s were lost. The enemy had paid a heavier price trying to stop TF-15 from linking up with the garrison: They suffered 304 KIA; ARVN captured 41 crew-served and 85 individual weapons, and destroyed two PT-76 tanks.[33]

Even before the link-up, toward the end of May, the situation in An Loc had considerably improved. Uninterrupted air strikes had taken a heavy toll on the enemy forces and in particular on their anti-aircraft weapons that ringed the city. Intelligence reports indicated that the NVA had even filled up their depleted units with Cambodian Khmer Rouges soldiers, who, worst of all, often refused to fight. By early June, helicopters were able to land at An Loc for resupply and medevac. June 9, the day following the link-up, was the day when twenty-three helicopters were able to land safely and evacuate hundreds of wounded who had waited so long in the inferno of An Loc.

By mid-June, An Loc was secure enough for visits from VIPs. A few days after the link-up, General Hollingsworth and Sir Robert Thompson, Special Advisor to President Nixon—and the man in charge of the successful counterinsurgency campaign in Malaysia after WWII—came to An Loc. Colonel Nhut showed them the NVA tanks that had been destroyed inside the city. Sir Thompson told Nhut that An Loc was the biggest victory in the post-World War II era, far exceeding the battle of Dien Bien Phu.[34]

On June 16, Gen. Nguyen Van Minh and General Hollingsworth landed in An Loc. Colonel Nhut reported that on the way to 5th Division Headquarters, Hollingsworth suddenly stopped in front of Lt. Col. Art Taylor, senior advisor to the 1st Airborne Brigade, and pinned a U.S. Silver Star on his uniform. Taylor, perplexed and moved, started to cry; Nhut also felt tears swelling in his eyes.[35]

During his first visit to An Loc since the NVA offensive, General Minh pinned the colonel rank insignia on the uniform of Lieutenant Colonel Huan, the 81st Airborne Commando Group commander. On this occasion, Minh took time to explain that Huan was not the only person worthy of recognition, but that many more would be rewarded in due time. Afterward, Nhut invited General Minh to visit Dr. Quy's operating bunker to meet the famous surgeon, who had performed a total of 254 major operations under very primitive conditions. The visiting party was somewhat embarrassed to see a near-term pregnant woman lying in pain on Dr. Quy's operating table. Obviously, the enemy, defeated and demoralized, preferred to run away than to stay and fight and inflict casualties on ARVN troops, and Dr. Quy's operating room now had to deal with emergencies of a different nature.

Ten

End of the Siege

Immediately after the historic link-up between the 6th and 8th Airborne Battalions, ARVN troops launched a counter-attack to recapture the lost terrain in the city. In the north, the 81st Airborne Commando Group and the 3rd Ranger Group reoccupied the northern part of An Loc without encountering enemy resistance. On June 10, the commandos captured one soldier who was hiding under a deep underground bunker. He said he was a cook with a unit from the 5th Division. He also disclosed that there were so many soldiers killed in his unit that he was ordered to pick up a weapon and fight, but he was so scared that he kept digging a bunker to avoid Air Force bombs.[1]

The next day, the 3rd Ranger and the 81st Commando attacked northward in tandem to retake the high ground north of An Loc. On June 12, the 36th Ranger Battalion raised the national flag on the artillery dependents quarters. Subsequently, the 52nd Ranger Battalion seized the Dong Long airport and high ground next to Dong Long Hill to support the advance of the 81st Commando Group. The commandos took Dong Long Hill, the dominant terrain north of An Loc the same day, after a well-executed pincer movement.

The commando attacking units consisted of the 2nd and 3rd Commando Companies and four reconnaissance teams under Capt. Nguyen Son, Capt. Pham Chau Tai and Lt. Le Van Loi, respectively. During the night of June 11, the above units, advancing in three different columns, reached a location near the top of Dong Long Hill. At daybreak, the commandos launched a surprise attack on the enemy positions by shooting and throwing hand grenades into the enemy bunkers. The North Vietnamese panicked and fled into a nearby forest, leaving behind many dead and weapons. In the morning of June 12, Lieutenant Loi proudly raised the national flag on Dong Long Hill.[2] The same day, General Hung declared to a Viet Nam Radio reporter that the city of An Loc was completely liberated.

An officer who participated in the attack to recapture Dong Long Hill described the bloody battle of June 12 in the following terms: "My eyes were blurred by the heroic images of my friends. His right hand severed by a bullet, Thieu calmly raised his hand to slow down the bleeding and kept shooting with his weapon held against his body with his left hand, as if he were holding a torch while firing in the midst of smoke and dust. Y Muih Mlor, his hand bleeding profusely, standing calmly on the roof of the enemy bunker as if nothing happened to him; and this very morning Vosary, his lower jaw taken by an enemy bullet, pointing in the direction of the enemy bunker to his friends. A man with dark skin, his mouth full of red blood, a picture that frightened the little Viet Congs or at least made them shiver. These pictures in part reflected the bravery of the airborne commandos which can be seen only in times of crisis."[3]

During an ensuing pursuit operation, the commandos discovered a deep bunker on the edge of a neighboring forest. Hearing some noises coming from below, the commandos, instead of throwing hand grenades into the bunker as was normal procedure under the circumstances, called the suspected NVA soldiers to get out and surrender, because they believed the enemy was in no mood to put up a fight at this stage. The commandos were stunned to see two little girls emerging from the bunker. One commando later commented that they looked like two "moving skeletons." The two girls, may be six or seven years old, were indeed emaciated, dazed, and too weak to climb out of the bunker; their clothes were in tatters.

The commandos took the girls to their headquarters and gave them food and clothing. The two girls, named Ha Thi Loan, eight, and Ha Thi No, nine, finally explained that their father was RF Sergeant Ha Van Hien, who was a member of the RF unit defending Dong Long. When Dong Long was overrun on April 13, their mother took them and their younger brother and tried to flee toward the city. Their mother was killed by an artillery shell and their younger brother, seriously wounded, later died in the bunker where they were hiding. The two girls sustained themselves for two months with some vegetables and water from rain. They also ate raw chickens that were killed by artillery fire.[4]

Nguyen Cau, the army TV reporter embedded with the 5th Division, made arrangements to evacuate the two girls to Saigon where they were finally reunited with their father after the siege of An Loc. The Associated Press shortly thereafter interviewed Cau about the circumstances of the rescue of Thi Loan and Thi No. *Time Magazine* also published the story of the two girls. In 1974, an American couple adopted the girls with the permission of their father and the Vietnamese government.[5]

In the meantime, in the western sector, the 7th Regiment (-) retook the area that had fallen into enemy hands on May 11 during the NVA's third attack on the city. In the south, the paratroopers also expanded their control to effectuate a link-up with Task Force 15. Unit commanders reported that the enemy just ran away every time they were engaged by the ARVN troops.

In the mopping-up operations around An Loc, the units discovered the hulks of burned-out tanks scattered all over the battlefields, including a dozen tanks abandoned inside B-52 craters, which constituted unexpected obstacles to the movements of enemy armored vehicles. In an area three kilometers southwest of An Loc, previously targeted by B-52s, ARVN troops discovered 208 bodies with assorted weapons. In the area west of the perimeter, ARVN troops discovered an enemy headquarters which had been destroyed by C-130 gunships; inside the command post the soldiers found damaged communication equipment and many skeletons. On June 12, all areas two kilometers around the city that were occupied by NVA forces in the previous two months had been retaken, and as one senior ARVN officer in An Loc put it, "the national flag of South Viet Nam began to flutter in the winds over the sky of the newly liberated heroic Binh Long." [6]

Capt. Charles Huggins, an advisor with the 81st Airborne Commando, recalled that by that time most of the North Vietnamese had fled, leaving behind their dead, wounded, and weapons. "In the end," Huggins said, "the NVA were scared to death. They were crowded in bunkers, sometimes as many as 15 in a fighting position with only two firing points. They wouldn't fight."[7]

After the link-up of the 6th Airborne Battalion and TF-15 with the 1st Airborne Brigade at Thanh Binh hamlet, south of An Loc, Gen. Ho Trung Hau, 21st Division commander, declared his mission accomplished. Hau's optimism was somewhat premature because, despite the above link-up, the 21st Division was still bogged down north of Chon Thanh. On June 6, Lt. Col. Edward J. Stein and the 31st Regiment commander and his party were ambushed and cut off from the regiment. Stein was able to request tactical air support through a U.S. FAC. Two A-37s braved strong anti-aircraft fire to provide close support and save the entire party.[8]

Lt. Col. Burr M. Willey, senior advisor to the 32nd Regiment, and Lt. Col. Charles Butler, senior advisor to the 33rd Regiment, were not so lucky. On June 19, as the 32nd Regiment, supported by thirteen tanks, launched a new attack on NVA positions, it was hit by rocket and mortar fire. One rocket landed in the middle of the regiment command group; as Colonel Willey ran over to provide assistance, he was hit by another rocket and was killed instantly. Willey was on his third tour in Viet Nam.[9]

On June 21, Lieutenant Colonel Butler was killed while accompanying the 33rd Regiment during a fight along the highway.[10] A week later, Lt. Col. Nguyen Viet Can, the 33rd Regiment commander, was killed by artillery fire when his regiment reached Dong Phat hamlet, southeast of An Loc.[11]

It is true, in a final analysis, that the 21st Division had failed to carry out its mission of reopening Route 13, but its critics were quick to forget that the men from the 21st fought hard and incurred heavy casualties and that the NVA were forced to divert one entire division to cope with the new front, which would otherwise have been available to exert additional pressure on An Loc and, in all probability, capture the city. "At this time the enemy is more intent on preventing the 21ˢᵗ Division from reaching An Loc than they are on defeating friendly forces around the provincial capital," General Hollingsworth correctly assessed. "I believe that the enemy is incapable of applying pressure to both An Loc and Hwy. 13 simultaneously."[12]

The good news for the exhausted defenders of An Loc was that the improved situation around the city had allowed the arrival of fresh troops to replace them. On June 13, General Minh, III Corps commander, ordered the 2ⁿᵈ Battalion of the 31ˢᵗ Regiment/21ˢᵗ Division to be heliborne into An Loc to reinforce the 5ᵗʰ Division. (General Minh chose that battalion possibly because it had been commanded by then-Capt. Le Van Hung in the mid-1960s.) Also on the same day, the 48ᵗʰ Regiment from ARVN 18ᵗʰ Division, was brought into An Loc to replace other exhausted units of the garrison. One week later, the 32ⁿᵈ Regiment/21ˢᵗ Division, which had suffered heavy casualties, was replaced by the 46ᵗʰ Regiment of ARVN's 25ᵗʰ Division. But, according to Gen. Ngo Quang Truong, probably the best thing that happened to the defenders was that they were finally able to do what they could not do during the siege: take a bath and swim freely in the nearby creeks.[13]

The transportation of new troops into An Loc and the extraction of old units defending the city at one time were carried out by helicopters from the U.S. 229ᵗʰ Aviation. One American pilot later recalled that the soldiers he saw on the ground in An Loc were "in very rough shape." Another pilot observed, "Some of the South Vietnamese flown out were barefoot, some were dazed and some were too exhausted to do more than shuffle."[14]

Because the LZ for the helicopters involved in these troop movements was located south of the city within the 1ˢᵗ Airborne Brigade, it was secured by a unit of that brigade. Second Lt. Vu Van Hoi from the 5ᵗʰ Battalion—whose platoon was in charge of the security of the LZ—noticed that the new troops were somewhat nonchalant with regard to enemy indirect fire. Hoi advised Second Lt. Nguyen Van Xuan, his classmate at the Military Academy, and a platoon leader with the newly arrived 18ᵗʰ Division, about how to assemble his men under enemy artillery fire. Xuan took this opportunity to inform Hoi of the death of their common classmates: Huynh Huu Tri, 18th Division, and Truong Thanh Minh, 5th Division. Hoi bade farewell to his friend and wished him well. A few months later, he learned that Xuan had been killed in An Loc.[15]

Traditionally, cadets graduating at the top of their classes at the Military Academy chose to serve in the Airborne and Marine Divisions and other combat units. In 1971, for example, Second Lt. Nguyen Duc Phong, valedictorian of Class 22B, was killed by a recoilless rifle shell just a few months after graduation, when he charged on enemy positions at the head of his armored unit during the Cambodian invasion. Phong, an exceptionally gifted student and destined for a brilliant career, was selected to attend graduate schools in the United States in order to become an instructor at the academy. He declined the offer and chose instead to serve in a combat unit. In times of war, exceptional men, sadly, often die young.

The 1st Airborne Brigade left An Loc on June 18, but instead of being extracted from the city, it was ordered to attack and destroy enemy pockets of resistance between An Loc and Tan Khai. The paratroopers made heavy contact with the enemy in a few areas and suffered additional casualties, but succeeded in clearing that portion of Route 13. From Tan Khai, the paratroopers were transported by helicopters to their rear bases in Saigon, Bien Hoa, and Vung Tau for reorganization. Subsequently, they rejoined the Airborne Division north of Hue and participated in the counter-attack to retake the city of Quang Tri.

Before leaving An Loc, Colonel Luong, the 1st Airborne Brigade commander, asked Tran Van Nhut to help find the remains of the paratroopers who had given their lives while defending An Loc and to build a cemetery south of the city so that, in the future, people who entered An Loc would remember the 1st Airborne Brigade that had given so much for the freedom of its residents. Colonel Nhut shook Luong's hand and promised to do his best to satisfy his wishes. Alas, soon thereafter, Nhut had to leave An Loc to rejoin his new post in MRI.

On the morning of June 24, the 81st Airborne Commando Group received orders to leave An Loc. After a brief but moving farewell ceremony at the commando cemetery attended by the grateful people of An Loc, the 81st troops moved toward the pick-up point on Route 13 south of the city. The commandos noticed the remains of many dead civilians lying along the highway; they were An Loc residents killed by enemy artillery and rockets while fleeing the city. As the last helicopters were hovering over Route 13, the enemy started to fire artillery on the pick-up zone: one commando was seriously wounded, another was killed by shrapnel; he was the last commando killed in the battle of An Loc. After a short period of rest and reorganization in its rear base, the 81st Airborne Commando Group was also sent to MRI to reinforce the I Corp's counter-attack to recapture Quang Tri.[16]

The 81st Commando performed magnificently in An Loc, but it had also paid a heavy price: 68 KIA, and close to 300 WIA. These numbers were fortunately much lower than Colonel Huan's prediction. The day before the commandos assaulted into the Doi Gio Hill area southeast of An Loc on April 16, Colonel Huan had assembled his men to give them a somewhat somber assessment of the situation in An Loc. He told them he intended to take 550 men with him and predicted that about 300 of them would not return. He then asked for volunteers; all 1000 men or so raised their hands.[17]

On July 7, the 3rd Ranger Group left An Loc and was replaced by the 5th Ranger Group under Lt. Col. Ngo Minh Hang. On the same day, Lieutenant Colonel Corley, senior sector advisor, informed Colonel Nhut that he would receive a VIP's visit. Nhut went to the helipad to meet the visitor. Suddenly a column of helicopters landed while Cobra gunships circled the city to protect it from enemy artillery fire. Nhut was stunned when he saw President Thieu wearing his customary khaki safari suit and black baseball cap step out of one of the helicopters. Following President Thieu were Gen. Cao Van Vien, Chairman of the JGS, a French General named Vanuxem, General Hollingsworth, and a throng of Vietnamese and foreign reporters. (President Thieu originally had invited Prime Minister Khiem to come along, but decided at the last minute to let the latter stay in Saigon, in case "something happened" to him in An Loc.)[18]

Gen. Paul Vanuxem, a retired French general, was a good friend and advisor to President Thieu. When the then-Colonel Vanuxem had opened the *Cours d'Etat Major* (General Staff Course) in Hanoi in the early 1950s, President Thieu, then a captain, was one of his students. During the Indochina War, Vanuxem was one of those promising colonels Gen. De Lattre de Tassigny, commander-in-chief of French Forces in Indochina, selected to command a *Groupement Mobile* in North Viet Nam. The French press at that time dubbed these Groupement Mobile commanders "De Lattre's marshals," in allusion to Napoleon's field marshals during France's First Empire.

General Vanuxem was also a good friend of Viet Nam. He came to the country every year to see President Thieu and to watch the progress of the war. All his children were born in Viet Nam, which they considered their second country. Once, General Vanuxem sent his son to Viet Nam during a summer break to practice parachute jumping and to train with the Vietnamese Airborne Division. His daughter also volunteered at Cong Hoa General Hospital. It was reported that President Thieu, at one point, had even approached the French government to appoint General Vanuxem French ambassador to Viet Nam. During the An Loc visit, Vanuxem was presented with a Vietnamese flag that had withstood the enemy attacks and artillery bombardments.[19]

Colonel Nhut invited President Thieu and his party to visit 5th Division Headquarters. President Thieu was very moved when he saw General Hung, emaciated and haggard, emerging from his underground bunker to meet him. The President turned to one of his aides and jokingly asked: "Hung does not seem to see me. And why does he keep blinking his eyes?" The aide answered ceremoniously: "Mr. President, General Hung has not seen sunlight for a long time!"[20]

At the 5th Division headquarters, President Thieu awarded General Hung, Colonel Truong, 8th Regiment commander, and Colonel Nhut the National Order, Third Degree, which was normally awarded to high-ranking generals (the second degree and first degree were typically reserved for foreign dignitaries and chiefs of state). President Thieu also elevated Lt. Col. Nguyen Thong

Thanh, deputy sector commander, to the rank of colonel. On this occasion, President Thieu decreed that all defenders in An Loc would be promoted to the next higher rank.

Afterward, General Hung invited President Thieu to visit the northern sector, which had received the brunt of the NVA attacks. President Thieu stopped at the charred carcasses of five T-54s lying around the command post of the 8th Regiment and had his picture taken with the soldiers of the regiment. When informed about Colonel Vy, 5th Division deputy commander, being slated to attend a staff course in a service school in the U.S, President Thieu nominated Colonel Truong as the new 5th Division deputy commander. While President Thieu was visiting the 8th Regiment, the NVA fired artillery into the city. The President turned toward French General Vanuxem and said: "Maybe they know I'm visiting, and they want to salute me."[21]

When the official party passed by "Hoang Hon" (Dawn) Boulevard, President Thieu stopped and knelt in prayer before the statue of Jesus Christ that had remained intact after two months of constant artillery barrage and encirclement. Afterward, the President visited the 81st Airborne Commando Group cemetery and knelt in front of its memorial monument to commemorate the fallen commandos as well as the residents who had lost their lives during the siege. The President then asked Gen. Cao Van Vien, Chief of JGS, to create a special medal for the Binh Long campaign.

Concerned about the safety of President Thieu and his party, General Hung suggested to the President to visit the Binh Long Sector and its territorial units, because the fortified sector's underground headquarters could provide protection against sporadic enemy artillery fire. While waiting for the helicopters for the trip back to Saigon at the Binh Long Sector headquarters, President Thieu grabbed a grease pencil and wrote on the sector's operation map the four words "BINH LONG ANH DUNG" (GALLANT BINH LONG). The President then called Madame Thieu in Saigon to inform her that he was visiting An Loc and that she should not wait for him for dinner.

At that time, General Hung presented to the President the helmet he wore during the siege of An Loc as a token of his appreciation for the presidential visit. Visibly moved, President Thieu tapped Hung on the shoulder and shook his hand, then boarded his departing helicopter. The President must have treasured General Hung's gift because he kept it on his desk at the Independence Palace.[22]

Although the siege had been officially lifted with the visit of President Thieu, An Loc still remained a dangerous place because the enemy still occasionally executed direct and indirect fire into the city from hidden locations. And tragically, the latest and highest ranking soldier killed in An Loc was a U.S. general. On July 9, Brig. Gen. Richard J. Tallman, Hollingsworth's new deputy, landed in An Loc with several of his key staff officers to observe the progress of ARVN operations and assess their needs. When the general and his party left the helipad, they were hit by 75mm recoilless rifle fire. The helicopter took off and escaped possible destruction, but General Tallman was injured and some officers in his party died instantly.[23]

Doctor Nguyen Phuc, the senior doctor at Binh Long sector hospital, recalled that the wounded American officers were rushed to his underground operating room, but General Tallman's head injuries were very serious and all he could do was to temporarily bandage the wounds and administer saline solution infusion before the general was evacuated to the 3rd Field Hospital in Saigon, where he died on the operating table.[24]

In early July, due to the improvement of the situation in An Loc, the units started to give permission to their men to visit their families and loved ones. Dr. Quy recalled his first impression of the outside world after three months in the inferno of An Loc. "It was really different from the scenes of bunkers, tanks, bombs in the battle," wrote Quy. "In a very short period of time, I had left hell to return to the normal environment of a human being. I had discovered a very strange thing, and that was the air was so fragrant and so sweet. It was the first time in my life that I had felt the sweetness of the air."[25]

On July 11, the first units of the 18th ARVN Division under Col. Le Minh Dao were heliborne into An Loc. The following day, the entire division was in place and was ready to take over from the 5th Division.

In mid-July, the entire 21st Division returned to the Mekong Delta and was wildly cheered by the local populace for its contribution to the final victory of An Loc. Notably absent from these celebrations was Brig. Gen. Ho Trung Hau, the division commander: Hau had been sacked earlier by President Thieu for failure of leadership as a division commander in combat. His arrogance and rudeness had antagonized the officers of the 21st Division and his lack of tactical initiative had caused unnecessary loss of life during the attacks to remove the *chot* south of Tau O. [26]

The following statistics on the Battle of Binh Long, including the link-up operations, were published by ARVN/JGS on August 15, 1973.[27] (It should be noted that these statistics were only preliminary at the time of their publication and may not reflect the true losses on both sides.)

1. Losses in Personnel

	ARVN	Enemy
KIA	2,280	6,464
WIA	8,564	
MIA	2,091	
Captured		56

2. Total Hospitalized and Dead while in Hospital
(from 4/9 to 7/31/72)

Units	Hospitalized	Died in Hospital
5th Division	1,324	363
Airborne Division	1,203	222
15th Regiment/9th Division	592	15
3rd Ranger Group	154	58
81st Airborne Comm. Group	278	60
Binh Long Sector	376	119
21st Division	2,398	577
25th Division	545	102

3. Losses in Weapons

	ARVN	Enemy
Crew-served	118	596
Individual	1,846	1,623
Tanks and APCs	38*	72
Howitzers	32	

*1st Armored Squadron lost 60% and 9th Armored Squadron lost 30% of their armored vehicles.

4. Losses in Aircraft

VNAF		USAF	
C-123 Transports	2	C-130 Transports	2
Skyraider Fighters	3	A-37 Fighters	1
Light Observation	1	Chinook Helicopters	1
Helicopters	14	AC-119 gunships	1
		Cobra Armed Helicopters	3
		02 Observation	1
		UH-1 Helicopters	1

5. Fire Support (from 4/7 to 8/3/72).
    Fighters*

VNAF:	3,337 Sorties
USAF:	8,778 Sorties

Armed Helicopters:	6,473 Sorties
B-52:	268 Missions**

Artillery Support:***

105mm:	678,000 Rounds
155mm:	148,329 Rounds

* In addition to VNAF's 3rd Air Division based in Bien Hoa, the following units participated in providing air support to the Battle of Binh Long:

- 1 Helicopter Squadron from VNAF's 4th Air Division based in Can Tho.

- 2 U.S. Fighter Squadrons
- Fighters from two U.S aircraft carriers based in Vung Tau and Phu Quoc.
  ** One Mission consisted of 2 to 4 sorties. The total of B-52 sorties amounted to 865 broken down as follows: April: 361. May: 350 and June: 154.
  *** Artillery support was provided primarily to the relieving column moving on Highway 13.

6. Supply by Parachutes to An Loc (from 4/11 to 7/12/72).

C-130	305 Sorties
C-123	123 Sorties
Airdrops	3,336 Parachutes*

* Including 3,868 tons of food, ammunition, and medicines, and 118,600 liters of POL. Of all parachutes dropped into An Loc, only 1,182 (or one third) were recovered. These included 1,138 tons and 35,500 liters of POL. The balance was lost to the enemy or damaged.

7. Average Daily Supply Rate to the Battle of Binh Long.

Food	35 Tons
Gasoline	23,700 Liters
105mm Ammo	7,530 Shells
155mm Ammo	1,550 Shells
Other	91 tons
Personnel Transported	55 Persons

8. Average Daily Transportation Available.

Tank Trucks	4
Transport Trucks	35
Corder Trucks	20
Air Transportation:	
VNAF	9 CH-47s + 1 C-123
USAF	5 C-130s

9. Population Evacuated.

From An Loc to Binh Duong 36,179 Persons
From An Loc to Chon Thanh   7,723 Persons

Eleven

The ARVN 18th Division in An Loc

Colonel (later General) Le Minh Dao had a rather unremarkable career. In the early 1960s, he served as an *aide-de-camp* for a French-trained general who was one of the masterminds of the *coup d'etat* against President Diem. Dao subsequently attracted the attention of the "Delta Clan," which awarded him the position of province chief of Chuong Thien and Dinh Tuong provinces. Gen. Nguyen Van Minh, III Corps Commander, appointed Dao to the important position of 18th Division commander despite the fact that Dao had no combat experience.

Dao surprisingly rose to the occasion. He succeeded in transforming a young and ineffective division into a good fighting force. Dao also had a high sense of theatrics and public relations. It was reported that one day, as he was visiting his wounded soldiers at the Cong Hoa General Hospital, one soldier complained about the poor quality of his wheelchair, compared to the German-made wheelchair of a fellow soldier in his room. As the latter was willing to trade his for 30,000 *dong* (or about forty U.S. dollars), Dao pulled out his wallet and gave the money to the other soldier in front of about thirty patients in the room. The soldier straightened himself up in an erect posture in his wheelchair, saluted his division commander and, overwhelmed by emotion, started to cry.[1]

Every time he awarded decorations to soldiers who had distinguished themselves in battle, Dao never failed to give them a small envelope containing some cash and a lighter on which were engraved the words "Present from the 18th Division Commander." By all accounts, Dao's genuine concern for the welfare of his men had earned him their loyalty and respect.

The 18th Division was one of the youngest ARVN divisions. Created in 1963—first as the ARVN 10th Division—it consisted of three independent regiments: 43rd, 48th, and 52nd. The 10th Division became the 18th Division in 1967 because the number "10" was considered an unlucky number (as opposed to the number "9" or any multiple of that number).

From 1965 to 1969, the 18th Division was responsible for the 33rd Tactical Area consisting of the provinces of Bien Hoa, Long Khanh, Phuoc Tuy, Binh Tuy, and the Special Vung Tau Sector. In 1970, the 18th Division became a mobile force operating throughout MRIII. In the early months of that year, the 18th had participated in the III Corps-directed invasion of Cambodia; during that incursion, it had destroyed many COSVN secret bases after heavy engagements with the NVA forces in Chup, Pean Chaeng, Suong, Damber, Kandaol Chrum, and Phum Khuar.

Colonel Dao assumed the command of the 18th Division toward the end of March 1972, just two weeks before the NVA launched their Easter Offensive. In April 1972, while the garrison of An Loc was fighting for its life, Dao was busy fighting VC independent regiments and provincial units in Binh Duong and Phuoc Tuy provinces with the 43rd and the 48th Regiments. (The 52nd Regiment, which had been attached to the 5th Division and had suffered heavy losses during the battle of Loc Ninh, was being refurbished and reorganized in An Loc.)

The Communists' plan in MRIII at that time was to create a diversion in the north by attacking the border outposts in Tay Ninh province and to pin down the 18th Division in the south to prevent it from reinforcing An Loc by attacking ARVN bases in Binh Duong, Hau Nghia, and Phuoc Tuy provinces. In April 24, the 43rd Regiment of the 18th Division battled the VC independent 101st Regiment in Cha Ray and Trung Lap in Binh Duong province, killing a total of 321 enemies in five days of intense fighting.[2] During the same time, the Communists opened a new front in Phuoc Tuy province by attacking the district of Dat Do and occupying many hamlets of the district of Long Dien. Colonel Dao used the 48th Regiment and Phuoc Tuy territorial forces to engage the VC independent 274th Regiment and the provincial 445th Battalion. The enemy withdrew with heavy losses after a few days of combat.

Toward the end of June, as the situation in An Loc had considerably improved, III Corps ordered the remainder of the 18th Division to the city to replace the exhausted 5th Division. (By that time, the 48th and 52nd Regiments were already in An Loc.) It took Dao two weeks to assemble the remnant units of his division and to transport them by helicopters into An Loc. When the first elements of the division arrived on July 11, the entire city had been retaken by friendly forces, but the enemy still held the strategic Doi Gio-Hill 169 southeast of An Loc, the Quan Loi airport, and some important pockets of resistance outside the city, in particular in the southern area around Xa Cam hamlet. Furthermore, the NVA still occupied blocking positions in the vicinity of Tan Khai on Route 13, causing the 18th Division to rely mainly on VNAF for troop movements and resupply. (By the time the 18th Division moved to An Loc, the Vietnamization program was almost complete, but, according to General Dao, the small U.S. advisory team under Col. John Evans was still able to provide tactical air support and resupply missions.)[3]

More important, the strategic district of Loc Ninh was still in enemy hands, as III Corps had no reserves to push north to retake the city. It is noteworthy that the same situation happened in MRI after the successful recapture of Quang Tri in September 1972. At that time, due to the fact the Airborne and the Marine Divisions were overextended and had suffered heavy losses, and JGS had run out of strategic reserves, the South Vietnamese army was unable to cross the Thach Han River to recapture the city of Dong Ha and the territory extending from the Thach Han to the Ben Hai River. The last river comprised the southern limit of the old DMZ as specified by the 1954 Geneva Accords.

In the first few days after the 18th Division's arrival, Colonel Dao ordered the 43rd Regiment to attack enemy positions south of An Loc in an effort to widen the division's control area and eventually to link up with the town of Tan Khai. During that sweeping operation, the 2nd Battalion, 43rd Regiment, was ambushed and encircled by elements of the NVA 7th Division while operating five kilometers southwest of Xa Cam hamlet. The battalion held its lines and repulsed many enemy assaults, but Maj. Nguyen Van Thoai, the battalion commander, was killed during one of these assaults. Capt. Nguyen Huu Che, battalion executive, was finally able to extricate the battalion from the ambush site, thanks to the effective artillery protective fire and round-the-clock U.S. tactical air support, which created—in the words of Captain The—a "firewall" around his battalion position. The 2nd Battalion subsequently destroyed some of the NVA *chot* in its area of operation. In one of these encounters, the battalion captured about thirty weapons of all kinds abandoned on the terrain. Among the weapons captured was a piece of paper on which were hastily written the following words: "This is a present to you, we are going back North."[4]

The biggest problem facing the 18th Division, however, was that the enemy still controlled the high ground to the southeast—from which NVA observation posts still directed artillery fire into the city—and the strategic Quan Loi airport east of the city. Therefore, as soon as he had settled down at An Loc, brought in the division artillery, and consolidated the defense of the city, Colonel Dao ordered the recapture of the above two objectives in order to eliminate—or at least reduce—indirect enemy fire into the city and to increase the 18th Division's tactical control area. According to Colonel Dao's original plan, the 52nd Regiment and the 5th Ranger Group would be responsible for the defense of An Loc while the 48th Regiment and the 43rd Regiment would be assigned the mission of retaking the Doi Gio-Hill 169 area and the Quan Loi airport respectively.

On July 17, the 3rd Battalion, 48th Regiment, was ordered to capture Hill 169. On the way to the objective, the 3rd Battalion saw many foxholes and bunkers that had been recently abandoned by the enemy. As the forward elements arrived at the edge of the rubber plantation facing Hill 169, the battalion came under heavy artillery fire from the northwest and 82mm mortar fire from the east. The soldiers had to take cover behind rubber trees to avoid being hit by shrapnel. Capt. Nguyen Phuc Song Huong, the battalion commander, requested counter-battery fire, but his request was denied because An Loc was running low on artillery ammunition. Huong readied his battalion for a probable enemy assault after they had lifted their artillery fire in accordance with their customary *tien phao hau xung* tactic, but the expected assault didn't materialize; Huong inferred from the enemy's inaction that they didn't have any sizable unit left in the area.

Captain Huong then went to the frontline to study the terrain. Hill 169 consisted of a central hilltop and two lower crests on its northwestern and southern sides. At the foot of Hill 169, the wreckage of a Skyraider and three helicopters testified to the viciousness of the battle for the control of this strategic high ground between the 1st Airborne Brigade and NVA forces three months earlier. To attack Hill 169, his men would have to cross open terrain covered with tall elephant grass and would thus present an easy target for the enemy's 75mm recoilless rifles and machineguns. Huong was also concerned about a repeat of an earlier battle in Long Khanh province where his wounded soldiers were burned to death by elephant-grass fires caused by extensive summer heat and recoilless rifle fire. Consequently, he requested napalm bombs to burn the elephant grass, but was told by the regiment that they were not available and that he would be allocated, instead, two A-37 sorties to support the attack.

While the A-37 fighters were circling the target, Captain Huong ordered two platoons, one from the 1st Company and the other from the 3rd Company, to speed across the clearing and establish a foothold at the foot of Hill 169. The A-37s dropped their bombs on the top of the hill, but the NVA, dug in on the northern and southern slopes, fired their B-40 and B-41 weapons on the two platoons from the 3rd Battalion. Captain Huong grew increasingly concerned about the fate of his platoons as the latter didn't return fire, while the enemy rockets caused the elephant grass to burn and to engulf his men in a thick cloud of smoke. The platoon leaders finally reported two dead and five wounded but they had seized the stone bridge at the foot of Hill 169; they also requested reinforcements to expand their foothold.[5]

Captain Huong ordered his Headquarters Company to stay in place and be ready to support the battalion's attack with its two organic 81mm mortars. He then dashed across the burnt-out clearing with the rest of the battalion to assault Hill 169. The battalion, however, was pinned down in the open by heavy enemy recoilless rifle fire. Fortunately, Huong and his men were able to seek cover along small creeks originating from Hill 169. The radioman carrying the PCR-25 was killed at Huong's side by rocket shrapnel. As the casualties kept mounting, Huong ordered his battalion to retreat toward the rubber plantation.

Taking advantage of a big rainstorm that night, Captain Huong ordered a second attack. The 1st Company under Lieutenant Ly would seize the northwestern crest, the 3rd Company under Lieutenant Co would seize the southern crest, while the battalion headquarters and the two remaining companies would take care of the central hilltop. The battalion moved out in silence in the thick of the night and succeeded in reaching the hilltops undetected. The men from the 3rd Battalion simultaneously opened their fire and quickly overwhelmed the enemy who were sleeping in their bunkers and didn't expect a night assault during a big storm.

"They are on the top of the hill!" yelled the North Vietnamese soldiers who ran downhill in great panic.[6]

Master Sergeant Be and his intelligence squad jumped into the enemy command bunker and seized the Communist Chinese central switchboard, killing the North Vietnamese soldiers who were calling for help. During the night, the enemy command post switchboard was taken to An Loc for intelligence gathering purposes; the wounded soldiers were also evacuated to the city for treatment.

The 1st Company, however, reported that it was unable to progress to the top of the northern crest due to enemy recoilless rifles fire and that it was being attacked by enemy tanks moving uphill on the northern slope. Captain Huong requested air support. About half an hour later, a C-130 gunship arrived at the scene and started to strafe the enemy tanks. At the same time, the men from the 1st Company also fired their M-72s weapons at the approaching tanks and succeeded in stopping their attack. The NVA responded by firing their 120mm artillery on Hill 169 without interruption because they knew they had lost it to the 18th ARVN Division.

The following day, the 1st Company launched another attack to capture the northern crest but was met with furious resistance. Captain Huong was shot in the leg by sniper fire while following the progress of the 1st Company. Huong was evacuated to Saigon and the attack on the last enemy positions on Hill 169 lost momentum.[7]

On July 27, Lt. Col. Tran Ba Thanh, the 48th Regiment commander, decided it was time to take the remaining crest of Hill 169. He committed his reserves to attack this last North Vietnamese pocket of resistance. By 3:00 P.M., the enemy *chot* on the hill was eliminated; the only survivor raised his hands to surrender.[8]

The 48th Regiment's next objective was Doi Gio (Windy Hill). With an altitude of 150 meters, Doi Gio was located in a very difficult and dangerous terrain. Its name reportedly came from the nightly howling of the winds that reverberated through the neighboring thick rubber plantations. The relatively steep eastern and western slopes of Doi Gio made any attack from these directions a risky endeavor. The northern and northeastern slopes were more gradual but the enemy had good fields of fire in these directions. Furthermore, the 6th Airborne Battalion and the airborne 105mm artillery battery—which had previously occupied Doi Gio—had prepared strong defensive positions on the hill; and these reinforced structures had been further improved by the NVA forces defending Doi Gio.

Lt. Col. Tran Ba Thanh decided to launch a multi-directional assault on August 9, using the 48th Reconnaissance Company and the 1st Battalion. The battle raged all day long. From the top of the hill, the enemy threw grenades and explosives and fired machineguns and 75mm recoilless weapons toward the attacking columns of the 48th moving uphill. Around 5:00 P.M., the 48th Reconnaissance Company reached the top of Doi Gio from the western slope. Using their M-72 weapons and grenades, the men from the reconnaissance company destroyed the enemy bunkers one by one. Then, the men from 1/48 Battalion launched their final assaults and overran the remaining NVA pockets of resistance on the hill.

The enemy left thirty-one dead and eleven crew-served weapons. The 1/48 recovered the six 105mm howitzers from the airborne artillery battery that had been overrun on April 21.[9]

While the Airborne and Marine Divisions, the 81st Commando Group, and other ranger units in the Northern Front were advancing toward Quang Tri in their seemingly unstoppable counter-attack to recapture the fallen city, the 18th Division launched its attack to retake the Quan Loi airport east of An Loc. Colonel Dao assigned this difficult mission to the 43rd Regiment and the 5th Ranger Group. On August 8, these two units had cleared Route 303 linking An Loc to Quan Loi, but were stopped by well-bunkered NVA forces outside the airport gate.

Quan Loi airport was built by the 1st U.S. Cavalry Division to support operations near the Cambodian border. U.S. engineer units had leveled a small hill to build the runway and multiple fortified concrete structures and bunkers to protect the base; the latter were also surrounded by a fifty-meter-deep network of barbed wire. Except for the airport gate—which opened up on Route 303—the base was surrounded by relatively steep slopes, which constituted additional barriers for the defense of the airport. And now, the NVA defenders were using these structures to fight off ARVN troops assaults. Previous intelligence reports even indicated that these installations had been occupied by the headquarters of the NVA 9th Division and COSVN during the earlier attacks on An Loc.

On August 9, the 5th Ranger Group launched the attack on the airport with the 30th and 38th Battalions. The Rangers met furious resistance from enemy units manning the concrete structures surrounding the runway. The following day, the enemy counterattacked, causing heavy losses to both battalions. The Rangers were able, however, to beat back the attack with effective close tactical air support.

In the next two weeks, the 43rd Regiment and the 5th Ranger Group took turns attacking Quan Loi, but were able to occupy only one-third of the airport. One officer from the 30th Rangers later reported that when the battalion began the attack, his company had more than 100 soldiers, but after it was withdrawn from the battle there remained only about forty fighting men.[10]

Finally, Lt. Col. Le Xuan Hieu, 43rd Regiment commander, ordered the 2nd Battalion, reinforced with the 43rd Reconnaissance Company, to bypass enemy blocking positions on the southern perimeter of defense and to attack Quan Loi airport from the northwest. The men from the 2nd Battalion had to use their M-72s and hand grenades to destroy multiple pockets of enemy resistance. In particular, one company-size *chot* was overrun after a short engagement. The documents captured indicated the enemy company involved was down to only twenty-five men.

Maj. Nguyen Huu Che, the newly promoted 2nd Battalion commander, recalled that around noon, when his battalion seized the small hill on the western edge of the airport in preparation for the assault on the runway, it met strong resistance from the North Vietnamese defenders. With effective artillery and tactical air support, the battalion succeeded in eliminating the last pockets of enemy resistance. Many prisoners were captured; most of them were very young and the majority asked to be accorded the *Chieu Hoi* status under the government "Open Arms" policy. It was obvious that, despite intense political indoctrination and propaganda, the North Vietnamese soldiers did indeed listen to Radio Saigon and believed in the truthfulness of the South Viet Nam government's "Open Arms" program.

In one of the *chot* positions that had been overrun, the 2nd Battalion discovered one wounded North Vietnamese soldier whose leg was tied to other soldiers with Chinese-made telephone wire. One battalion medic, without hesitation, jumped into the foxhole to try to save the wounded enemy soldier. One grenade exploded; the medic was killed instantly.[11]

At 5:00 P.M., the 2nd Battalion was in complete control of the small hill facing the airport runway. However, from the hill the battalion had to move through a small valley covered with dense vegetation, then cross a flat plateau on the other side of the valley before reaching the runway. That small valley constituted the "meat grinder" for the 2nd Battalion as it was covered by a dense net of *chot* that offered fierce resistance in spite of heavy artillery and air support. Because an unusually high number of soldiers were killed in that valley, the men from the 2/43 Battalion dubbed it "The Death Valley."

Major Che decided to conduct night attacks to remove enemy *chot*. He selected the most experienced soldiers in the battalion and formed three-man teams that he equipped with a good supply of hand grenades and a cane similar to those used by blind people. At nightfall, these teams started to operate. They used their canes to find their way forward and each time their canes detected a hole or depression, they threw a grenade into it. In one single night, all *chot* had been eliminated while the battalion suffered no casualties.

Finally, the 2nd Battalion succeeded in seizing the western end of the runway, which ran about one kilometer in a northeasterly direction. To the south of the runway were a few scattered civilian houses. Immediately north of the runway were heavily built defensive structures previously occupied by elements of a U.S. Cavalry brigade. Farther north were gently rolling hills leading toward a narrow valley and past that a chain of high mountains covered with dense forests. The terrain was favorable to NVA's defense and re-supply and would also provide protection and cover for their withdrawal.

As the 2nd Battalion was pinned down at the western end of the runway, Colonel Dao, the 18th Division commander, and Lieutenant Colonel Hieu, the 43rd Regiment commander, went to the front to assess the situation. The next day, Major Che attacked enemy positions north of the runway, using two companies from his battalion and the 43rd Reconnaissance Company under Capt. Nguyen Tan Chi, after an intense artillery barrage. The enemy put up a strong resistance, firing their 12.7mm machineguns and mortars at the 2nd Battalion men charging in the open across the runway and causing many casualties to the attackers. Major Che stopped the attack and requested help from the 43rd Regiment. That night, Colonel Hieu, the 43rd Regiment commander, sent Che a few cans of beer. Che told his orderly to crawl to the frontline to give some to Captain Chi.

The next day, the 18th Division dispatched to the 2nd Battalion the TOW platoon that was detached by ARVN/JGS to the 18th Division to conduct tests on the use of TOW against enemy fortifications.[12] TOW (Tube-launched, Optical-tracked, Wire-guided) missiles are crew portable or installed on vehicles. The TOW antitank missile was introduced for service in the U.S. Army in 1970; it had an effective range of three kilometers. Colonel Dao allocated seven TOWs to the 2nd Battalion to be used against reinforced concrete bunkers that had previously withstood artillery fire. In Major Che's estimate, each TOW cost about three million Viet Nam *piasters* (or 2,500 U.S. dollars) at the time. Although the target was not enemy tanks, in Che's opinion the use of TOWs in this case was appropriate because it could save a lot of his men's lives.

The platoon under Second Lieutenant Phuong fired two TOW missiles in conjunction with a four-barreled XM-202 antitank weapon at the enemy-occupied bunkers located on the north side of the runway. Unable to stand the intense heat generated by the antitank missiles, the frightened enemy defenders ran in all directions like—in Major Che's words—"bees whose hive has been broken."[13] The survivors escaped into the adjacent valley, leaving behind their wounded and dead comrades. Che ordered a frontal assault on the enemy positions. The enemy offered no resistance. Many wounded and dead North Vietnamese soldiers lay inside and around the bunkers. The 2nd Battalion captured many weapons, including one 12.7mm machinegun and two 61mm mortars. Quan Loi airport, the last strategic objective and the important link to the outside world, was finally under the control of ARVN troops. A few days later, deserving soldiers from the 2nd Battalion were awarded the Vietnamese Gallantry Cross for this important victory. Major Che, the battalion commander, was awarded the Vietnamese National Order and the Gallantry Cross with palm, the highest decoration for valor in combat. He was also awarded the U.S. Bronze Star with "V" Device by General Hollingsworth, the III Corps senior advisor, for this outstanding achievement.[14]

Brig. Gen. Ly Tong Ba, former 23rd Division commander, recalled his interesting experience regarding the use of TOWs to remove NVA *chot* during the 1972 Easter Offensive in Kontum in the Central Highlands. Ba, an armor officer, skillfully used his armor units to beat back repeated assaults from two NVA divisions. However, he was unable to destroy a battalion- size *chot* well protected by the fortified chapel of Kontum; he was particularly concerned that the enemy would reinforce and expand the above enclave in order to launch new attacks. Ba had already used a combined tank-infantry task force to try to destroy the enemy *chot*, but the narrow streets leading to the chapel left little room for his tanks to maneuver. As a result, he had lost one infantry company and one M-41 tank in that failed mission.

Ba called Colonel Rhotenberry, senior division advisor, and asked for TOW missiles because he was convinced that only this weapon could destroy the intended target. Rhotenberry refused, arguing that it would be against the rules because TOW must be used against tanks and not fortifications. Ba was not ready to give up. He called Mr. John Paul Vann, the senior II Corps advisor, and reiterated his request. He explained to Vann that he needed to "solve" the battlefield that very night because the situation may become dangerous if the enemy *chot* were not removed. Vann again refused because it would be against the rules.

"In case Kontum is lost tonight," replied Ba, "then Mr. Vann, would you sit there and wait to meet Hoang Minh Thao[15]to drink coffee with your TOW missiles."[16]

Vann finally relented and agreed to release the TOW missiles. Ba directed his infantry units and the 1/8 Tank Company to be ready to assault the chapel, a fortified structure of Kontum Cathedral, then he moved a jeep mounted with the TOW system to a discrete location near the objective.

"The TOW missile left the launching pad like a magic arrow, a white and bright trace lunged forward in the direction of the chapel," Ba later recalled, "A thunderous noise! The chapel exploded, smoke, dust, tiles, structures shot skyward. The entire fortified chapel complex suddenly disappeared. No weapon fire was heard from the enemy position. The 75mm recoilless rifles, B-40s, B-41s and the entire battalion were put out of combat in the nick of time. Our tanks and infantry launched the assault and overran the objective. The last NVA *chot* in Kontum was removed before the city was shrouded under darkness and the Central Highlands rain."[17]

The Kontum experience, no doubt, had made the use of TOW in the destruction of enemy fortifications more acceptable and this was probably the reason ARVN/JGS created a TOW platoon to conduct tests on the use of TOWs on reinforced bunkers and fortifications. And Colonel Dao, the 18th Division commander, was fortunate to have at his disposition the TOW missiles to deal with the American-built structures at Quan Loi airport.

A few days after the 43rd Regiment's success in Quan Loi, the 52nd Regiment, in turn, scored another victory: two battalions of the regiment operating in the vicinity of Phu Kien hamlet west of An Loc engaged an enemy battalion. After one day of fierce fighting, the NVA soldiers withdrew, leaving behind sixty-seven dead.[18] However, the NVA were not ready to give up after these successive setbacks. In a last-ditch effort to isolate the newly lost Quan Loi airport, the enemy used a sizable force to establish blocking positions between the airport and the city of An Loc. On September 8, the 2nd and 3rd Battalions, 43rd Regiment, received orders to eliminate the enemy *chot*. The enemy blocking forces were rapidly overrun, leaving sixty-five dead on the terrain.[19] Obviously, after five months of tough fighting and constant bombardment, the few remaining NVA forces were exhausted and had no stomach for another deadly—and futile—resistance.

In late September, the 48th Regiment, which had replaced the 43rd at Quan Loi, launched a sweeping operation to eliminate the last pockets of enemy resistance in the area. On September 23, the 3rd Battalion engaged a battalion-size enemy force and forced the last remaining NVA unit to withdraw from the outer perimeter of An Loc.

Meanwhile, some good news from MRI that lifted the morale of the whole country! On September 15, ARVN troops, after bloody combat, had retaken the Citadel of Quang Tri, the last NVA bastion south of the Thach Han River. The previous night, under cover of artillery fire, the 3rd Marine Battalion from the 147th Brigade blew a hole in the Citadel wall from which the attacking forces rapidly gained a foothold on the southeastern corner of the fortress. During the night, the Marines fought block by block and used hand grenades to annihilate the last pockets of resistance. Finally, the following morning, after forty-eight days of uninterrupted fighting, the Vietnamese Marines—like their U.S. counterparts in World War II in Iwo Jima—raised the national flag on the main headquarters of the Citadel and its surrounding walls.

Without question, the recapture of Quang Tri was a personal victory for Gen. Ngo Quang Truong, the I Corps commander and the rising star in the Vietnamese Army. With that victory, Truong reached the zenith of his military career. Sir Robert Thompson, who directed the successful counter-insurgency campaign against the Communist guerillas in Malaysia after World War II and was now an advisor for President Nixon, openly called General Truong one of the world's finest generals. He stated that he would not hesitate to put British troops under General Truong's command. An article in *Time* magazine even speculated that Truong was a likely candidate to replace President Thieu. Of course, President Thieu was not amused. A suspicious man, Thieu began to keep Truong under his watchful eyes.

While all this transpired, the negotiations in Paris appeared to be heading toward some kind of peace accord. In November 1972, President Thieu, expecting a post-Paris agreement "land-grabbing" period, in which both sides would try to occupy as much land as possible before an international control organization was put in place, ordered the corps commanders to take necessary actions to counter the enemy effort to grab more land. Consequently, General Minh, III Corps commander, decided to pull the 18th Division out of An Loc and to use it as the Corps reserve. On November 29, the 18th Division was replaced by three Ranger groups (3rd, 5th and 6th) under the command of Col. Nguyen Thanh Chuan, commander of Ranger forces in III Corps.

Twelve

Assessing the Battle of An Loc

Historians and even generals seem to have a tough time categorizing a siege as "successful" or "unsuccessful" from the defenders' perspective. The authors of *Valley of Decision*, for example, mentioned that during a meeting of the National Security Council on March 27, 1968, Gen. Earl Wheeler, Chairman of the JCS, seemed to suggest that Hanoi had achieved its goal at Khe Sanh—that is, the NVA may have lured U.S. troops away from Hue and Saigon, their main objectives during the Tet Offensive. General Westmoreland, the former MACV commander, on the contrary, stated in a 1968 interview that he was proudest of his decision to hold Khe Sanh, implying that Khe Sanh constituted an important U.S. victory.

What then are the yardsticks for measuring the success or failure of a siege? General Wheeler seemed to suggest that Khe Sanh was a failure because the U.S. had forfeited the *initiative* and had fallen to NVA's stratagem of holding U.S. forces in Khe Sanh with ambushes and limited attacks on outposts on surrounding hills while launching all-out assaults on Hue and major urban centers. Deceiving and outwitting the enemy are as old as warfare itself. In *Art of War*, fourth-century B.C. Chinese strategist *Sun Tzu* called it "practice of dissimulation" or "artifice of deviation." One of its forms is dubbed the *duong dong kich tay* (or show off in the east and strike in the west) strategy. It is not clear whether or not the NVA intended to apply this strategy at Khe Sanh. Some military analysts believe that the enemy initially wanted to take both Khe Sanh and Hue but later decided to abandon the first objective and to concentrate on the second. In any event, the attack on Hue forced General Westmoreland to use three U.S. Marine battalions to help recapture the city and raised concerns in Washington about the vulnerability of the Khe Sanh base.

With regard to assessing the siege of Khe Sanh, General Wheeler and General Westmoreland, as seen earlier, had opposite views. While General Wheeler viewed it as a strategic failure, General Westmoreland considered it a victory, possibly because by applying overwhelming U.S. airpower, he had inflicted heavy *casualties* on NVA forces.

It is clear, however, that neither initiative nor casualties can be used to assess the success or failure of a siege because initiative is rather an elusive concept and the number of casualties is but one of many factors contributing to the final outcome of the siege.

In a final analysis, the only logical yardstick to measure the success or failure of a siege, in my opinion, is "objective." In other words, a siege is successful or unsuccessful depending upon whether or not it helps achieve the objectives that have been clearly set forth.

In this regard, the siege of Nasan in 1953 was a success for the French because it thwarted the Viet Minh's plan to take over the Thai Highlands while inflicting heavy casualties on the enemy regular forces. Dien Bien Phu, on the other hand, was a strategic blunder with grave geopolitical consequences for the French. The surrender of the *camp retranché*, in effect, marked the beginning of the end of French presence in Indochina. It was also the beginning of the dismantlement of the French colonial empire as its defeat and humiliation at Dien Bien Phu encouraged organized armed insurrections in its African colonies.

In the case of Khe Sanh, General Westmoreland's main objectives were not clearly stated; but, based on documents which have been made available, they appeared to be: a) protect the DMZ; b) support his barrier concept to cut off the battlefields in the south; c) support an eventual invasion of Laos; and d) inflict heavy casualties on the NVA with overwhelming U.S. airpower.

Under mounting pressure from President Johnson and his military advisor, Gen. Maxwell Taylor—who were concerned about a possible repeat of Dien Bien Phu—General Westmoreland evacuated Khe Sanh in April 1968. The abandonment of Khe Sanh defeated General Westmoreland's first three objectives because it exposed the left flank of the two northern provinces of Quang Tri and Thua Thien south of the DMZ,[1] aborted the barrier concept to interdict NVA's supply lines to the south, and annulled the MACV commander's cherished dream of invading Laos. The heavy casualties suffered by the enemy may have delayed but didn't stop the General Offensive: In 1972, the NVA hurled their finest divisions supported by armor and artillery regiments across the DMZ to attack Quang Tri province while making deep envelopments in the south in an effort to capture Kontum in MRII and An Loc in MRIII.

History will probably record the failure of Khe Sanh to achieve U.S. objectives and agree with General Wheeler's suggestion that Hanoi may have accomplished its goals in that siege (deceiving the enemy and securing its supply lines to its forces in the South).

While the siege of Khe Sanh was somewhat controversial in that its assessment depends upon the criteria used to measure its outcome, and Dien Bien Phu was a severe military setback which caused the French to lose the Indochina War itself, An Loc was undeniably the greatest feat of ARVN's arms. On the other hand, unlike the sieges of Nasan, Dien Bien Phu, and Khe Sanh, where the battle sites were chosen by the French and the American generals, the reverse was true for An Loc. The NVA leaders chose An Loc as the main objective in their thrust toward the capital city of South Viet Nam. As such, ARVN's objectives were self-evident: a) hold An Loc at all costs; and b) inflict maximum casualties on the enemy and destroy their will to fight. By all accounts, An Loc had achieved these goals. Like the Russian stand at Leningrad during World War II—which had saved Russia from the German invasion—the battle of An Loc had practically saved the capital city of South Viet Nam from the onslaught of the NVA's divisions rushing from their sanctuaries in Cambodia.

Also, because Nasan and Khe Sanh had never been completely surrounded by the enemy—they could be resupplied and reinforced by air anytime during the siege—they were not true sieges in the strict definition of the word. They may be called a "semi-sieges," and consequently, it is not appropriate to compare them to the other two sieges. The following comparison between Dien Bien Phu and An Loc, on the other hand, would reveal the following similarities and differences.

The French had 15,000 men defending Dien Bien Phu whereas at the beginning of the battle, ARVN had only about 7,500 men at An Loc.

The attacking forces were two divisions, plus a number of independent regiments, totaling about 30,000 troops in the case of Dien Bien Phu. In the case of An Loc, the attacking forces were also two divisions supported by armored and artillery regiments. The total enemy force amounted to some 21,000 troops—excluding one division engaged against ARVN's rescuing forces moving from the south.

At Dien Bien Phu, there was no civilian population, whereas in An Loc there were many thousands of civilians who needed food, medical care, and physical protection.

At Dien Bien Phu, the French had a perimeter of defense measuring sixteen kilometers by nine kilometers, but An Loc had a defense perimeter only a tenth as large. In other words, in the early stages of the siege there were points within Dien Bien Phu well beyond enemy artillery range, which was never the case in An Loc.

Dien Bien Phu had the disadvantage of being on a valley floor, subjected to deadly artillery fire from the enemy batteries well bunkered inside the surrounding hills. Although the topography of An Loc was somewhat different, the city of An Loc itself was no less vulnerable as it is the only open terrain in the middle of a forest of impenetrable bamboo and rubber plantations.

At Dien Bien Phu, the French had twenty-eight artillery guns (twenty-four 105mm and four 155mm) and twenty-four 120mm mortars. In An Loc, during the most crucial days of the battle, only one 105mm gun was available to provide close support. (The other guns had been destroyed by enemy artillery during the first attack.) The French had tanks at Dien Bien Phu whereas the Viet Minh had none. In the case of An Loc, the reverse was true.

What then were the causes of success of the defense of An Loc? First, it was the air support available that made the biggest difference between An Loc and Dien Bien Phu. Day after day, B-52 sorties hit NVA assembly areas, logistical installations, even the first echelon assault units. B-52 strikes were so accurate that they could hit enemy troops less than one kilometer from the An Loc perimeter and disrupt enemy offensive schemes.

Second, it was the determination of ARVN troops. The French had at Dien Bien Phu some of their best units (paratroopers and legionnaires), but they also had many hill tribe paramilitary units called *partisans* who deserted en masse after the first waves of attack in which they were exposed to the Viet Minh's deadly artillery fire. (It is significant to note that the garrison of An Loc received some 80,000 artillery rounds, or three times the number that were fired into Dien Bien Phu.)

With regard to ARVN's performance in An Loc, Lewis Sorley reported that General Abrams responded vigorously to critics who said that South Viet Nam had defeated the invaders only because of American air support. "I doubt the fabric of this thing could have been held together without U.S. air," Abrams told his commanders. "But the thing that had to happen before that is the Vietnamese, some numbers of them, had to stand and fight. If they didn't do that, ten times the air we've got wouldn't have stopped them."[2] According to senior ARVN commanders in An Loc I interviewed, General Hung, undoubtedly, was the man who was instrumental in holding together the "fabric" of the defense of An Loc against vastly superior enemy forces—and in spite of a deteriorating relationship with his American advisor. While French General De Castries requested Hanoi's permission to surrender when the situation in Dien Bien Phu became hopeless, General Hung doggedly fought on, even when enemy forces were converging on his command post and were firing B-40 rockets directly at his underground bunker. Hung's vow to his men that he would never be taken alive had galvanized the spirits of the defenders during the darkest hours of the siege.

Noteworthy is the fact that the only information about the uneasy relationship between General Hung and Colonel Miller and about Hung's depicted "inability to handle the stress of high-intensity combat" came from only one source: Colonel Miller himself. Willbanks readily admitted that "the discussion of the relationship between Hung and Miller was based on interviews and communication with Colonel Miller. It was impossible to get General Hung's side of things because he committed suicide shortly after the fall of Saigon in 1975."[3]

Colonel Ulmer, who replaced Colonel Miller as 5th Division senior advisor on May 10, had probably a fresher and more objective view of General Hung's conduct. Ulmer later recounted that Hung seemed weary and cautious, but he was clearly in command. Ulmer also recalled that "Hung never buckled, though he was clearly very concerned."[4]

A senior officer who had witnessed General Hung's conduct during the siege of An Loc is Col. Bui Duc Diem, a veteran of the Indochina War who had fought in a paratroop battalion in North Viet Nam. Three times wounded at An Loc, Colonel Diem was awarded two U.S. Silver Stars for heroism during the siege. As Assistant for Operations to General Hung, he was the number three man in the command structure of the 5th Division and the only high-ranking officer who survived the siege of An Loc and the fall of the South—the number two man, Col. Le Nguyen Vy, deputy division commander, also committed suicide in 1975. Colonel Diem told this author that General Hung was always calm under pressure. Diem also reported that when NVA tanks were closing in on the 5th Division command post, General Hung sent a number of his staff officers to man the defensive positions around the underground bunker; two young staff officers were killed by cannon shells from a T-54 tank before the tank was destroyed by other defenders. General Hung, wearing a flak jacket, a steel helmet and carrying a M-16 rifle, often visited the frontline talking to the troops and making sure they knew how to use their M-72 antitank weapons.

Brig. Gen. Mach Van Truong, who, as a colonel, commanded the 8th Regiment, Col. Nguyen Cong Vinh, former 9th Regiment commander, and Col. Pham Van Huan, former commander of the 81st Airborne Commando Group, told me that Hung never panicked and was in full control of the situation.

Finally, the third cause of the success of the defense of An Loc, in my opinion, was the errors committed by the NVA in the planning and execution of their 1972 Easter invasion. "There were mistakes on both sides, plenty of them," recalled Colonel Miller about the NVA's first attack on An Loc, "but we must have made fewer because we were still there when it quieted down, and that meant we were there from then on in my opinion."[5] The NVA, indeed, had made quite a few mistakes during their 1972 invasion. The failure of their Nguyen Hue campaign and, in particular, its bitter defeat in the battle of An Loc, were, in fact, the results of flawed intelligence, strategic errors, and tactical shortcomings.

Sun Tzu, the famous Chinese strategist, wrote: "Know your enemy, know yourself: one hundred battles engaged, one hundred battles won." Obviously, the Communists didn't know their enemy well when they decided to launch their Easter Offensive; they had, indeed, misjudged the resilience of the South Vietnamese army and the American commitment to support its ally, even at a time when U.S troops were disengaging from the country.

In the view of some military analysts, General Giap's biggest mistake in launching the 1972 Eastern invasion was to trust the antiwar activists and communist sympathizers in Saigon, who assured him that the South Vietnamese people were ready to overthrow the Saigon government and would acclaim the North Vietnamese troops as liberators.

It has also been suggested that the North Vietnamese underestimated the staying power of the South Vietnamese forces because they concluded from the lessons of Operation LAM SON 719 that ARVN units would break and run under pressure. If this was true, then the Communists had indeed grossly misjudged ARVN'S performance. In that fateful Laotian campaign, in fact, the South Vietnamese troops' movements, logistical preparations, and most of all, the speculations of the American press, had alerted the enemy to the incoming attack. (The attack didn't start until February 7, 1971, but by February 1, the *Washington Post,* the *Baltimore Sun,* and the *New York Times* reported the possibility that a strike into Low Laos was imminent.)[6] As a result, the NVA had concentrated a powerful anti-aircraft defense system in the area. Over one hundred U.S.

helicopters were shot down during the first week and consequently, the Americans substantially cut down on the number of helicopters available for troop transport, resupply, and medical evacuation. Although on March 6, the ARVN launched a successful air assault on Tchepone and discovered a large number of enemy bodies, the attacking forces also suffered heavy casualties. Ambushed and overwhelmed by far superior enemy forces while lacking adequate air support, logistical supply, and medical evacuation, ARVN units had to retreat without accomplishing their mission of searching for and destroying enemy logistical installations around this important staging area on the Ho Chi Minh trail. The pictures in the U.S. media depicting isolated cases of panicking soldiers clinging to the skids of helicopters gave to the enemy—and also to the world—the wrong impression that ARVN units would fold under pressure.

The enemy, on the other hand, appeared not to have learned one of the lessons of the 1968 Tet Offensive, and that is, ARVN would stand and fight when defending South Vietnamese towns and cities—even when taken by surprise. No cities fell, no ARVN units defected or fled during the above offensive. The VC did occupy a large area of the city of Hue, but they were ultimately driven out after tough house-to-house fighting. The Communists also seemed to overlook the fact that almost half of the war-making potential of the VC was destroyed in this failed offensive and that the NVA had to send North Vietnamese troops to replenish the VC units or, in some instances, to replace them entirely.

Moreover, Hanoi had misjudged President Nixon's resolve to support South Viet Nam in the middle of this crucial Vietnamization period and to bring the formidable U.S. airpower in-country and in the theater to bear upon the North Vietnamese aggressors. While Cobra gunships were very effective against enemy infantry and tanks in the open, the AC-119 Stingers, AC-130 Spectres, A-37s, and F-4s provided accurate close air support and had on many occasions broken enemy assaults. The most important tool in the U.S. arsenal, no doubt, were the B-52s, which, day after day, went after enemy logistical installations, assembly areas and even enemy attacking formations less than one kilometer from ARVN positions. In many instances, the B-52s' timely and accurate strikes had saved some ARVN units from possible annihilation. As reported in an earlier chapter, a preplanned B-52 strike scored a direct hit on an NVA regiment headquarters and one battalion—which began to deploy in formations for the final assault during the second attack on An Loc—forcing the enemy to cancel the attack on the western wing entirely.

With regard to strategy used by the NVA during their Easter Offensive, as mentioned earlier, Hanoi hoped that by launching a simultaneous three-pronged attack on Quang Tri, Kontum, and Binh Long, it would sow confusion within ARVN/JGS as to the main thrust and would force the latter to commit the general reserves prematurely. This multi-pronged offensive would also allow for strategic flexibility, as a successful attack on Quang Tri would open the door to the Imperial City of Hue, while a successful attack on Kontum would cut South Viet Nam in half. A successful thrust on Binh Long, in the other hand, would allow for the installation of the Provisional Revolutionary Government (P RG) in An Loc and would pose a threat to the capital city of Saigon itself.

A three-pronged attack, however, has its drawbacks because the NVA had to disperse all their forces to three distant fronts, and thus were unable to reinforce—and resupply in a timely manner—any of them when the need arose. In MRI and MRII respectively, with additional troops and logistical supplies, the NVA could have exploited their initial successes at Quang Tri and Tan Canh by attacking Hue and Kontum, which were lightly defended at that time. By the time the attacking forces regrouped and were ready to resume the attack, ARVN had already brought in reinforcements to mount a counter-attack to retake Quang Tri and to beat back the NVA's attack on Kontum.

Likewise, had the NVA received fresh troops with adequate supplies, they could have taken An Loc right after the fall of Loc Ninh on April 7, because at that time An Loc was defended only by Binh Long territorial forces, a ranger battalion, and the depleted 7th Regiment of the 5th Division. By the time the NVA 5th Division, the main attacking force—in conjunction with the 9th Division, which was already in place—was ready to resume the attack after its victory at Loc Ninh, ARVN III Corps had been able to reinforce An

Loc successively with the two remaining ranger battalions from the 3rd Ranger Group, the 8th Regiment of the 5th Division, the 1st Airborne Brigade, and the 81st Airborne Commando Group.

Further, because of the lack of reinforcements, the enemy had to stop after each attack to regroup, be resupplied, and be replenished before resuming the attack. Consequently, the NVA not only had lost the momentum for failing to exploit and reinforce the initial successes, but also had allowed the defenders to reorganize and III Corps to bring in reinforcements. Worse, during the lulls between two attacks, VNAF and USAF conducted round-the-clock air strikes on enemy regiments and armored units assembled around An Loc with disastrous consequences for the morale of the troops and the combat worthiness of the attacking forces.

By contrast, the South Vietnamese had a far superior strategic mobility, thanks to VNAF and USAF's airlift capacity, that had allowed ARVN/JGS to quickly bring in reinforcements in accordance with the development of the situation on the three fronts. When the decision was made to reinforce An Loc at the war council in Saigon on April 7, for example, it took ARVN only four days to move the entire 21st Division by air from the Mekong Delta to Bien Hoa airbase and from there by trucks to Chon Thanh, south of An Loc. When it was decided to reinforce the counter-offensive of I Corps to recapture Quang Tri after the siege of An Loc had been lifted in July, it took less than a week to complete the airlift of the 1st Airborne Brigade and the 81st Airborne Commando Group to Phu Bai airport, south of Hue.

With regard to the battle of An Loc, Tran Van Nhut was convinced that the NVA's failure to launch a surprise initial attack on the capital city of Binh Long at the beginning of the offensive constituted a strategic blunder. In *Unfinished War*, General Nhut, indeed, believed that had NVA used their 9th Division to launch a surprise attack on An Loc during the first days of the offensive, then encircled Loc Ninh with the 5th Division, while at the same time interdicting Route 13 with the 7th Division, they could have easily captured An Loc because the city was very lightly defended at that time.[7] From a strategic standpoint, he might be right. However, from the logistical point of view, this could hardly be done because the enemy had to build up its supply bases before launching a large-scale offensive on three different fronts. And this was not an easy task given the fact that their supply lines had been interdicted and their logistical installations damaged or destroyed without interruption by USAF and VNAF warplanes. For this reason, first, they had to take Loc Ninh—which stood on their lifeline—so that they could bring in their supplies in food and ammunition before the 9th Division was finally able to launch their first attack on An Loc, six days after the fall of Loc Ninh. It took the 5th Division an additional twenty-eight days to participate with the 9th Division in the third attack on An Loc.

In his memoir, Brig. Gen. Mach Van Truong, former 8th Regiment commander, reported that during the first NVA attack on An Loc on April 13, 1972, his regiment captured the executive officer of a tank company. The NVA officer disclosed that his unit moved to the South immediately after it was activated in Hanoi and the officers were required to go through a political indoctrination session in which they committed themselves to implement the following three-phase campaign: a) Take Loc Ninh, capture materials and equipment from ARVN 9th Regiment and the district of Loc Ninh, resupply in fuel and food, then attack An Loc; b) Take An Loc, resupply in fuel and food from ARVN 5th Division and Binh Long Sector then attack Binh Duong; c) Occupy Binh Duong, resupply as above then launch a coordinated attack on Saigon.[8]

According to General Truong, the prisoner's revelation explained why dried rice and rations issued by ARVN quartermasters were found on the bodies of dead NVA soldiers. The fact that Communist troops bought or confiscated canned and dry foods at the local markets around An Loc in early April showed that, even with the supplies captured at Loc Ninh, the NVA's logistical lines were not keeping pace with their front units.

A similar situation developed in MRI and also in MRII. In MRI, the days following the collapse of the city of Quang Tri on May 1, as the remnants of ARVN's 3rd Division and attached units were fighting their way back toward the lightly defended My Chanh line amid thousands of refugees fleeing south, NVA's three attacking divisions could have launched a pursuit operation to capture the Imperial City of Hue. Instead, they had to stop to consolidate their new positions and to await resupply in order to build up their logistics before continuing the offensive. This gave ARVN time to regroup, refurbish, and bring in reinforcements in order to launch the successful counter-offensive to recapture the city of Quang Tri in September.

In his memoir *25 Nam Khoi Lua* (25 Years of War),[9] Brig. Gen. Ly Tong Ba, former 23rd Division commander in MRII, reported that, after the capture of the town of Dac To about twenty miles north of Kontum, the two attacking NVA divisions stopped to celebrate their victory. Had they continued their offensive, reasoned Ba, they would have been able to capture the city of Kontum, because his division, located at Ban Me Thuot south of Pleiku, wouldn't have had enough time to replace the 22nd Division, which had been defeated earlier in Dac To.

Both the enemy offensives in MRI and in MRII seemed to indicate that the North Vietnamese were often too cautious and too slow in exploiting their early tactical successes, but the reality was that the constant pounding of their supply lines by B-52 strikes prevented the timely build-up of their logistical bases necessary for any successful pursuit operation. In MRII, by the time the commander of the NVA's B3 Front resumed the offensive fifteen days after the fall of Dac To , General Ba had been able to bring his entire division to Kontum and to conduct a well prepared and well executed defense plan, which thwarted the enemy's ambition to control the Central Highlands and to cut South Viet Nam in half.

According to ARVN field commanders in An Loc, the major tactical mistake of the NVA was the lack of coordination between the attacking forces. Due to constant tactical and strategic air interdiction or due to the inability of Communist military leaders to direct a multi-divisional offensive, the different wings launched their assaults at different times; this allowed the defending units to support each other and the 5th Division to focus air support to the units being attacked.

On the other hand, the enemy's failure to sustain the momentum of attack in An Loc was due not only to the NVA's failure to reinforce the attacking forces to exploit their initial successes, but also to the absence of clear objectives for the tankers and the lack of coordination between armor and infantry units. During the first attack on An Loc, enemy tanks casually rolled down the main thoroughfares of the city without infantry protection, because the tankers were told that the defenders would flee in panic and the population would greet them as liberators. Some defenders did panic—ARVN soldiers had never faced enemy tanks in battle before—but they did not flee, and the civilian population fled instead of welcoming the northern "liberators." After the defenders had recovered from their initial shock and discovered the effectiveness of the M-72 antitank weapon, they started to hunt down the enemy tanks all over the city.

During the succeeding waves of attack, the North Vietnamese tankers were more cautious, but their unit commanders—who lacked experience in combined arms tactics—ordered their units to be split in small elements to support various attacking columns. This "piecemeal" tactic violated the principles of mass and maneuver inherent in the use of armor in battle. Instead of striking en masse deep on weak points in the ARVN's defense to produce shock and surprise, the use of a few tanks on each wing to support the infantry was a recipe for disaster: to avoid being destroyed as sitting ducks alongside the slow-advancing infantry, the tanks continued to progress deep into ARVN positions without infantry protection, and thus were easy prey for the defenders and U.S. Cobra gunships.

The enemy's ineffective employment of armor resulted in great part from the fact that the control of the armor branch was centralized at COSVN and, consequently, tank and infantry units in An Loc were operating under two different chains of command with little or no combined arms coordination.

On the other hand, the enemy's inflexible tactic of launching frontal human-wave assaults on ARVN positions following the lifting of artillery barrages, proved damaging to their infantry. ARVN defenders, in fact, were instructed by their unit commanders to rest, even relax, in their foxholes or bunkers during the artillery barrage and to stand up and shoot at enemy human waves at close range, when the North Vietnamese stopped or shifted their artillery. Many enemy units were decimated by this costly—and recurring—tactic.

Although every indication points to the fact that the Communists had lost the battle of An Loc, Viet Nam critics brushed aside the staggering losses suffered by the North Vietnamese Army, focusing instead on the devastation done to the city. "Perhaps the best that can be said is that the city died bravely," commented an American reporter, "and that—in a year that included the fall of Quang Tri and Tan Canh—is no small achievement."[10] But An Loc didn't die; it stood proudly amid its rubbles as a testimony to its unshakable determination to overcome adversity.

Viet Nam war critics also argued that the South Vietnamese needed American assistance in order to prevail. Lewis Sorley convincingly responded to that: "No one seemed to recall that some 300,000 American troops were stationed in West Germany precisely because the Germans could not stave off Soviet or Warsaw Pact aggression without American help. Nor did anyone mention that in South Korea there were 50,000 American troops positioned specifically to help South Korea deal with any aggression from the north. And no one suggested that, because they needed such American assistance, the armed forces of West Germany and South Korea should be ridiculed or reviled. Only South Viet Nam (which by now was receiving only air support, not ground forces as in Germany and Korea) was singled out for such unfair and mean-spirited treatment."[11]

In spite of the American self-appointed pundits' assessments and analyses, one thing is clear: An Loc may have been destroyed but when the fighting ended, the South Vietnamese troops still controlled the city. "Two and two-thirds divisions [of enemy troops] is one helluva rent to pay for twenty-five percent of a small inconsequential province capital for less than thirty days of occupancy by two battered companies," General Hollingsworth wrote in a letter.[12] Andradé summed it up best when he wrote: "In war as in law, possession is nine-tenths of ownership and after the smoke has cleared An Loc remained in Saigon's hands. Despite all the armchair analysis and polemic excuse-making, the North Vietnamese attack in III Corps had indeed been thwarted. As one anonymous American advisor observed, 'The only way to approach the battle of An Loc is to remember that the ARVN are there and the North

Vietnamese aren't. To view it any other way is to do an injustice to the Vietnamese people."[13]

Thirteen

The Aftermath

The Paris Agreement

After the ARVN's victory in Kontum in May, the recapture of Quang Tri and the liberation of An Loc in September, Hanoi finally realized they had lost the 1972 Easter Offensive. Their best divisions had been convincingly defeated—some of them badly mauled—by the South Vietnamese Army. The debacle of the NVA's Nguyen Hue campaign pushed Hanoi to sign the Paris Peace Agreement in January 1973 to save what was left of its invading army from attacks by ARVN units and bombardments by the USAF and VNAF. On the other hand, for the Communists, peace is considered only as a temporary phase of relative military quiescence, an expedient breathing space to be used for revising tactics and refurbishing arms for renewed fighting under more favorable conditions. Thus, shortly after the signing of the Agreement, the NVA feverishly prepared for a new invasion.

The Paris Agreement was an American creation that allowed the United States to disengage "with honor," but didn't solve the basic issue over which the war had been fought for a quarter of a century. The issue, according Arnold Isaacs, a noted author on Viet Nam, was who would rule in South Viet Nam. "And this was not decided," wrote Isaacs, "just deferred to negotiations between two sides whose perceptions contained no basis for compromise. To negotiate a settlement would require bridging a gulf of hate and suspicion that was as wide as a million graves."[1]

Worse, the Paris Agreement failed to require the withdrawal of an estimated 125,000 to 145,000 NVA troops from the South. (The Agreement had only this to say on the matter: "The question of Vietnamese armed forces in South Viet Nam shall be settled by the two South Vietnamese parties in a spirit of national reconciliation and concord, equality and mutual respect, without interference, in accordance with the post-war situation. Among the questions to be discussed by the two South Vietnamese parties are steps to reduce their military effectives and to demobilize.")

Because the North Vietnamese were allowed to leave their troops in South Viet Nam, they continued to try to occupy as much land as possible, and to use these "liberated" zones as springboards for renewed offensives. Right after the Agreement, the Communists also began building a sophisticated network of routes across mountains and creeks to bring supplies to the South. Their engineer units worked day and night to cut roads through forests and hills. Echoes of detonations could be heard every day beyond the range of mountains west of RN1 in MR1. Three engineer and transportation divisions, under the NVA High Command, were activated to hasten the building of more roads and to expedite the flow of supplies moving south.

President Thieu was aware of the danger posed by the presence of a large NVA force in the South, but he had to sign the Agreement under heavy pressure from the White House. "If the South Vietnamese had shunned the Paris Agreement," explained Lewis Sorley, "it was certain not only that the United States would have settled without them, but also that the U.S. Congress would then have moved swiftly to cut off further aid to South Viet Nam. If, on the other hand, the South Vietnamese went along with the agreement, hoping thereby to continue receiving American aid, they would be forced to accept an outcome in which North Vietnamese troops remained menacingly within their borders. With mortal foreboding, the South Vietnamese chose the latter course, only to find—dismayingly—that they soon had the worst of both, NVA forces ensconced in the south and American support cut off."[2]

Dr. Henry Kissinger—who co-authored the Paris Agreement with Hanoi's Politburo member Le Duc Tho—readily admitted

NVA's violations. As preparation for his post-Agreement meeting with Le Duc Tho, for example, Kissinger had this to say:

> To make our point, I had brought along a compilation of North Vietnamese violations in the two weeks since the signature of the Paris Agreement. The list left no doubt that Hanoi accepted no constraints of any of the provisions it has signed so recently. We had incontrovertible evidence of 200 major military violations. The most flagrant were the transit of the Demilitarized Zone by 175 trucks on February 6 and the movement of 223 tanks heading into South Viet Nam through Laos and Cambodia. Transit of the DMZ by military vehicles violated Article 15(a), on the working of which we had spent nearly two months and which banned all military traffic, as well as requiring the concurrence of the Saigon government. It also violates the explicit stipulation that new military equipment could be introduced into South Viet Nam only on the basis of one-for-one replacement through previously designated international checkpoints (Article 7). The movement of tanks through Laos and Cambodia violates Article 20, according to which all foreign troops were to be withdrawn from Laos and Cambodia and the territory of these countries was not to be used as a base for encroaching on other countries. When the tanks reached South Viet Nam, they would be also violating Article 7's prohibition of new materials. [3]

The situation was particularly critical in MRIII where the reorganized NVA 5th, 7th, and 9th Divisions began attacking ARVN outposts near the Cambodian border to open new corridors to bring personnel and supplies into South Viet Nam from their sanctuaries on the other side of the border. The refurbished ARVN 5th Division, headquartered at Lai Khe, was the only force available to deal with the above three NVA divisions after the Paris Agreement. Consequently, ARVN forces, overextended and without U.S logistical and air support, were unable to conduct cross-border operations to destroy enemy units and their logistical installations—as they used to do before 1970.

The Siege of Tong Le Chan (May 1972–April 1974)

In the early stage of the NVA 1972 Easter invasion, III Corps had ordered all ranger units along the Cambodian border, such as in Ben Soi, Thien Ngon, Katum, Bui Gia Map, to withdraw to more defensible locations. Tong Le Chan was left alone because the 92nd Border Ranger Battalion, which was defending that camp, volunteered to stay and fight.

Like other border ranger camps, Tong Le Chan was formerly occupied by a unit of the Civilian Irregular Defense Group (or CIDG), a paramilitary organization consisting mostly of ethnic Montagnards. It was created by the U.S. Special Forces in 1967 to detect and interdict the infiltration of VC units from their safe sanctuaries in Laos and Cambodia. The CIDG program was under the direct control of the U.S. 5th Special Forces Group headquartered in Nha Trang. The organization, administration, and training of the CIDG bases were assumed by the U.S. Special Forces. The first CIDG base was located at Buon Enao in Darlac province in MRII. In 1965, there were about eighty CIDG bases established in isolated mountainous areas along the Laotian and Cambodian border. Each base was built like a fortress capable of both self-defense and infiltration interdiction.[4]

Since 1965, with the massive introduction of U.S. forces into Viet Nam and the consequent "Americanization" of the Viet Nam War, the CIDG program was intensified and the border outposts had evolved into Special Forces Fire Support Bases equipped with powerful weapons and capable of conducting deep patrols into enemy territory. By 1967, there were about 100 Special Forces bases throughout South Viet Nam. Because of the strategic importance of these FSBs, the VC tried to eliminate them at all costs and many important battles took place at Lang Vei, Thuong Duc, Kham Duc and other places in MRI; Duc Co, Plei Me, Plei Djering, Plateau Gi, Dong Xoai and others in MRII; Ben Soi, Tong Le Chan, Trang Sup, Chi Linh and others in MRIII; Cai Cai, Thuong Thoi, Tinh Bien and other places in MRIV.

Since 1970, along with the drawdown of U.S. troops in connection with the Vietnamization of the war, the CIDG Forces were transferred to ARVN and became what was known as Border Rangers. Because each Special Forces camp had from 300 to 400 members of CIDG, these units were transformed into border ranger battalions. From August 27, 1970, to January 15, 1971, forty-nine Special Forces camps, out of a total of 100, had officially become ARVN border ranger battalions; the rest of the camps were closed and their effectives were distributed among the newly created battalions.[5]

Because Tong Le Chan was established near the enemy "War Zone C," it constituted a threat to the enemy line of communication and supply. As a consequence, it had been constantly harassed and attacked. The Tong Le Chan camp was transformed into the 92nd Border Ranger Battalion on November 30, 1970. The battalion had 318 men, consisting of the original 292 members of CIDG and newly assigned ARVN officers and NCOs. Most of the men were ethnic Stieng Montagnards.[6]

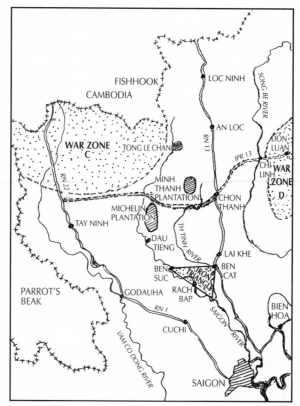

Map 13: Tong Le Chan

The Tong Le Chan camp, about fifteen kilometers south-west of An Loc, was built on a small hill overlooking Road 246 linking VC's "War Zone C" and "War Zone D." It also sat between the Fishhook and Parrot's Beak areas—which had been the Communist secret bases dating back to the Indochina War—and also on the vital line of communication between the COSVN headquarters in Cambodia and the VC-controlled "Iron Triangle" farther south. Because all artillery units in An Loc and Doi Gio Hill had been destroyed during the siege of An Loc, III Corps had moved two 155mm howitzers into Tong Le Chan in order to provide artillery support to the embattled garrison. It was obvious that, from the VC's perspective, this choke point must be removed at all costs.

On May 10, 1972, the NVA, using 130mm guns and mortars, unleashed a powerful artillery barrage on Tong Le Chan. The barrage was followed by direct 75mm recoilless rifle fire. At the same time, intense enemy anti-aircraft fire from 37mm and 57mm weapons, and even SA-7 missiles, prevented tactical air support to the besieged outpost. After the enemy lifted their artillery barrage, the VC 200th Independent Battalion, supported by direct fire from T-54 tanks' 100mm cannons, launched their usual human wave assault. Maj. Le Van Ngon, the 92nd Border Ranger Battalion commander, waited until the attackers were about to cross the thick system of barbed wire—which was previously set up by the U.S. Special Forces around the camp—to order fire. The VCs, believing the outpost had been already annihilated by their massive artillery barrage, were taken by complete surprise. They were decimated in the open before reaching the well-protected border rangers' defensive positions. After launching a few futile attacking waves, the enemy decided to withdraw, leaving about 100 bodies on the barbed wire.[7]

The brilliant victory of the 92nd Border Ranger Battalion, however, was barely noticed because bigger and more important battles were taking place at Quang Tri, Kontum, and An Loc. In early 1973, Maj. Le Van Ngon was promoted to lieutenant colonel. As was the case for French General De Castries at Dien Bien Phu, Ngon's new rank insignia had to be dropped by parachute. At twenty-five, Ngon was the youngest lieutenant colonel in the South Vietnamese Army.

After the debacle of the VC 200th Independent Battalion, the NVA focused their attention on An Loc. In the meantime, they applied their usual "strangulation tactics" at Tong Le Chan with occasional sapper attacks, frequent shelling to inflict casualties, and murderous anti-aircraft fire to interdict air supply and medical evacuation. The NVA believed that once An Loc was taken, Tong Le Chan would fall without fighting. The longest—but least noticed—siege in contemporary military history had begun.

Due to the thick ring of anti-aircraft weapons around Tong Le Chan, the resupply of the garrison was by parachute drops carried out by VNAF C-130s. As in the case of An Loc during the first phase of aerial resupply operations, a high percentage of the drops landed outside the camp and were recovered by the VC, as the C-130s had to fly at high altitudes to avoid being hit by enemy anti-aircraft fire. With regard to medical evacuation, many helicopters had braved anti-aircraft fire to land at Tong Le Chan, but most of them were severely damaged by enemy fire. From October 1973 to the end of January 1974, only six helicopters—out of twenty medevac and resupply missions—were able to land at the camp, but three were destroyed at the LZ. In December 1973, a Chinook CH-47 was also destroyed while attempting to land at Tong Le Chan. It was the thirteenth helicopter hit by enemy anti-aircraft fire during the single month of December. VNAF casualties included nine KIA and thirty-six WIA. In January 1974, or one year after the signing of the Paris Agreement, twelve seriously wounded border rangers still remained at Tong Le Chan.[8]

During 1973, the VC continued their strangulation tactics with sporadic shelling, occasional sapper attacks, and shooting at incoming aircraft. All this took a toll on the defenders; by year's end, the 92nd Rangers were down to 255 men, including many unevacuated wounded. Tong Le Chan had also become a burden for III Corps, which had to divert scant VNAF resources for the aerial resupply of the garrison.

As Saigon was too busy or unwilling to act to save Tong Le Chan, the situation at the camp worsened every day. Food and ammunition were running low and the number of casualties kept mounting due to frequent shelling and sapper attacks. The enemy used loudspeakers to urge the defenders to surrender but Colonel Ngon vowed to defend Tong Le Chan to the last man. Ngon told his men if the enemy overran the base, he would request air strikes on the camp so he would die with them.

Furthermore, on April 10, 1973, elements of NVA's 7th Division attacked and overran Chi Linh outpost on Inter-Provincial Route (IPR) 13, about twenty-five kilometers southeast of An Loc. As a result, Tong Le Chan was the only outpost left in the northern area of Binh Long province.

To alleviate the pressure on Tong Le Chan, on July 23, 1973, the VNAF, marshalling its dwindling resources, flew over thirty missions of bombardment on NVA positions around the besieged garrison, but the results were minimal due to intense anti-aircraft fire.

Toward the end of March 1974, the NVA renewed their attacks on Tong Le Chan. During the night of March 24, the refurbished 271st Regiment, 9th NVA Division, launched a four-pronged assault on the ranger camp after three days of intensive artillery preparation. At that time, the garrison of Tong Le Chan consisted of 254 rangers, 4 artillerymen, 12 LCDB (convicted deserters), and 7 airmen from a downed helicopter.[9] Most of the defenders had been wounded at least once. At one point, the attackers were able to reach the second ring of barbed wire, but they were stopped and decimated by well-placed claymore mines. Although some rangers had collapsed from exhaustion and uninterrupted fighting during the battle, the rest used hand grenades to stop the following attacking waves—which had succeeded in reaching the last ring of barbed wire just in front of the defenders' positions. The enemy finally gave up and the last survivors quickly disappeared under the cover of darkness. Although Lieutenant Colonel Ngon had beaten back the last attack, he knew that he couldn't hold out any longer without resupply and reinforcements.

On April 11, 1974, the NVA launched new attacks on Tong Le Chan after unleashing more than 1,000 rounds of artillery on the outpost, destroying most of the bunkers that had been heavily damaged by previous artillery barrages. Once again, the rangers held their ground, but Colonel Ngon knew the end was near. The battalion ran low on ammunition, the casualties kept mounting, and the men, totally exhausted from continuous fighting, were deemed unable to sustain another attack. Ngon requested III Corps' permission to withdraw before the camp was overrun by the enemy. But Lt. Gen. Pham Quoc Thuan, III Corps commander, ordered Ngon to defend the camp "at all costs," although, in all probability, Thuan knew very well the 92nd Rangers were in no position to carry out his order.

For Colonel Ngon, however, the choice was clear: if he stayed, the battalion would be annihilated because his men were too weak to fight; on the other hand—unlike what General De Castries did at Dien Bien Phu—Ngon vowed he would never surrender to the enemy. The only choice left was to break out of the encirclement and to fight his way back toward An Loc.

Around midnight on April 12, 1974, Tong Le Chan reported it was on the verge of being overrun. Afterward, Ngon ordered the destruction of all important papers and documents. All radio communication with III Corps was also shut down. Ngon requested the VNAF aircraft that circled high above the camp to stop dropping illuminating flares so his battalion could leave the base under cover of darkness. Under the skillful leadership of the young ranger commander, the brave men of the 92nd Ranger moved out in combat formation, bringing with them all their wounded.

During the night, the 92nd Rangers engaged the enemy at a few locations on its itinerary and suffered twenty-four killed and thirty-four wounded. The main body of the battalion reached An Loc on April 14. The siege of Tong Le Chan ended officially the next day when the last rangers made it back to An Loc. Four rangers who formed the rearguard were killed while trying to stop the enemy's pursuit.[10]

On April 13, VNAF warplanes strafed elements of the NVA 9th Division, which were occupying the abandoned ranger camp, and destroyed most of the remaining structures.

The battle of Tong Le Chan showed that the ARVN was not an army of cowards or incompetents. When well led, ARVN units fought with great courage, not only in big battles such as the recapture of Quang Tri and the siege of An Loc, but also in multiple little battles whose names didn't appear on U.S. literature on the Viet Nam War. The epic siege of Tong Le Chan was one of these battles. A South Vietnamese reporter probably summed it best when he wrote: "This was the longest siege in contemporary military history, a battle in which there was the biggest imbalance between the opposing forces and finally a withdrawal operation commanded by a young and most courageous battalion commander."[11]

The 1975 Invasion

In the middle of NVA's frantic build-up in preparation for a new invasion, the U.S. Congress, on April 4, 1974, cut military aid to South Viet Nam for the fiscal year 1974–75 from one billion to $750 million. Out of this $750 million, $300 million was appropriated as salary for the personnel employed by the Defense Attaché Office (DAO) in Saigon. Interestingly, Israel received $2.1 billion in military aid during the three-week Yom Kippur War in 1973. In other words, South Viet Nam, over one year, received 21% of what Israel obtained for three weeks. President Thieu, on a TV broadcast, complained that South Viet Nam had to fight a "poor man's war."

Toward the end of 1974, the NVA was ready to strike. On January 1, 1975, the NVA's 7th Division, supported by T-54 tank units, overran the provincial capital of Phuoc Long province in MRIII, 115 kilometers north of Saigon. Although the fall of Phuoc Long would put the enemy at striking distance from the capital of South Viet Nam, President Thieu and the Joint General Staff decided it was too risky to inject an adequate force to save the garrison. American inaction in face of this blatant violation of the Paris Agreement, on the other hand, sent a clear signal to Hanoi that they had *carte blanche* to launch their spring offensive.

NVA's next objective was in the Central Highlands. The Communists knew that they would pay a heavy price by attacking Pleiku, the seat of II Corps Headquarters. Instead, applying their traditional "strategy of indirect approach," they moved their troops as if they were about to attack the above city. Then on March 10, 1975, one division reinforced by one reserve infantry regiment and one armored regiment launched a coordinated attack on the main objective: Ban Me Thuot. The city fell on March 16, despite a heroic defense by elements of ARVN's 53rd Regiment at Hoa Binh base near Phuong Duc airport. The fall of Ban Me Thuot prompted President Thieu to order the evacuation of Pleiku, which, in turn, triggered the collapse of the entire MRII.

Because this strategy of indirect approach was so crucial in the Viet Nam War—it is safe to say that the collapse of South Viet Nam in 1975 was nothing more than a series of successful envelopments—it begs further discussion at this point. First, in 1972, the NVA launched their Easter Offensive with a frontal attack on Quang Tri and two deep envelopments in Kontum and An Loc; as we have seen earlier, this offensive had failed because the NVA lacked the strategic mobility to reinforce three separate fronts. The reverse was true in 1975, when this strategy of indirect approach was made easier for the Communists, not only because of a new system of roads built after the Paris Agreement, but also because the ARVN, by that time, had lost its strategic mobility to reinforce the areas under attack.

In MRI, instead of launching a frontal assault on Hue and Danang, the NVA massed superior forces to attack the Truoi area south of Hue and the Quang Tin area south of Danang. The collapse of MRII, on the other hand, made the defense of MRI more precarious. Judging the situation untenable, Gen. Ngo Quang Truong, I Corps commander, ordered the evacuation of Hue on March 23 and the evacuation of Danang, the second biggest city of South Viet Nam, on March 27.

It was unfortunate, in retrospect, that during the Viet Nam War the United States preferred to adopt a strategy of static defense by building a chain of fire support bases along the Laotian border— including Khe Sanh—instead of seizing the initiative by applying the strategy of indirect approach that General MacArthur had so brilliantly implemented in the daring landing in Inchon, Korea, in September 1950. This envelopment by sea had allowed the United Nations' troops to recapture Seoul and to inflict irreparable losses to the North Korean Army. Recently, an American author commented that political realities in the U.S. and the world would never have permitted an invasion north of the DMZ. But one wonders why these "political realities" had permitted the heavy bombing raids around Hanoi and the mining of Hai Phong harbor.

Bui Tin, a former NVA colonel and editor of *Nhan Dan*, the Communist Party's official newspaper,[12] recently disclosed that Gen. Le Trong Tan, Chief of Staff, Viet Nam People's Army, told him in 1977: "The Americans needed to deploy no more than a division to occupy the Dong Hoi panhandle temporarily, China would have sat idly by while our troops were pinned down, defending our rear in the North—our unavoidable priority. The configuration of the war would have been flipped completely."[13]

Bui Tin reported, on the other hand, that Gen. Vo Nguyen Giap was very concerned about North Viet Nam's vulnerability should the United States and ARVN forces occupy the panhandle area south the Gianh River and that every year he conducted military exercises to counter that possibility.

In other words, had the United States executed envelopments by sea north of the DMZ in the late 1960s, NVA's supply lines to the South would have been cut off, the sieges of Khe Sanh and An Loc—with the attendant staggering losses in human lives—could have been avoided, the enemy rear would have been threatened, the North Vietnamese people might have risen up against the Communist dictatorial regime, the war could have been won, or at least some kind of armistice similar to the one in Korea could have been reached, and peace may have been a possibility.

The Battle of Xuan Loc (April 8–April 20, 1975)

To exploit their successes in the northern MRs, the North Vietnamese hurled their entire IV Corps—consisting of three divisions and supporting tank and artillery regiments—against the 18th Division defending Xuan Loc. After the collapse of MRI and the northern part of MRII, Xuan Loc, Bien Hoa, and Cu Chi, in fact, became the last defense line against the NVA's advance toward the capital. The city of Xuan Loc, in particular, took on a special strategic importance. Situated about eighty kilometers northeast of Saigon, Xuan Loc controlled the vital junction of RN1 and RN20, the two paved highways into Saigon from the coastal cities and from the Central Highlands. The fate of the capital—and of the Republic—

thus hinged on this last vestige of South Vietnamese resistance.

To prepare for the NVA's attack on Xuan Loc, Brig. Gen. Le Minh Dao, 18th Division commander, deployed his units as follows:

-Task Force 43 (Col. Le Xuan Hieu), consisting of 43rd Regiment (- 2/43 Battalion), 5th Armored Squadron, 2/52 Battalion, 82nd Ranger Battalion, and Long Khanh Territorial Forces, was responsible for the defense of Xuan Loc.
-Task Force 48 (Lt. Col. Tran Minh Cong), consisting of 48th Regiment and supporting units, was assigned the task of securing RN1 east of Xuan Loc.
-Task Force 52 (Col. Ngo Ky Dung), consisting of 52nd Regiment (-2/52 Battalion) and supporting units, was responsible for the defense of the western sector along RN 20.

In mid-March 1975, elements of NVA's IV Corps overran Dinh Quan District on RN20 and Binh Khanh District on RN1, effectively isolating Xuan Loc from the Central Highlands and the coastal areas. In early April, the enemy seized important areas within Long Khanh province.

The first attack on Xuan Loc began at 5:40 A.M. on April 8. After intense artillery preparation, all three divisions of NVA's IV Corps assaulted South Vietnamese positions from three directions:

- The 6th Division attacked Tran Hung Dao hamlet from the north in an effort to secure RN1 in the vicinity of the latter's junction with RN20, and to interdict ARVN rescuing columns from the south.
- The 7th Division attacked Xuan Loc from the northeast; its mission was to seize the town of Tan Phong located at the junction of RN1 and IPR2, just south of the city.
- The newly formed 341st Division attacked the western sector of Xuan Loc in order to secure RN20 from the town of Kien Tan to the junction of RN1 and RN20.

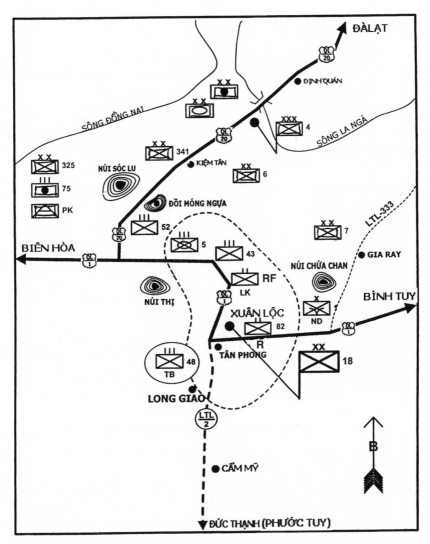

Map 14: Battle of Xuan Loc

The NVA 274th Regiment/ 6th Division succeeded in capturing the high ground north of RN1 but was stopped by the 1st Battalion, 52nd Regiment. The other prong of the 6th Division, led by the 33rd Regiment, met furious resistance from the territorial forces of Long Khanh province and had to withdraw.

On the northeastern sector, ARVN's 43rd Regiment threw back repeated assaults from the 165th Regiment/7th Division. Four T-54s and one PT-76 tank were destroyed inside the barbed wire.[14] On the right flank of the 43rd Regiment, the 82nd Ranger Battalion, defending Xuan Loc airstrip, inflicted heavy casualties to the NVA's 209th Regiment, which attacked across open terrain.

On the west, the NVA's 270th Regiment/341st Division launched an attack on Nui Thi Hill west of An Loc, but was stopped by 2/43 Battalion. Regiment 266/341st Division, attacking in the direction of Long Khanh High School, was beaten back by the 18th Reconnaissance Company and two RF battalions. However, one battalion of the 266th Regiment succeeded in infiltrating through the defenders' lines and establishing an enclave in the market and church area.

At around 11:00 A.M., General Dao used his reserve—consisting of two infantry battalions and two RF battalions, supported by elements of the 5th Armored Squadron—to launch a counter-attack to regain the areas occupied by elements of NVA's 341st Division in the morning. The North Vietnamese offered furious resistance but the penetrating units were destroyed in the afternoon and left many dead.

During the two-day attack on An Loc, ARVN artillery provided effective fire support because Colonel Hung, the division artillery commander, had dispersed his units to avoid enemy counter-battery fire and prepared planned missions on expected enemy avenues of approach. VNAF's F-5 Freedom Fighters (single-seat fighter-attack aircraft) and Skyraiders from Bien Hoa-based squadrons, on the other hand, were very effective against enemy units attacking in the open and identified enemy formations around Xuan Loc. C-130s dropping illuminating flares also helped the defenders detect enemy movements at night and destroy them with artillery.

On April 12, ARVN/JGS reinforced the 18th Division with the 1st Airborne Brigade. General Dao ordered the paratroopers to replace the 48th Regiment on the eastern sector; the latter became the reserve for the division.

On April 15, the NVA's 341st Division launched multiple human-wave assaults on the 3rd Battalion, 52nd Regiment, which was securing the high ground in the western sector. Two companies of the 3/52 were overrun and the rest of the battalion had to withdraw. The attacking forces, reinforced with elements of the 6th Division, broke through the perimeter of defense of the 52nd Regiment the night of April 15. General Dao used his reserve to counterattack to stop the enemy's advance toward Xuan Loc. Dao also requested permission to use the BLU-82B, also named "the Daisy Cutter," on enemy attacking formations. The BLU-82 bomb, originally used to create an instant clearing in the jungle, had also been used as an anti-personnel weapon because of its large lethal radius (300–900 feet).

On April 16, the VNAF, assisted by technicians from DAO, dropped one BLU-82 bomb from a C-130 transport aircraft on an enemy concentration north of Xuan Loc. JGS's intelligence report indicated that the bomb inflicted heavy casualties to the staff of NVA's IV Corps and wiped out one regiment nearby.[15] For an instant, NVA, thinking that the U.S. had resumed B-52 strikes in support of ARVN, momentarily stopped the offensive to reassess the situation.

On the eastern sector, meanwhile, the 1st Airborne Brigade threw back the attacks of two regiments from the 7th NVA Division during the night of April 15. The enemy left many bodies in front of the paratroopers' perimeter. On April 18, the 1st Airborne Brigade, reinforced with an M113 armored company, attacked enemy positions in the forested areas east and southeast of Xuan Loc. The enemy suffered about 200 KIA. Three paratroopers were killed, eighteen wounded, and one M113 APC was damaged.[16]

Xuan Loc, against heavy odds, stood its ground after twelve days of repeated assaults from vastly superior forces. By that time, the NVA leadership, stunned by the unexpectedly fierce defense of the garrison, concluded that it was futile—and too expensive—to try to take the city. They decided instead to bypass Xuan Loc and to launch a direct attack on Bien Hoa, the northern gate to the capital city of South Viet Nam.

To cope with the new development, on April 20 Lt. Gen. Nguyen Van Toan, the new III Corps commander, ordered the 18th Division to fall back to the new defense line: Trang Bom-Long Thanh. There, it continued to fight until Gen. Duong Van Minh, the new President of the Republic, ordered the surrender of all ARVN units.

According to the 18th Division's after-action report, the respective losses in the battle of Xuan Loc were as follows:

Friendly: 30% for all participating units.
            60% for Task Force 52.
Enemy: 5,000 to 6,000 casualties.
            37 tanks and armored vehicles destroyed.
            1 mounted anti-aircraft weapon captured.[17]

Undeniably, the public reputation of the South Vietnamese Army was, to a great extent, redeemed by the heroic stand of the 18th Division. "Despite the public image of corruption and incompetence," wrote George J. Veith and Merle L. Pribbenow, "the ARVN, as shown in the battle of Xuan Loc, was not an army of bumblers and cowards as it is so often portrayed. It was an army that stood and fought with great courage not only on a few well-known occasions like the siege of An Loc, but also in hundreds of little battles whose names most Americans never knew."[18]

One captured Communist document in the late 1960s boasted that "Saigon's Infantry + American Firepower = National Liberation Army (NLA)" An Loc and ARVN's successful defense of Kontum and recapture of Quang Tri in 1972 unequivocally demonstrated that, with American air support, the ARVN could defeat both VC and NVA forces in conventional warfare, or—to put it under a codified format that was often used in Communist propaganda literature—that "Saigon's Infantry + American Firepower > NLA + NVA."

And to this day, I am convinced that, had we continued to receive American fire support, we would have stopped and crushed the NVA offensive during the critical months of February, March, and April 1975. Unfortunately, that was not to be the case, and although we had won many battles in 1972, because one critical variable was missing in the above strategic equation, we inexorably ended up losing the war; and hundreds of thousands of ARVN officers and government officials of the former regime had to bear the brunt of the victors' post-war politics of hatred and violence.

Losers are pirates

There is a Vietnamese saying: *"Duoc lam vua, thua lam giac"* (Winners are kings, losers are pirates.) The Communists had every intention of applying that law after their 1975 victory. A 2001 study by California's *Orange County Register*, based on interviews of former inmates, both in the United States and Viet Nam, and hundreds of pages of documents, including testimony from more than 800 individuals sent to jails, found that:

—An estimated 1 million people were imprisoned without charges or trials.

—165,000 people died in the Socialist Republic of Viet Nam's "re-education camps," according to published academic studies in the United States and Europe.

—Thousands were abused or tortured: their hands and legs shackled in painful positions for months, their skin slashed by bamboo canes studded with thorns, their veins injected with poisonous chemicals, their spirits broken with stories about relatives being killed.

—Prisoners were incarcerated for as long as seventeen years, according to the U.S. State Department, with most terms ranging from three to ten years.

—At least 150 re-education prisons were built after Saigon fell twenty-six years ago.

—One in three South Vietnamese families had a relative in a re-education camp.[19]

Fortunately, after their release, ARVN officers who spent more than three years in these "re-education" camps were allowed to emigrate with their families to the United States under a U.S. Congress-approved humanitarian resettlement plan that benefited all Vietnamese who had sided with the United States during the Viet Nam War.

Maj. Gen. Le Minh Dao, former 18th Division commander, spent seventeen years in re-education camps. Dao was interned longer than most other generals probably because, as seen earlier, his division inflicted heavy casualties on the NVA's IV Corps at Xuan Loc in April 1975, and temporarily thwarted their rush toward Saigon.

Brig. Gen. Mach Van Truong, former 8th Regiment commander in An Loc, also spent seventeen years in Communist concentration camps. Truong was elevated to brigadier general and commanded the 21st Division in the last few months of the Viet Nam War. After the siege of An Loc, a team of U.S. military doctors operated on his neck to remove the shrapnel that was lodged there since the second NVA attack on the city. By Truong's account, the Communist prison officials told him they could spare his life but his "war crimes" could not go unpunished. In Truong's case, the war crimes consisted of the timely reinforcement of the besieged garrison with his regiment and upsetting NVA's attempt to take An Loc in order to establish the seat of the PRG in that city. Truong later confided that, had the U.S. doctors not removed the shrapnel in his neck, he would have likely died in the Communist concentration camps because the harsh manual labor in the camps would have caused the rupture of sensitive nerves in his neck by the unremoved shrapnel. General Truong now lives in Texas. He still complains about recurring headaches due to his old neck wound.

Lt. Gen. Nguyen Vinh Nghi, former 21st Division commander during the An Loc rescuing operation, was detained for thirteen years: as commander of a task force defending the strategic city of Phan Rang, south of Nha Trang, he was captured by the NVA when his headquarters at Phan Rang air base was overrun on April 16, 1975. General Nghi was the highest-ranking prisoner of war in the Indochina Wars. Brig. Gen. Pham Ngoc Sang, commander of the

6th Air Division—which was relocated to Phan Rang after the evacuation of Pleiku—was also captured with General Nghi. (General
Sang refused to be airlifted out of Phan Rang after the fall of that
city; he volunteered instead to stay with General Nghi's headquarters to provide air support to the retreating units. Sang also spent
thirteen years in a re-education camp; he died in California shortly
after emigrating to the United States.)

Brig. Gen. Ho Trung Hau—who succeeded Gen. Nguyen Vinh
Nghi as 21st Division commander—also spent thirteen years in a
Communist concentration camp. He died in Saigon shortly after
his release.

Brig. Gen. Tran Van Nhut was more lucky: In September 1972,
Nhut was appointed commander of the 2nd Division in Quang Ngai
in MRI. After the fall of MRI, the remnants of his division were put
under General Nghi's operational control. While Nghi and his staff
were captured by the NVA, Nhut was rescued by a naval ship off
the coast of Phan Rang, after he jumped into the sea from his C&C
helicopter. (His controversial escape in face of the enemy had, to a
certain extent, tarnished his reputation as a good soldier and com-
petent province chief during the siege of An Loc.) Generals Dao,
Nghi, and Nhut now live in the United States.

Lt. Gen. Nguyen Van Minh, III Corps commander during the
siege of An Loc, was later reassigned as commander of the Capital
Special District. He safely emigrated to the United States in 1975
and died in California in 2006.

Brig. Gen. Le Quang Luong, former 1st Airborne Brigade commander, assumed the command of the Airborne Division after An
Loc and successfully participated in the counter-offensive to recapture Quang Tri. In April 1975, when this author visited him at his
headquarters in Saigon, Luong was very frustrated that President
Thieu had committed all his brigades "piece-meal" by attaching
them to II and III Corps, while he just sat at his headquarters and
could do nothing to save them from annihilation. Luong emigrated
to the United States in 1975 after the fall of Saigon; he died in
2007 in California.

ARVN senior officers were typically incarcerated for thirteen
years in the average. Some were detained twice in Communist

camps. Col. Nguyen Cong Vinh, former 9th Regiment commander at Loc Ninh, belonged to the last category. After the fall of Loc Ninh, Vinh was incarcerated in a Communist concentration camp in Cambodia. Released after the Paris Agreement, he was sent back to a re-education camp in North Viet Nam in 1975. Colonel Vinh now lives in California.

Colonels Pham Van Huan, former 81st Airborne Commando Group commander, and Nguyen Van Biet, 3rd Ranger Group commander, and Lt. Col. Le Van Ngon, the hero of Tong Le Chan, also spent time in a North Vietnamese re-education camp after the war. Colonel Huan now resides in California, Ngon died in a concentration camp, and Biet died in Saigon after his release. Col. Bui Duc Diem, former Assistant for Operations to the 5th Division commander, reported that, after his release from a re-education camp in North Viet Nam, the Communist government denied his request for an exit visa, but thanks to the intervention of the U.S Embassy in Thailand—to which he had sent copies of his two Silver Star awards earned in An Loc—he was able to come to the United States. Diem now lives in Oregon.

Col. Ho Ngoc Can, whose task force T-15 was the first, along with the 6th Airborne Battalion, to effectuate the link-up with the besieged garrison of An Loc, had a dramatic and heroic ending. After An Loc, Can was appointed province chief of Chuong Thien, a VC-infested province in MRIV. One of the most decorated officers in the South Vietnamese army whose courage was legendary in the Mekong Delta, Can fought to the very end in 1975 in defiance of Gen. Duong Van Minh's order of surrender. He was taken prisoner by the VC after his RF and PF units ran out of ammunition. The Communists took him to Can Tho, the seat of IV Corps, and executed him at the city's soccer field on August 14, 1975. According to the people who witnessed his execution, Colonel Can shouted "Long Live the Republic of Viet Nam!" before he was felled by the bullets of the VC firing squad.

Pham Phong Dinh, a military historian, disclosed that Can had thought about committing suicide to comply with the traditional view of a "*Quan Tu*" (virtuous leader)—who rather dies than surrenders to the enemy—but his Christian faith had prevented him from doing so. Brig. Gen. Le Van Hung, the former 5th Division commander and the hero of An Loc, and his former deputy, Col. Le Nguyen Vy (later general), were not restricted by these religious considerations.

In April 1975, General Hung was deputy IV Corps commander in the Mekong Delta. On the morning of April 30, Gen. Duong Van Minh, the new President of the Republic, ordered all ARVN units still fighting in the capital city and in MRIV to lay down their weapons and to await the arrival of Communist military authorities to hand over their military bases. In the evening, General Hung bade farewell to his wife. He then went to his room and shot himself in the heart with his pistol. According to Pham Phong Dinh, the historian, General Hung died at 8:45 P.M. on April 30, 1975. At around 11:00 P.M., Maj. Gen. Nguyen Khoa Nam, IV Corps commander, called to offer his condolences to Mrs. Hung; afterward, Nam went to his office and shot himself in the head with his Browning pistol.

Generals Nam and Hung could have fled the country on a navy ship or flown in their personal helicopters to the U.S. 7th Fleet off the coast of the Mekong Delta, but they had decided to stay and die because time-honored Confucian tradition requires that "if a citadel is lost, the general must die with the citadel."

Col. Le Nguyen Vy, former 5th Division deputy commander in An Loc, was elevated to brigadier general and assumed the command of that division after the siege. On April 30, after hearing on the radio Gen. Duong Van Minh's order of surrender, General Vy bade farewell to his officers, then he went to his trailer that served as his office, put a Beretta 6.35 pistol under his chin and pulled the trigger. (The same day, Gen. Phan Van Phu, former II Corps commander and General Tran Van Hai, 7th Division commander, also committed suicide.)

"*Sinh vi tuong, tu vi than*" (General in lifetime, saint in death) goes a Vietnamese saying. By fighting their whole life for their country and at the end, by choosing to die instead of surrendering to the enemy, the above generals are worshiped as "*than-tuong*" (general-saints) by the adoring Vietnamese people, and every thirtieth of April—dubbed "black April"—the members of the overseas

Vietnamese communities gather at pagodas or other worship places to pay respects and to commemorate the memories of these fallen heroes.

Not content with executing, incarcerating, and torturing their living enemies, the Communists, in their relentless pursuit of a policy of hatred and retribution, also went after the dead. "The new rulers failed to bring anything resembling true reconciliation with those who had been on the losing side," wrote Arnold Isaacs. "In an act of ugly vengeance, the victors bulldozed dozens of military cemeteries and obliterated their dead enemies' graves—in Vietnamese culture, a devastating loss for the families of the dead."[20] The 81st Airborne Commando Group's cemetery in An Loc didn't escape the Communist wrath. Following is the story of a former resident of An Loc who had returned to her native city after the war:

> As for me, at the one time I had come back to visit my country, I had returned to An Loc to look for the echoes of those unforgettable troubled times, and most of all, to kneel before the cemetery of those 68 heroes of the Airborne Commandos, who had given their life for the nation, to pay tribute and burn incense in their memories. I couldn't hold my tears when I saw that the old scenery had changed. The old cemetery, that served as the symbol of loyalty and heroism, had become an urban center. Those vengeful "atheists" had dug out the remains of our brothers and dumped them outside Xa Cam Gate. With a heavy heart, I found my way to Xa Cam Gate, but in front of me, there were only a sad and quiet rubber tree forest, and the dusty red soil routes on which I used to play with my friends, kicking up the red dust, those same roads on which the frightened residents of An Loc had fled away, those roads that were soaked up with the blood of my brothers and of the enemy; I whispered a prayer for your spirits—our national heroes—for the spirits of all Vietnamese who had died during this atro-

cious war, for the early liberation of the Fatherland
from this incarcerated life. [21]

Since the implementation of the cultural liberation period
known as *Doi Moi* (Renovation) in the late 1980s, the Vietnamese
Communist regime has invited the members of overseas Vietnamese
communities to come back and to use their financial resources and
technological know-how to help rebuild the country. But political
reconciliation would require overcoming the simmering ill will and
animosity and, as Isaacs Arnold has appropriately put it, "bridging
a gulf of hate and suspicion that was as wide as a million graves."

Nature has an admirable way of regenerating itself—even after
a destructive war; and if there were ever a positive note concern-
ing the old battlefields and sanctuaries, it probably would be the
restoration of the wildlife in a 1,160-square-mile area just across
from Binh Long province. In an article titled, "Endangered species
thrive along Ho Chi Minh Trail" (*San Jose Mercury News*, March
4, 2007), Jerry Harmer, an Associated Press reporter, said that, according to New York-based Wildlife Conservation Society, at least
forty-two threatened species and an estimated half of the world's
population of a rare species of primate now live in this area—which
used to be the safe haven for NVA units involved in the 1972 Binh
Long campaign.

"Four decades after the U.S. warplanes plastered it with bombs,"
wrote Harmer, "a remote corner of the old Ho Chi Minh Trail in
Cambodia is making a comeback as treasure trove of endangered
wildlife... Today, the sounds of war have given way to the mes-
merizing pulse of soft tropical sounds: the calls of yellow-cheeked
crested gibbons fill the cold dawn air, and birds such as blue-eared
barbets and white-rumped shamas sing through the day."

It is no small consolation to know that the U.S. airplanes that
devastated the Cambodian forests along the Ho Chi Minh trail forty years ago had, in their own way, contributed to the comeback
of the wildlife in these areas: today, elephants are seen shepherding
their young to drink at the multiple jungle water holes created by
old B-52 bomb craters.

Epilogue

After the fall of South Viet Nam in 1975, politicians and military analysts predicted that Viet Nam's pro-Western neighbors would fall like dominoes in the face of seemingly unstoppable North Vietnamese divisions equipped with the latest Soviet and Chinese weaponry. Thirty-three years later, no dominoes have fallen. Instead, the Soviet Union has collapsed along with the international Communist system.

Bui Tin, a former colonel in the North Vietnamese army and the editor of Nhan Dan, the VCP's mouthpiece, believed that the Vietnamese Communist regime will also die because heaven is no longer on their side. He wrote: "I believe that although heaven was on the side of the North Vietnamese during the war, the Communist utopia will not last long. Heaven is just. When living kindly, one will reap goodness. When sowing wind, one will reap tempest. Communism has reached its glorious goal, but in the process, it has bankrupted itself, both in theory and in deed. Its goal to build a society without exploitation is contradicted by its cruel and inhumane practices, its violence against its opponents, and its embrace of class struggle and war."[1]

I agree that the Vietnamese Communist regime will not last, but for more earthly reasons. It very existence in fact, is being threatened, not only by insurmountable geopolitical and economic dilemmas, but also by the tremendous advances in information technology.

Although it doesn't publicly proclaim it, China—as in the case of Taiwan—historically has considered Viet Nam a renegade southern province. They named it An Nam, or "the Pacified South." China's occasional killings of Vietnamese fishermen in Viet Nam's Vinh Bac Bo (Gulf of Tonkin), in fact, has added to a consistent pattern of Chinese southern expansionism: conquest of the Paracel Islands in 1974; invasion of the northern provinces of Viet Nam in 1979 and subsequent annexation of 6,000 square kilometers of borderland; occupation of the Spratley archipelagoes the same year and acquisition of 12,000 square kilometers of territorial waters in the Vinh Bac Bo conceded by Hanoi under the 2000 Vinh Bac Bo Pact.

Concerns about Beijing's new aggressiveness have sparked new military re-alignments in the strategic Asia-Pacific region. Despite the Free World's professed commitment to "constructive engagement" with China, the post-World War II policy of "containment" remains a popular ploy in today's global, political chess game. Viet Nam has thus regained its strategic value in U.S. eyes as a missing link in the containment scheme and a counterbalance to the even graver threat of Chinese expansionism.

But effective and lasting strategic cooperation, such as in NATO or the U.S.-Japan alliance, requires that the partners share the same moral values and political ideology. In other words, only a free and democratic Viet Nam, enjoying popular support and the support of the community of free nations, can stand up to the aggression of its former allied and historical enemy and effectively contribute to regional security.

Viet Nam is also facing daunting odds on the economic front. To foster economic growth necessary to generate jobs for a population that is expected to increase to 100 million by 2010, Viet Nam needs to export its products and attract foreign investments. In other words, in order to survive, Viet Nam needs to participate in the global economy. The country's recent admission to the World Trade Organization (WTO) is a good start in that direction, but participating members, on the other hand, are required to provide an environment of fair competition and safe investment or, in other words, the institution of the rule of law, the eradication of corruption and bureaucracy, and most of all, the dissolution of government-subsidized state enterprises.

In an age where innovation and pluralism have become interdependent, to succeed, economic reform must be implemented concurrently with political reform. But for authoritarian regimes, political reform means the erosion of the government's grip on power, and its ultimate demise. "The fatal dilemma of the communist system," correctly predicted Dr. Zbigniew Brzezinski in The Grand Failure: The Birth and Death of Communism in the Twentieth Century (New York: Scribner's, 1989), "is that economic success can only be purchased at the cost of political stability, while political stability can only be sustained at the cost of economic failure" (102).

Moreover, in the view of political scientists, the Communist regime can hang on to power only if it can control three things: food, movement, and ideas. In today's Viet Nam, food tickets and travel permits are no longer required. In the meantime, the Viet Nam Communist leadership is desperately struggling to control the free flow of information; but the last bulwark of the regime is being threatened by the explosion of information technology. For younger generations of Vietnamese—80% of the Vietnamese population were born after the war—Marxist ideology is a thing of the past and gone are the endless political indoctrination sessions in which they were required to recite Ho Chi Minh's slogans like parrots. For them now, money is their goal in life and Bill Gates has dethroned Ho Chi Minh to become their new hero.

One of the ironies of the Viet Nam War is that the losing side—those who fled the country after the fall of Saigon, and their descendants—are doing quite well in their adopted countries. Based on statistics published by the Organization for Economic Co-operation and Development for 2005, it is estimated that the total purchasing power parity (PPP)—a measure often used to compare the standards of living between countries—of three million Vietnamese overseas is about two times the total PPP for the 84 million Vietnamese at home (which, at 620 U.S. dollars per capita, ranked 145th in the world). The Vietnamese communities overseas also have gained considerable political clout in their new countries. The second generation of Vietnamese immigrants has, in recent years, actively participated in the political process of their countries of adoption. In the United States, quite a few have been elected to local offices, two have been elected to state legislatures, and recently, for the first time, a young Vietnamese-American attorney in Louisiana won a seat in the U.S. House of Representatives.

In the last few years, several U.S. cities and states have adopted resolutions recognizing the former South Viet Nam flag—three horizontal red stripes on a yellow background—as the official flag of the Vietnamese American communities. The resolutions also permit the flag to be ceremoniously displayed on public properties.

These remarkable political and psychological achievements culminated in the unveiling of a Joint Viet Nam War Memorial, the first of its kind in the world, in April 2003 in Westminster City, California. An eleven-foot-high bronze monument portrays a soldier from the former Republic of Viet Nam and an American GI standing side by side with their countries' flags behind them. The dedication ceremony was attended by an estimated 10,000 people, most of them Vietnamese Americans—many of them coming from other parts of the world.

It was no coincidence that the American speaker, who represented the U.S. Viet Nam veterans at the unveiling, was retired Lt. Gen. Walter Ulmer, former senior advisor to the 5th ARVN Division during the last stage of the siege of An Loc. Nor was it a coincidence that the main member of the joint organizing committee was retired Lt. Col. Mandela Craig, former advisor to the 15th Regimental Task Force—which was one of the first units to link up with the besieged city.

In his speech, General Ulmer recalled the victory of An Loc and expressed his belief that the war could have been won had South Viet Nam continued to receive U.S. support. An Loc obviously was on everybody's mind and remained a lasting source of pride and inspiration for Vietnamese veterans and their former U.S advisors.

As one of the guest speakers at the unveiling, I expressed my hope that similar monuments would someday be built in the cities of a free and democratic Viet Nam. I also expressed my conviction that the fallen Vietnamese and American heroes had not died in vain because I believe that the Viet Nam War had bought time for the Free World to win the Cold War and to liberate hundreds of millions of people of Eastern Europe from Communist oppression. I further believe that the sacrifices of the U.S. and South Vietnamese soldiers had allowed the people of Thailand, the Philippines, and Indonesia to live today under democratic regimes.

In retrospect, I believe that the battle of An Loc—by saving the former Republic of Viet Nam in 1972—had bought three precious additional years for the Free World to muster other assets to bring the former USSR to its knees and to ultimately prevail in the Cold War. I also like to believe that An Loc had bought time for President Nixon to go to Beijing in February 1972 to seek China's cooperation in containing Russian influence in Asia. This diplomatic breakthrough and the resulting U.S.-China rapprochement, combined with Moscow's excessive cost of military assistance to Hanoi during the Viet Nam War, the disaster of its 1979 invasion of Afghanistan, its inability to compete with the U.S. in the field of military space technology, and the failure of its obsolete economic system to compete with the Western World in the new global economy, in turn, had ultimately brought about the dismantlement of the Soviet Empire and the collapse of the antiquated Marxist ideology.

In assessing the battle of An Loc, General Hollingsworth declared: "I think it will go down in history as the greatest victory in the history of warfare."[2] This may be an exaggeration, but, somehow from the bottom of my heart, I tend to agree.

Appendix

SENIOR ARVN COMMANDERS AND U.S. COUNTERPARTS

III Corps
Lt. Gen. Nguyen Van Minh   Maj. Gen. James F. Hollingsworth

Battle of Loc Ninh (April 4–April 7, 1972)
Col. Nguyen Cong Vinh   Lt. Col. Richard S. Schott
    9th Regiment commander
Lt. Col. Nguyen Huu Duong
    Task Force 1-5 commander
Lt. Col. Nguyen Ba Thinh   Lt. Col. Walter D. Ginger
    Task Force 52 commander
Major Nguyen Van Thinh   Capt. George Wanat (Acting)
    Loc Ninh District Chief

Battle of An Loc (April 13–June 8, 1972)
Brig. Gen. Le Van Hung   Col. William Miller (April 13–May 10)
    5th Division commander

                      Col. Walter Ulmer (May 10–June 8)

Lt. Col. Ly Duc Quan
    7th Regiment commander

Col. Mach Van Truong
    8th Regiment commander
Col. Le Quang Luong   Lt. Col. Art Taylor
    1st Airborne Brigade commander
Lt. Col. Pham Van Huan   Capt. Charles Huggins
    81st Airborne commander
Lt. Col. Nguyen Van Biet   Lt. Col. Richard J. McManus
    3rd Ranger Group commander
Col. Tran Van Nhut   Lt. Col. Robert Corley
    Binh Long province chief

Relief Operation (April 12–July 15 1972)

Maj. Gen. Nguyen Vinh Nghi   Col. J. Ross Franklin
    21st Division commander (April 12–May 3 1972)
Brig. Gen. Ho Trung Hau
    21st Division commander (May 3–July 15)
Col. Nguyen Huu Kiem   Lt. Col. Edward J. Stein
    31st Regiment commander
Col. Nguyen Van Biet   Lt. Col. Burr M. Willey (KIA)
    32nd Regiment commander
Lt. Col. Nguyen Viet Can (KIA)   Lt. Col. Charles Butler (KIA)
    33rd Regiment commander

18th Division at An Loc (July 11–November 28)

Col. Le Minh Dao   Col. John Evans
    18th Division commander
Lt. Col. Le Xuan Hieu
    43rd Regiment commander
Lt. Col. Tran Ba Thanh
    48th Regiment commander
Lt. Col. Ngo Ky Dung
    52nd Regiment commander

Notes

Introduction

1. *Reader's Digest*, March 1973, p. 151.

2. James H. Willbanks, *The Battle of An Loc* (Bloomington: Indiana University Press, 2005), 164.

3. Lam Quang Thi, *The Twenty-Five Year Century. A South Vietnamese General Remembers the Indochina War to the Fall of Saigon* (Denton: University of North Texas Press, 2002*)*.

4. Robert G. Kaiser, "The Arrogance of Power Revisited," *San Jose Mercury News,* January 21, 2007.

5. William M. Hammond, *Reporting Viet Nam: Media and Military at War* (Lawrence: University Press of Kansas, 1998), 269, 270.

6. Hammond, 115.

7. Tran Van Nhut, *Cuoc Chien Dang Do* (Unfinished War) (Santa Ana, CA: An Loc Publishing, 2003.)

8. Nguyen Ngoc Anh, *Chien Thang An Loc* (The Victory of An Loc) (Austin, TX: Self-published, 2007).

Chapter 1

1. John Prados and Ray W. Stubbe, *Valley of Decision: The Siege of Khe Sanh* (Boston: Houghton Mifflin, 1991).

2. *"Quan Luc Viet Nam Cong Hoa." Quan Su 4,* 1972 (ARVN, Military History 4, 1972), p. 124.

3. ARVN, Military History 4, p. 125.

4. Ibid., 128.

5. Martin Windrow, cont., *Rolling Thunder in a Gentle Land,* ed. Andrew Weist (Oxford UK: Osprey Publishing, 2006), 43.

6. ARVN, Military History 4, 147.

7. Ibid.,151.

8. ARVN, Military History 4, 152, 153.

9. Ibid., 154, 155.

10. Ibid., 155.

11. Ibid., 160.

12. Ibid., 172.

13. Ibid., 209.

14. Ibid., 109.

15. "Battle of Khe Sanh," Wikipedia, accessed October 21, 2007.

16. Ibid., 4.

17. Ibid., 5.

18. Ibid., 8.

19. Ibid., 9.

20. Ibid., 10.

21. Prados and Stubbe, 297.

22. "Battle of Khe Sanh," Wikipedia.

Chapter 2

1. There is a Vietnamese proverb: *Phep vua thua le lang* (Royal decrees are worth less than the village's customs).

2. Lewis Sorley, cont., *Rolling Thunder in a Gentle Land,* 185.

3. Willbanks, 62.

4. Dale Andradé, *America's Last Vietnam Battle* (Lawrence: University Press of Kansas, 2001), 389.

5. Ibid.

6. Andradé, 391.

7. Willbanks, 67.

8. Frances FitzGerald, *Fire in the Lake* (Boston: Little, Brown & Co., 1972), 369.

9. Edward Metzner, *More than a Soldier's War* (College Station: Texas A&M University Press, 1995), 193.

10. Willbanks, 10.

11. Andradé, 373.

12. Ibid.

13. Mach Van Truong, "*Trung Doan 8 Bo Binh va Tran Chien An Loc*" (8th Regiment and the Battle of An Loc) unpublished memoir; copy in author's possession, p. 6.

14. By naming their offensive in honor of a national hero who routed the Chinese invaders in the nineteenth century, the North Vietnamese showed a remarkable lack of political savvy as they needed massive Chinese military assistance for their planned invasion.

15. Andradé, 384.

16. Ngo Quang Truong, *The 1972 Easter Offensive* (Reprinted in Vietnamese in *Ranger Magazine* 21, Sept. 2007), p. 137.

17. Ibid., 136.

18. Andradé, 384, 385.

19. Nguyen Duc Phuong, *Chien Tranh Viet Nam Toan Tap* (Comprehensive Narrative of the Viet Nam War) (Toronto, Canada: Lang Van, 2001), 568.

20. Lewis Sorley, "Reassessing ARVN," A Lecture Delivered at the Viet Nam Center, Texas Tech University, March 17, 2006, p. 23.

21. Ibid., 22.

Chapter 3

1. Ngo Quang Truong, *The 1972 Easter Offensive*, 140.

2. Tran Van Nhut, 118.

3. Colonel Nhut was later elevated to brigadier general and assumed command of the 2nd Division in I Corps after the Easter Offensive.

4. Lt. Col. Nguyen Thong Thanh was one of my best battalion commanders when I commanded the 9th Division in the Mekong Delta.

5. Tran Van Nhut, 118.

6. Nguyen Ngoc Anh, 24, 25. The details of the demise of TF 1-5 were based on an interview of the author with Lt. Col. Nguyen Huu Duong., the former task force commander. Colonel Duong

currently lives in Australia.

7. Willbanks, 47.

8. FAS Military Analysis Network, CBU-87/B Combined Effects Munitions (Website: 66.218.69.11).

9. Willbanks, 47.

10. Ibid.

11. Tran Van Nhut, 120.

12. Andradé, 399.

13. Willbanks, 46.

14. Nguyen Cong Vinh, Letter dated June 16, 2006; copy in author's possession.

15. Tran Van Nhut, 120.

16. Ibid., 121.

17. Mach Van Truong, 5.

18. Ibid., 6.

19. Willbanks, 41.

20. Ibid.

21. Ly Tong Ba, *25 Nam Khoi Lua* (25 Years of War) (np: Self-published, 1995), 162, 163.

22. Willbanks, 58.

23. Mach Van Truong, 5.

24. Conversation with Maj. Gen. Le Minh Dao, former 18th ARVN Division.

25. Willbanks, 51.

26. Ibid., 52.

27. Willbanks revealed that most of the description of the "Battle of Loc Ninh" comes from Captain Smith's *Battle of Loc Ninh, RVN 5-7 April 1972*, unpublished narrative (Fort Bragg, North Carolina, 21 October 1976). See the *Battle of An Loc*, 193 n15.

28. Willbanks, 193 n 24.

29. Nguyen Cong Vinh, *Cau Chuyen Suy Tu Cua Mot Cuu Tu Nhan Chinh Tri* (Reflections of a Political Prisoner) (San Jose, CA: Mekong-Ty Nan, 1996), 122.

30. Ibid.

31. Colonel Vinh spent thirteen years in Communist re-education camps. He currently lives in California.

32. Tran Van Nhut, 122.

33. Ngo Quang Truong, *The 1972 Easter Offensive*, 146.

34. Colonel Bui Duc Diem now lives in Oregon.

35. Willbanks, 54.

36. In his letter, Colonel Vinh alleged that the district had evacuated before the NVA attack on Loc Ninh. This contradicts Nhut's statement that he still had radio contact with Major Thinh, the district chief, on April 7.

37. Willbanks, 42.

38. Ibid., 53, 54.

39. Nguyen Ngoc Anh, 29.

40. Nguyen Quoc Khue, *3rd Ranger Group and the Battle of An Loc* (reprinted in *Ranger Magazine* 7, Feb. 2003), 89.

41. Willbanks, 81.

Chapter 4

1. Nguyen Ngoc Anh, 55.

2. Ngo Quang Truong, *The 1972 Easter Offensive*, 143.

3. General Truong replaced Gen. Hoang Xuan Lam as I Corps commander after the fall of Quang Tri on May 1, 1972.

4. Ngo Quang Truong, *The 1972 Easter Offensive*, 143.

5. Tran Van Nhut, 123.

6. Ibid.

7. Nguyen Quoc Khue, 78.

8. Ibid., 2.

9. Ibid., 3.

10. Ibid., 5, 6.

11. Tran Van Nhut, 124.

12. Ibid., 181.

13. Conversation with General Mach Van Truong, former 8th Regiment commander in An Loc.

14. Nguyen Duc Phuong, 571.

15. "*Muoi Chin Ngay Trong An Loc* (Nineteen Days in An Loc)," *KBC Army Magazine* 12 (Nov. 1994): 12.

16. Ngo Quang Truong, *The 1972 Easter Offensive*, 144.

17. Mach Van Truong, 5.

18. Tran Van Nhut, 124.

19. Willbanks, 70.

20. Mach Van Truong, 7.

21. Ibid., 8.

22. Ibid., 9.

23. *KBC Army Magazine* 12 (Nov. 1994): 13.

24. Nguyen Quoc Khue, 95.

25. Ibid., 89.

26. Ibid.

27. Ibid., 92.

28. Tran Van Nhut, 132.

29. Willbanks, 65.

30. Ibid., 72.

Chapter 5

1. Nguyen Huu Chinh, *Phi Doan 237 Tham Du Mat Tran An Loc* (237th Squadron in the Battle of An Loc) Unpublished report, October 2006, copy in author's possession.

2. Tran Van Nhut, 133.

3. Mach Van Truong, 9.

4. Ibid., 10.

5. Tran Van Nhut, 134.

6. Mach Van Truong, 10.

7. Willbanks, 72.

8. Ngo Quang Truong, *The 1972 Easter Offensive*, 145.

9. Nguyen Ngoc Anh, 71.

10. Mach Van Truong, 10.

11. Ibid.

12. Ibid., 11.

13. Ibid.

14. Ibid.

15. Telephone conversation with Nguyen Cau, who currently lives in San Jose, California.

16. Mach Van Truong, 11.

17. Nguyen Quoc Khue, 97.

18. Tran Van Nhut, 135.

19. Willbanks, 76.

20. *81st Ranger Magazine,* July 1998, p. 72.

21. Willbanks, 78.

22. Philip C. Clarke, "The Battle that Saved Saigon," *Reader's Digest*, March 1973.

23. Tran Van Nhut, 136.

24. Clarke, *Reader's Digest*.

25. Phan Nhat Nam, *Mua He Do Lua* (Red Burning Summer) June 1972 (Reprinted in Tieu Lun Online Library), p. 12.

26. Ibid., 9.

27. Ibid., 11.

28. The Phoenix program was a national campaign aimed at the elimination of the VC political and administrative infrastructure.

29. Tran Van Nhut, 136.

30. Nguyen Ngoc Anh, 121.

31. Nguyen Quoc Khue, 100.

32. Ibid., 103.

33. Willbanks, 78.

34. Mach Van Truong, 13.

35. ARVN, *Tran Binh Long* (The Battle of Binh Long), 109.

36. Willbanks, 83, 84.

37. Mach Van Truong, 13.

Chapter 6

1. ARVN, *Tran Binh Long* (The Battle of Binh Long), 112.

2. Mach Van Truong, 14.

3. Tran Van Nhut, 154.

4. ARVN, *Tran Binh Long* (The Battle of Binh Long), 112.

5. The VC's B3 Front encompassed the provinces of the Central Highlands.

6. Le Khac Anh Dao, *Nhung Tran Danh Khong Ten* (The Nameless Battles) January 2003, pp. 186, 187.

7. Ibid., 193.

8. *Tran Chien An Loc* (The Battle of An Loc), online Tieu Lun Library (Website: tieulun.hopto.org), p. 7.

9. Nguyen Quoc Khue, pp. 98, 99.

10. *KBC Army Magazine* 12 (Nov. 1994): 13.

11. Willbanks, 80.

12. Nguyen Quoc Khue, 108.

13. Ibid., 109.

14. Nguyen Van Quy, *Hoi Ky An Loc: 86 Ngay cua mot Bac Si Giai Phau tai Mat Tran* (Memoirs of An Loc: 86 Days of a Surgeon in Battle) (Westminster, CA: Van Nghe Pub., 2002).

15. Phan Nhat Nam, *Red Burning Summer*, Tieu Lun online library (Website: tieulun.hopto.org), p. 3.

16. Telephone conversation with Col. Bui Duc Diem.

17. Andradé, 458.

18. Nguyen Ngoc Anh, 206.

19. Ibid., 207.

20. Andradé, 453.

21. Ibid., 454.

22. Willbanks, 106.

23. Andradé, 457.

24. Ibid., 456.

25. Ibid., 462.

Chapter 7

1. Nguyen Ngoc Anh, 151, 152.

2. Nguyen Duc Phuong, *Chien Tranh Viet Nam Toan Tap* (Comprehensive Narrative of the Viet Nam War), 571.

3. *Dac San Hoa Du* (Airborne Magazine, 2003), p. 125

4. Nguyen Ngoc Anh, 89.

5. Ibid., 91.

6. *M202A1 Flame Assault Shoulder Weapon: Gary's U.S. Infantry Weapons Reference Guide* (Website: inetres.com).

7. Truong Duong, *Mot Canh Hoa Du* (One Parachute Flower) (Np: Tu Huynh Publishing, 1999), 235.

8. *81ˢᵗ Airborne Commando Group Magazine*, July 1998, p.84.

9. *KBC Army Magazine* 12 (Nov. 1994): 27.

10. Tran Van Nhut, 160.

11. Vu Van Hoi, *Viet Ve An Loc* (Narrative on An Loc), Nov. 2006; unpublished essay in author's possession , p. 4.

12. ARVN, *Tran Binh Long* (The Battle of Binh Long), 115.

13. Ibid., 116.

14. Vu Van Hoi, 5.

15. Ibid.

16. Truong Duong, 235.

17. Tran Van Nhut, 161.

18. *81ˢᵗ Airborne Commando Group Magazine*, May 2006, p. 11.

19. *81ˢᵗ Airborne Commando Group Magazine*, July 1998, p. 83.

20. Ibid., 74.

21. Ibid.

22. Ibid., 84.

23. ARVN, *Tran Binh Long* (The Battle of Binh Long), 117.

24. Mach Van Truong, *Trung Doan 8 Bo Binh va Tran Chien An Loc* (The 8ᵗʰ Infantry Regiment and the Battle of An Loc, May 2007), p. 16.

25. *Dac San Hoa Du* (Airborne Magazine), 2003, p. 126.

26. Tran Van Nhut, 164.

27. Willbanks, 97.

28. *81ˢᵗ Airborne Commando Group Magazine,* July 1998, p. 89.

29. Telephone conversation with Brig. Gen. Mach Van Truong.

30. Hoang Khoi Phong, *Cay Tung Truoc Bao* (The Pine Tree Facing the Storm), Reprinted in the *81ˢᵗ Airborne Commando Group Magazine,* July 2007, p. 14.

31. Ngo Quang Truong, 148.

32. Tran Van Nhut, 169.

33. Ibid., 170.

34. Vu Van Hoi, 4.

35. Tran Van Nhut, 171.

36. Andradé, 441.

37. *Dac San Hoa Du* (Airborne Magazine), 2003, p. 126.

38. Vu Van Hoi, 6.

39. Mach Van Truong, 18.

40. Willbanks, 107.

41. Tran Van Nhut, 143.

42. Bui Duc Diem, unpublished account of the battle of An Loc, Aug. 2006; copy in author's possession.

43. Nguyen Quoc Khue, 120.

44. Willbanks, 109.

45. Ibid.

46. Tran Van Nhut, 171.

Chapter 8

1. *81ˢᵗ Airborne Commando Magazine*, July 1998, p.77.

2. Tran Van Nhut, 181.

3. Ngo Quang Truong, 155.

4. Andradé, 472.

5. In his memoir, Nhut reported that he and General Hollingsworth continued using their own code names to talk on the telephone after 1975, in the United States.

6. *The Battle of An Loc*, Tieulun Online Library (Website: tieulun.hopto.org), p. 9.

7. Letter from Lt. Col. Nguyen Phu Chinh, former 237ᵗʰ Squadron commander, dated October 17, 2006; copy in author's possession.

8. Willbanks, 116.

9. Ulmer later retired as a lieutenant-general.

10. Andradé, 472.

11. Ibid., 477.

12. *81ˢᵗ Airborne Commando Magazine*, July 1998, p. 93.

13. Nguyen Quoc Khue, 115.

14. Nguyen Ngoc Anh, 172, 173.

15. Willbanks, 116.

16. *KBC Army Magazine* 12 (Nov. 1994): 27.

17. Willbanks, 155.

18. Ibid., 121.

19. Tran Van Nhut, 188.

20. Ibid.

21. Ibid., 189.

22. Willbanks, 123.

23. Tran Van Nhut, 189.

24. Mach Van Truong, 20.

25. Andradé, 477.

26. *81ˢᵗ Airborne Commando Magazine*, July 1998, p. 93.

27. Truong Duong, *Mot Canh Hoa Du* (One Parachute Flower) (Np: Tu Huynh Publishing, 1999), 236.

28. ARVN, *The Battle of Binh Long*, 156.

29. Mach Van Truong, 21.

30. Ibid.

31. Tran Van Nhut, 191.

32. Ly Tong Ba, *25 Years of War* (Np: Self-published), 179

33. Le Khac Anh Dao, *Nhung Tran Danh Khong Ten* (The Nameless Battles), (Vancouver: Nguyet San Viet Nam, 2003), 201.

34. Ly Tong Ba, 183.

35. Tieu Lun Online Library (Website: tieulun.hopto.org), p. 12.

36. Vu Van Hoi, 6.

Chapter 9

1. Willbanks, 129.

2. Nguyen Dinh Sach, *Binh Long Anh Dung* (Heroic Binh Long), unpublished account of 21st Division in Binh Long in 1972; copy in author's possession.

3. Nguyen Dinh Sach, 8, 9.

4. Tran Van Nhut, 175.

5. Ibid., 176.

6. Ibid., 177.

7. ARVN, *Tran Binh Long* (The Battle of Binh Long), 128.

8. Willbanks, 132.

9. Nguyen Dinh Sach, 10.

10. Tran Van Nhut, 192.

11. ARVN, *Tran Binh Long* (The Battle of Binh Long), 158.

12. Andradé, 485.

13. Nguyen Dinh Sach, 11.

14. Willbanks, 130.

15. Nguyen Van Quy, 431.

16. Nguyen Dinh Sach, 14.

17. Long Phi (or Flying Dragon) was a name given to all 9th Division operations.

18. Nguyen Dinh Sach, 14.

19. Tran Van Nhut, 194.

20. Ibid., 195.

21. ARVN, *Tran Binh Long* (The Battle of Binh Long), 163.

22. Nguyen Ngoc Anh, 166.

23. Ibid., 171.

24. Ibid., 172.

25. ARVN, *Tran Binh Long* (The Battle of Binh Long), 163.

26. Nguyen Ngoc Anh, 173.

27. Ibid.

28. Phan Nhat Nam, *Mua He Do Lua* (Red Burning Summer), 4.

29. Ibid.

30. Ibid., 5.

31. Ibid., 6.

32. Ibid.

33. ARVN, *Tran Binh Long* (The Battle of Binh Long), 164.

34. Tran Van Nhut, 196.

35. Ibid., 198.

Chapter 10

1. *81ˢᵗ Airborne Commando Magazine,* May 1998, p. 78.

2. Ibid., 79.

3. Nguyen Duc Phuong, 574.

4. *81ˢᵗ Airborne Commando Magazine,* May 1998, p. 79.

5. When he came to the United States after the war, Nguyen Cau tried in vain to get in touch with the two girls.

6. Mach Van Truong, 22.

7. Willbanks, 142.

8. Ibid., 141.

9. Ibid., 135.

10. Ibid., 136.

11. Lt. Col. Nguyen Viet Can was the younger brother of Maj. Gen. Nguyen Viet Thanh, former IV Corps commander; General Thanh was killed in 1972 while directing his troops during an incursion into Cambodia.

12. Andradé, 485.

13. Ngo Quang Truong, 163.

14. Willbanks, 142.

15. Vu Van Hoi, 7.

16. *81ˢᵗ Airborne Commando Group Magazine,* May 1998, p. 96.

17. Ibid., 22.

18. Mach Van Truong, 23.

19. General Vanuxem died shortly after the Viet Nam War; his daughter returned the An Loc flag to the Vietnamese veterans in France.

20. Ngo Quang Truong, 164.

21. Mach Van Truong, 24.

22. Ibid., 25.

23. Ibid.

24. Nguyen Van Quy, 397.

25. Ibid., 386.

26. Nguyen Dinh Sach, 13.

27. ARVN, *Tran Binh Long* (The Battle of Binh Long), 202–4.

Chapter 11

1. *Su doan 18 Bo Binh Dac San* (18th Infantry Division Magazine), July 2005, p. 46.

2. Ibid., 199

3. Conversation with Gen. Le Minh Dao.

4. *Su doan 18 Bo Binh Dac San* (18th Infantry Division Magazine), July 2005, p. 202.

5. Le Khac Anh Dao, 45.

6. Ibid., 46.

7. Ibid., 48.

8. *Su doan 18 Bo Binh Dac San* (18th Infantry Division Magazine), July 2005, p. 201.

9. Ibid.

10. Nguyen Duc Phuong, 577.

11. Ibid., 203.

12. Conversation with Colonel Hua Yen Len, former Assistant for Operations, 18th Division.

13. *Su doan 18 Bo Binh Dac San* (18th Infantry Division Magazine), July 2005, p. 203.

14. Ibid., 204.

15. Hoang Minh Thao was the VC general in charge of B3 Front in the Central Highlands.

16. Le Khac Anh Dao, 163.

17. Ibid., 165.

18. *Su doan 18 Bo Binh Dac San* (18th Infantry Division Magazine), July 2005, p. 205.

19. Ibid.

Chapter 12

1. Gen. Hoang Xuan Lam, former I Corps Commander, once told the author that the evacuation of Khe Sanh made it very difficult, if not impossible, to defend Quang Tri and Thua Thien provinces.

2. Lewis Sorley, "Reassessing Viet Nam," 26.

3. Willbanks, 192 n7.

4. Andradé, 474.

5. Willbanks, 79.

6. Hammond, 249.

7. Tran Van Nhut, 127.

8. Mach Van Truong, 12.

9. Ly Tong Ba, 164.

10. Andradé, 501.

11. Sorley, "Reassessing Viet Nam," 26, 27.

12. Andradé, 489.

13. Ibid., 502.

Chapter 13

1. Arnold Isaacs, *Without Honor* (Baltimore: The John Hopkins University Press, 1983), 64.

2. Lewis Sorley, "Remembering Viet Nam," 16, 17 .

3. Henry Kissinger, *Years of Upheaval* (Boston: Little, Brown & Co., 1982), 32, 33.

4. Tran Do Cam, *Special Forces Airborne Commando Magazine* (Orange County, California, July 2004), p. 161.

5. Ibid., 162.

6. Ibid.

7. Ibid.,164.

8. Ibid.

9. Ibid., 167.

10. Ibid., 169.

11. Ibid.

12. Bui Tin defected to the West after 1975 and now lives in Paris.

13. Bui Tin, cont., 68.

14. *Dac San Su Doan 18 Bo Binh* (18th Infantry Division Magazine), July 2005, p. 26.

15. Ibid., 72.

16. Ibid., 31.

17. Ibid., 37.

18. George Veith and Merle Pribbenow, "Fighting Is an Art," *The Journal of Military History*, January 2004.

19. *Orange County Register* (website: http://www.darcenter.org)

20. Arnold Issaacs, cont., *Rolling Thunder in a Gentle Land,* ed. Andrew Wiest, 308.

21. Nguoi An Loc, *81ˢᵗ Airborne Commando Group Magazine,* p. 62.

Epilogue

1. *Rolling Thunder in a Gentle Land,* 73.

2. Andradé, 502

Glossary

AAR	After-Action Report
APC	Armored Personnel Carrier
ARVN	Army of the Republic of Viet Nam
CBU	Cluster Bomb Unit
C&C	Command & Control
CIDG	Civil Defense Group
COSVN	Central Office for South Viet Nam
CP	Command Post
FAC	Forward Air Controller
FLSVN	Front for the Liberation of South Viet Nam
FSB	Fire Support Base
GVN	Government of Viet Nam
HALO	High Altitude, Low Opening
IPR	Inter-Provincial Road.
JGS	Joint General Staff
KIA	Killed in Action
LCDB	*Lao Cong Dao Binh* or Convicted deserters
LZ	Landing Zone
MAF	Marine Amphibious Forces
Medevac	Medical evacuation
MIA	Missing in Action
MR	Military Region
NCO	Non-Commissioned Officer

NLA	National Liberation Army
NLF	National Liberation Front
NVA	North Vietnamese Army
NVN	North Viet Nam
PAVN	People's Army of Viet Nam
PF	Popular Forces
PRG	Provisional Revolutionary Government
PSDF	People's Self-Defense Forces
RC	Route Coloniale
RF	Regional Forces
RN	Route Nationale
RVN	Republic of Viet Nam
TOC	Tactical Operation Center
TRAC	Third Regional Assistance Command
VC	Viet Cong
VM	Viet Minh (Viet Nam Dong Minh Hoi or League of Vietnamese Alliance)
VNAF	Vietnamese Air Force
WIA	Wounded in Action

Bibliography

INTERVIEWS AND CORRESPONDENCE
(Ranks as of April 1972)

Bui Duc Diem, Colonel, Assistant for Operations, 5th ARVN
    Division

Hua Yen Len, Colonel, Assistant for Operations, 18th ARVN
    Division

Huynh Thao Luoc, Colonel, Chief of Staff, 18th ARVN Division

Le Minh Dao, Colonel (later major general), division commander,
    18th ARVN Division

Le Quang Luong, Colonel (later brigadier general), airborne
    brigade commander, 1st Airborne Brigade

Ly Tong Ba, Colonel (later brigadier general), division
    commander, 23rd ARVN Division

Mach Van Truong, Colonel (later brigadier general), regiment
    commander, 8th Regiment/5th Division

Nguyen Cau, TV reporter at An Loc

Nguyen Cong Vinh, Colonel, regiment commander, 9th
    Regiment/5th Division

Nguyen Dinh Sach, Colonel, former Chief of Staff, 21st ARVN
    Division

Nguyen Phu Chinh, Lieutenant Colonel, VNAF, squadron
    commander, 237th Helicopter Squadron

Pham Van Huan, Colonel, commando group commander, 81st Airborne Commando Group

Pham X. Quang, a former lieutenant colonel in the U.S. Marines and author of *A Sense of Duty: My Father, My American Journey,* whose father, the late VNAF Lt. Col. Pham V. Hoa, had participated in the air resupply missions in An Loc

Tran Van Nhut, Colonel (later brigadier general), province chief, Binh Long province

Vu Van Hoi, Second Lieutenant, platoon leader, 5th Airborne Battalion

PUBLISHED DOCUMENTS

Andradé, Dale. *America's Last Vietnam Battle.* Lawrence: University Press of Kansas, 2001.

Braestrup, Peter. *Big Story.* Boulder, CO: Westview Press, 1977.

FitzGerald, Frances. *Fire in the Lake.* Boston: Little, Brown & Co., 1972.

Hammond, William M. *Reporting Viet Nam: Media and Military at War.* Lawrence: University Press of Kansas, 1998.

Isaacs, Arnold. *Without Honor.* Baltimore: The John Hopkins University Press, 1983.

Kissinger, Henry. *The White House Years.* Boston: Little, Brown & Co., 1979.

———. *Years of Upheaval.* Boston: Little, Brown & Co., 1982.

Le Khac Anh Dao, *Nhung Tran Danh Khong Ten* (Nameless Battles). Vancouver: Nguyet San Viet Nam, 2003.

Ly Tong Ba, *25 Nam Khoi Lua* (25 Years of War). Np: Self-published, 1995.

Metzner, Edward. *More Than a Soldier's War.* College Station: Texas A&M University Press, 1995.

Nguyen Cong Vinh. *Cau Chuyen Suy Tu Cua Mot Cuu Tu Nhan Chinh Tri* (Reflections of a Former Political Prisoner). San Jose, CA: Mekong Ty Nan Publishing, 1996.

Nguyen Duc Phuong. *Chien Tranh Viet Nam Toan Tap*

(Comprehensive Narrative of the Viet Nam War).
Toronto, Canada: Lang Van, 2001.

Nguyen Ngoc Anh. *Chien Thang An Loc* (The Victory of An Loc). Austin, TX: Self-published, 2007.

Nguyen Quoc Khue. *3rd Ranger Group and the Battle of An Loc.* Reprinted in *Ranger Magazine 7*, 2003.

Nguyen Van Quy. *Hoi Ky An Loc: 86 Ngay cua mot Bac Si Giai Phau tai Mat Tran* (Memoir of An Loc: 86 Days of a Surgeon in Battle). Westminster, CA: Van Nghe Publishing, 2002.

Phan Nhat Nam. *Mua He Do Lua* (Red Burning Summer), June 1972. Reprinted in Tieu Lun online Library (Website: tieulun.tohop.org).

Prados, John, and Ray W. Stubbe. *Valley of Decision: The Siege of Khe Sanh.* Boston: Houghton Mifflin, 1991.

Tran Van Nhut. *Cuoc Chien Dang Do* (Unfinished War). Santa Ana, CA: An Loc Publishing, 2003. This book was translated into English and the edited version was published by Texas Tech University Press in May 2009 under the title *An Loc: The Unfinished War.*

Truong Duong, *Mot Canh Hoa Du* (One Parachute Flower). Tu Huynh Publishing, 1999.

Wiest, Andrew, ed. *Rolling Thunder in a Gentle Land.* Oxford, UK: Osprey Publishing, 2006.

Willbanks, James H. *The Battle of An Loc.* Bloomington: Indiana University Press, 2005.

Studies, Reports, Periodicals

Su doan 18 Bo Binh Dac San (18th Infantry Division Magazine), July 2005.

81st Airborne Commando Group Magazine, Issues 1998, 2001, and 2006.

ARVN. *Tran Binh Long* (The Battle of Binh Long), 1973.

ARVN. *Quan Su 4* (Military History 4), June 1972.

Dac San Hoa Du (Airborne Magazine), Special Issue, 2003.

Battle of Khe Sanh, Wikipedia. Accessed October 21, 2007.

Clarke, Philip C. "The Battle That Saved Saigon." *Reader's Digest*, March 1973.

Gary's U.S. Infantry Weapons Reference Guide (Website: inetres. com).

Harmer, Jerry. "Endangered Species Thrive along Ho Chi Minh Trail." *San Jose Mercury News*, March 4, 2007.

Kaiser, Robert G. "The Arrogance of Power Revisited." *San Jose Mercury News*, Jan. 1, 2007.

KBC Army Magazine 12, Nov. 1994.

Ngo Quang Truong. *The 1972 Easter Offensive* (Reprinted in Vietnamese in *Ranger Magazine* 21, May 2007).

Orange County Register (Website: www.darcenter.org).

Sorley, Lewis. "Remembering Viet Nam." A Lecture delivered at the National Archives, Washington D.C, April 30, 2002; and "Reassessing Viet Nam." A Lecture delivered at the Viet Nam Center, Texas Tech University, March 17, 2006.

Veith, George, and Merle Pribbenow. "Fighting Is an Art." *The Journal of Military History*, January 2004.

Unpublished Source Material

Bui Duc Diem, Colonel, Assistant for Operations, 5th ARVN Division. Unpublished manuscript on An Loc; copy in author's possession.

Mach Van Truong, Brigadier General, former 8th Regiment commander, 5th Division. *Tran Chien An Loc* (The Battle of An Loc); unpublished memoir on An Loc; copy in author's possession.

Nguyen Dinh Sach, Colonel, former chief of staff, 21st Division. *Binh Long Anh Dung* (Heroic Binh Long), July 31, 2007; unpublished manuscript in author's possession.

Nguyen Cong Vinh, Colonel, 9th Regiment commander, 5th Division. Letter on the battle of Loc Ninh, June 16, 2006; copy in author's possession.

Nguyen Huu Chinh, *Phi Doan 237 Tham Du Mat Tran An Loc*

(237th Squadron in the Battle of An Loc) Unpublished report, October 2006, copy in author's possession.

Vu Van Hoi. "Narrative on An Loc"; unpublished manuscript; copy in author's possession.

Index